CW00506116

REFLECTIONS IN BLUE

To Jock & Liz,

It's all a long time ago, but I still remember... Jock, did you ever find the lost bits of that door? I've suffered with my stomach ever since!

Best Wishes

David Hodges

A former senior officer with Thames Valley Police, David Hodges gained wide operational and management experience in his thirty years with the force, serving in all ranks from constable to superintendent and retiring as head of corporate communication.

During his service, he achieved several successes in the prestigious Queen's Police Gold Medal Essay Competition, including the first prize and award of the Gold Medal, and, as press, public relations officer, was for a time editor of the force's newspaper, *Thames View*.

Now a prolific crime novelist, he has several gripping thrillers to his credit. His first two novels, 'Flashpoint' and 'Burnout', published by Pharaoh Press, won critical media acclaim and he has followed up these earlier successes with a further novel, 'Slice', published by Robert Hale Ltd. His next novel, 'Firetrap', is to be published by Robert Hale later this year.

David lives with his wife, Elizabeth, on the edge of the Somerset Levels, where he can fully indulge his passion for writing and enjoy some 'retirement' time with his two married daughters and four grandchildren.

REFLECTIONS IN BLUE

DAVID HODGES

To my wife, Elizabeth, for all her love, patience and support over so many wonderful years.

Text © 2011 David Hodges

First published by Pharaoh Press 2011

ISBN: 978-1-901442-33-5

Typeset by Mousemat Design Limited

Printed in Great Britain by the MPG Books Group, Bodmin and King's Lynn

CONTENTS

CHAPTER 1

BEDPACKS AND DRILL-PIGS

He was not a particularly big man, but with the shotgun in his hands he took on the stature of a giant. For a second I froze on the narrow staircase and threw a swift sidelong glance at Andy, the young constable who had accompanied me on this so-called routine commitment. I didn't have to ask him what he was thinking; it was written all over his tense white face. As for me, I felt suddenly dizzy and very sick.

It was the sort of incident that every police officer fears he will have to face sooner or later and on that cold January night we had walked into it with our eyes wide open. The terse radio message had suggested nothing other than an ordinary run of the mill disturbance call, simply stating that a couple were having trouble with their twenty-seven year old son at an address on a Slough housing estate. No one had breathed a solitary word about shotguns, but to be fair, no one could possibly have foreseen that the man in question would try to back up his argument with his father's twelve-bore.

Now that he had, however, common sense and police firearms policy dictated a quick withdrawal to safer quarters and maybe we would have done just that if the man with the gun had not taken the initiative and retreated into an adjacent bedroom.

Thoughts of a stand-off or a probable suicide bid spurred us to immediate action and we went for the door together, bursting it open even as he tried to lock it from the inside. The gun was still in his hands as he backed away from us into a corner and his finger was hovering dangerously close to the trigger.

I swallowed hard. I had already been on a police firearms training course and had seen first-hand what a shotgun could do to a heavy car door from several yards. The effect on a human body at a range of just a few feet did not bear thinking about.

'Don't be silly,' I found myself saying to him in a cracked voice. 'Give it to me.'

He didn't answer, but studied me with a peculiar look in his eyes. Then my flesh began to crawl as I saw the barrel start to come up very slowly towards my stomach.

There was no time for hesitation and, stepping forward quickly, I pushed his gun hand down and away from me, at the same time grasping the weapon tightly by the stock with the other hand. Andy had moved too – he had to be telepathic – and was standing behind but slightly to one side of me. He immediately took hold of the barrel with both hands and firmly pulled the weapon from the gunman's grasp.

I had fully expected the thing to go off, but it didn't and it was only when we examined it afterwards that we learned the truth – the shotgun was actually empty. It turned out that our man had been unable to find any ammunition for the weapon because his father kept the cartridges locked away in a separate place. Suddenly our armed incident had turned into something of a damp squib, but I felt no embarrassment, only a tremendous sense of relief. A damp squib is a whole lot better than a shooting match any day of the week and I was certainly not about to complain. I was a bit peeved when I was summoned to see the sub-divisional chief inspector the following day, however. Instead of being told a commendation was in the wind, I was actually castigated for failing to comply with police firearms policy by tackling an armed offender rather than withdrawing and calling for armed back-up. Still, the man with the gun fared a lot worse. When he subsequently appeared in court, the magistrates were not at all amused and sent him to prison for six months.

That single terrifying incident serves to illustrate how unpredictable the role of an ordinary beat copper can be and how even the most routine commitment can turn into just the opposite at the drop of a hat. It is the uncertainty of the job that attracts so many different types of people to a police career – from plumbers to solicitors, soldiers to university graduates – and it was this that had attracted me as a fresh-faced school leaver of seventeen way back in the early sixties. But realising my ambition proved to be a lot more difficult than I had ever imagined.

Mathematics was the problem, but then it always had been. Even after leaving school, I still nursed smarting recollections of dreary afternoons spent in stuffy classrooms, trying to fathom how long it would take X number of men to fill a hole with sand – each time finishing up with a blank paper and a swift cuff round the ear. My most notable achievement was six out of a hundred in one end of term examination and even now I can hear my classmates' howls of derision when it was disclosed that three of the marks had been awarded for trying.

Nevertheless, until I passed through the school gates for the last time I was not unduly worried about my poor skills. English had always been my particular bent and with a sort of tragic naivety, I naturally assumed I would immediately embark on a journalistic career once I had thrown the school books aside. Consequently mathematics had no place in my preconceived life's plan.

The fact that the newspaper industry was not awaiting the onslaught of my pen with baited breath hit me with all the cruel force of a cold shower. The nearest I ever got to my goal was a three week job as a messenger in an obscure advertising firm in central London, which involved hauling sizeable parcels of advertising material all over the city for a salary that would disgust a youngster delivering newspapers today. I estimated that if I played my cards right I could make office junior in around three years.

I don't know what first attracted me to the police. Maybe it had something to do with the uniform and the fact that *Dixon of Dock Green* was being shown on the television at the time. Whatever the reason, the spectre of mathematics haunted me even here. If X number of men weren't filling a hole with sand they were filling a tank with water. Some educationalist seemed to be obsessed with this army of labourers marching backwards and forwards with spades and buckets. I had to face up to things; I would not make a police cadet until I came to terms with my particular problem. In fact, I wouldn't make anything.

It took nearly three years and a longish spell in a drab Civil Service department to make up the lost ground and by then I was too old for consideration as a police cadet. Tongue in cheek, I applied to take the entrance examination for police constable and, after three unsuccessful attempts (maths again), I came down to breakfast one morning to find the letter from the chief constable of the Berkshire County Constabulary lying on the doormat. I read it over and over again, my excitement mounting. I was through. It seemed unbelievable, but I had done it!

Other formalities, including a medical, interview and induction course, followed. Then in early January 1965, I finally headed for Sandgate in Kent and No 6 District Police Training Centre, staggering under the weight of two enormous suitcases bulging with personal effects and uniform equipment. I think if I had realised then what awaited me at the place I later came to know as Stalag Luft 3, I would have jacked the whole thing in there and then, but as it was, I went like the proverbial lamb to the slaughter.

There were about twenty of us waiting at the local railway station when the uncomfortable navy blue coach collected us to take us to our new home and the apprehension was palpable as we climbed aboard. Sadly, there was not a pretty female face among the new intake to lighten our mood, but that was to be expected. In those days women police officers generally attended separate training centres. Even when they qualified they didn't actually do the same job as the men. Policing then was a male dominated profession and the policewomen's department was in the main a specialist unit restricted to dealing with matters involving female offenders, minor criminal offences and children and young persons.

The staff were taking down the remains of the Christmas decorations when we all finally reached the training centre and filed into the shining entrance hall and it seemed to me like an omen; I think I must have been psychic.

The uniformed sergeant seated behind the desk just inside the door did little to allay my fears, but barked out our names as if we were a new batch of prisoners of war, slapping an identity tag into each nervous palm as we filed past and castigating anyone foolish enough to forget to call him sergeant.

Doubts crowded my mind as I followed a young constable from the senior course up the stairs and I was certainly not reassured when he showed me my dormitory. It was a lean, hungry looking place with a floor polished like new leather and rows of grim iron-framed beds. I was surprised to see a chart on the wall showing where each student was required to sleep, but I was soon to learn that everything in this place was regimented like an army barracks and that most of the instructors were ex-army or navy personnel with the old national service mentality to go with it. There was even a rumour going round that students had only just stopped using the loos by numbers!

The system of police training has changed substantially over the years, in line with the changing values and attitudes of society itself. The rigid militaristic flavour has virtually gone and attitudes towards discipline are much more relaxed. Whether that is a good or bad thing depends upon your point of view. However, to coin a phrase used a lot in those politically incorrect days, the hard traditional approach certainly separated the men from the boys.

In fact, some recruits didn't even get beyond the first few weeks before they decided to pack their bags and disappear – usually a lot faster than they had arrived. Others were found to be unsuitable for one reason or another and had their bags packed for them. It was all part of the natural weeding out process and it took a particular kind of forbearance to endure the rigours of that intense training school environment.

Even now, after forty-five years, some things remain indelibly etched on my memory. The standard training school haircut that left heads looking like dried thistle flowers, the eternal spit and polish normally associated with national service and the strict discipline that either made or broke a would-be recruit. To the ex-servicemen on the course it all came as no real surprise and they settled in quite naturally, but to those more used to the niceties of civvy street, a twelve stone sergeant screaming obscenities at them across a windswept parade square was the realisation of their worst nightmare.

I found it particularly hard. For a start, I didn't much care for sport and I couldn't swim a stroke. That put me right on the spot, because sport occupied a large slice of the curriculum and a non-swimming policeman was regarded as a total liability. I spent most of the time set aside for games trying to avoid concussion on the football field or a chlorine hangover in the swimming pool.

My attitude towards sport certainly didn't endear me to the physical training instructor (PTI) and he went to great pains to emphasise the fact. He had plenty of opportunity too, for he also took us for self-defence training – a subject dear to his clockwork heart. I will say one thing for the experience, I had never realised the human body was capable of bending in so many places before.

Drill turned out to be another problem because I was one of those unfortunate people with two left feet. No matter how hard they tried, no one could keep in step with me. This was rather unpleasant for the heel of the man in front and the toe of the man behind. It was even more unpleasant for me, for our aficionado of the parade square – an ex Royal Navy drill-pig – became quite obsessed with the idea that I had been visited on him for failing to go to church. He was only a small man, but he had the sort of voice and imaginative vocabulary that could be heard half a mile away and his opinion of me and my parentage was delivered frequently with the full strength of his vocal chords from a distance of around three feet.

The course was not just an endless round of physical pursuits, however. There was still plenty of time for the academic side of things and legal theory and police procedure actually formed the bulk of the curriculum. I was relieved to find that mathematics was not included, but it was not easy going back to school anyway, especially as the subjects then covered – such as larceny, judges' rules, police powers of arrest, goods vehicles and betting, gaming and lotteries – were totally alien to me and formed a colossal jigsaw, which seemed to be composed of completely unrelated pieces.

Then there were the dreaded definitions, to be learned verbatim in much the same way as I had learned my twelve times table in my first years at school. The idea of the definition was to provide in a nutshell a description of a particular offence under the criminal law or an important legal term or power of arrest. There were scores of the little horrors, ranging from just a couple to a dozen lines in length, and the unfortunate student was expected to know them all by heart.

The offence of stealing under the now obsolete Larceny Act was the most memorable of them. It ran: A person steals who, without the consent of the owner, fraudulently and without a claim of right in good faith, takes and carries away anything capable of being stolen, with intent at the time of such taking permanently to deprive the owner thereof. Provided that a person may be guilty of stealing any such thing notwithstanding that he has lawful possession thereof, if, being a bailee or part owner thereof, he fraudulently converts the same to his own use or to the use of any person other than the owner...'

The penalty for loss of memory on the regular Monday morning test was an appointment with the instructor for recitations on the Tuesday, half an hour before breakfast. If that didn't work then on the Wednesday there was another appointment earlier still. So it went on, until by Friday it was hardly worth going to bed in the first place.

After a few weeks, the student developed a phobia about these definitions. They became the *raison d'être* for his very existence. Every spare moment during the day, in between lectures, practical exercises and sport, was utilised. After the evening meal, once the spit and polish for the following day's drill had been done, there was a mad scramble for vacant rooms, niches in dormitories, even the occasional cupboard – anywhere that held the slightest promise of peace and quiet for a couple of hours cramming before the mass exodus to sample the fleshpots of Folkestone began.

I found that the best place to study was the toilet until someone else cottoned on to that idea as well. In no time at all the engaged signs were going up everywhere and it is hard to imagine anything more grotesque than lines of trainee coppers crouching in the cubicles of toilet blocks, reciting in a low monotone the definition of burglary or wounding – as if it were some kind of religious chant – to the accompaniment of the occasional flushing cistern.

The recruit of today does not have to worry so much about definitions and the old method of learning things parrot fashion has been replaced by what is said to be a more innovative approach. Maybe this is a step in the right direction and there again, maybe it is not. One thing is certain, however. That punitive method of teaching may have been primitive, but it got results. In short, you learned what you were told because you were too scared to do anything else. I know – I carried the impression from those circular wooden toilet seats for a long time afterwards.

The learning process was not confined to the official

curriculum either. There were other so-called unwritten laws to be learned too, which were in some respects even more important to commit to memory. Perhaps the most important of these was that of tongue control – as one of my compatriots discovered to his cost on the very first day of the course. The deputy commandant in his intimidating regalia had only just delivered the standard introductory chat to his petrified audience, detailing the rigid standards required of all students at the centre, when he made the classic error of rounding off with the usual: 'Any questions?' Of course, most of those crammed into the small room knew instinctively that this invitation was merely a formality and never actually expected to be taken up. But there is always one in every group who fails to appreciate the obvious.

'Is breakfast reasonably informal, sir?' a nervous voice suddenly queried.

There was a stunned silence. No one dared look at the young man standing at the back. Big Cheese winced, started to answer, then hesitated, eyeing the speaker up and down warily. 'What do you mean by "informal"?' he parried with that 'I know I shall be sorry I asked' expression in his eyes.

The recruit glanced round at the apprehensive faces of his colleagues and swallowed hard. 'Dressing gown and socks,' he blurted.

Big Cheese never did answer that question. In fairness to him he did try, but something seemed to stick in his throat and though he opened his mouth, no sound came out. Then as the whole building seemed to shudder, he cleared his throat, turned on his heel and stalked out, leaving the unfortunate student still standing at the back and the sergeant instructor studying him with a fixed cobra-like smile.

Silly questions and unguarded comments can get you into big trouble in an organisation like the police and straight after the incident one of my colleagues, an ex-matelot nicknamed Rowdy, gave me what turned out to be a very sound piece of advice: 'Always remember,' he warned, 'the mouth is designed for breathing and eating. At all other times it should be kept shut.' It was a pity he didn't stick to that golden rule himself though, for he became the very next casualty.

'Anyone here ex-RAF?' the class instructor queried shortly after the departure of the deputy commandant.

Several recruits stirred uneasily in their seats, but after what had just happened no one was prepared to say a word.

'Army then?' he went on.

Still no takers.

The sergeant sighed. 'What about the Royal Navy?' he persisted.

To my astonishment, Rowdy instantly snapped to attention.

The sergeant smiled. 'Excellent,' he murmured. 'What were you in?'

'HM Submarines,' Rowdy answered proudly.

'Were you indeed?' the sergeant commented with an air of triumph. 'Then you must be an early riser – just the man to sound the gong in the mornings!'

The gong was sounded as a form of reveille at a particularly indecent hour and the volunteer did his duty with commendable fervour over the next few weeks. The hideous booming reverberated right through the building, penetrating a mound of bedclothes and a couple of pillows with ease. You just couldn't escape from the sound and if you did manage to drift off to sleep again afterwards you soon regretted it when the sergeant burst in on you. The trouble with the man was that he had no finesse.

The weeks dragged by and at last I reached the stage when I felt I could not take any more. I was sick of leaping out of bed at the crack of dawn to the reverberations of the gong, lining up in a bitterly cold bathroom to shower and shave in water that seemed to have come straight from the Arctic and rushing back to the dormitory to make a stupid military style bedpack out of my sheets and blankets. I was browned off staring at my own reflection in toe caps that had taken me half the previous evening to polish – only to be told by the drill sergeant that my boots were filthy – marching round and round a windswept parade square, tripping over my own feet and charging after a ridiculous ball on a concrete hard playing field in a sleet storm. Most of all, I was tired of the mind-boggling lectures, the endless definitions and the nightly cramming sessions that left me virtually too tired to enjoy anything save a good sleep.

When one of the lads jacked it in altogether and packed his bags, I was on the verge of doing the same. Then the following morning I made my first successful bedpack and managed to earn some praise for my turnout at drill practice. Simple, almost childish accomplishments that did the trick. From that moment on I never looked back. The jigsaw pieces of the lectures started to fit into place and I actually found myself enjoying drill and football. The discipline and spit and polish I had once despised so much now made sense. I even saw wisdom in the remark our class instructor had made right at the start of the course: 'You're going to graft as you have never grafted before, because if you can't take it here you'll never take it outside on the street.' With understanding came the certain conviction that I would make it after all.

Shortly after the final pass-out parade, which signified the end of the thirteen week ordeal, the long awaited postings came through from the gods of each of the forces represented on the course. The chief constable of the Berkshire County Constabulary had decreed that I was going to a place called Didcot and I packed my bags and said my goodbyes with a feeling of nervous excitement. I was a proper policeman at last and I could hardly wait to be put to the test.

My naive enthusiasm was soon to receive a nasty jolt, however, for I was to find that it is one thing playing at being a policeman in the secure environment of the training centre and quite another doing the job for real on an unsympathetic street.

CHAPTER 2

BEATS AND BOOZERS

My helmet was a little on the large size and my boots creaked despairingly at every step. If I had been strolling through the town stark naked, I could not have felt more conspicuous. 'Right, lad,' the sergeant had said within an hour of my arrival for my first duty, 'I want you to go out there and terrify them. You certainly terrify me!'

My transition from training school student to beat patrolman was as quick as that. No preliminaries, no guided tour of the area to show me where everything was. Just a couple of welcoming handshakes, a mug of tea and then out to face the world.

My experience was by no means unique either. In those days the operational side of police training was almost primeval. As a rookie, you received very little practical instruction. There were no tutor constables to show you the ropes; they were to be an innovation of the distant future. Instead, you learned the job by a crude method of trial and error – mainly error. Success or failure depended largely on your own efforts, for you were on two year's probation and you could be required to resign at any time, without right of appeal, if it was considered that you were unsuitable.

You had as much to contend with inside the station as outside too. Unlike the police force of today where most stations are awash with raw recruits, there were very few probationary constables in comparison with the number of experienced bobbies – maybe just a couple per station – which meant that the new arrival stuck out like a sore thumb. You were never allowed to forget your lowly position either and you ended up making the tea, running errands, cleaning out the stray dog kennels and enduring the inevitable practical joke cooked up by the station wag. If you made a mistake, you became the object of ridicule for weeks afterwards and if you had the audacity to offer an opinion, you were immediately silenced with the comment: 'What do you know? Your numbers aren't dry yet!'

The method of policing was also a lot different then. When I stepped out on to the street, patrol duties in the cash-strapped Berkshire County Constabulary were generally carried out on foot or by means of a bicycle, which you had to buy yourself and then claim reimbursement through a monthly cycle allowance. The most that could be expected in the way of motorised transport was a couple of vans, one designated for use by the CID and the other for general purpose duties. Even those lucky enough to get a driving course within the first four years of service seldom got permission to slide behind the wheel. On the odd occasion that it did happen it was like being granted the freedom of the city.

As for personal radios, they were the sort of luxury that dreams were made of. Contact with the local station was maintained by a system of telephone kiosk 'points' kept by the bobby at hourly intervals. You simply stood outside the kiosk for ten minutes and resumed patrol if the station did not ring you. One of the worst sins that could be committed was to be late and it was a hanging offence to miss a point altogether.

With things the way they were, assistance was largely dependant on the pedal power of the nearest colleague – assuming it was possible to get to a telephone to call one in the first place – and the golden rule was to weigh up every situation before diving in, because what you started on your own you usually had to finish the same way. That in itself was a sobering enough thought and to make things even worse, you could be sure that if you handled a situation badly your armchair critics would make no allowances for your youth and inexperience afterwards, but simply throw the book at you.

In those days it was certainly a lonely existence for the trainee bobby. Even when you got home after a particularly bad day, unless blessed with the luxury of a wife, you had no one to confide in, except maybe another probationer over a pint in the local who was in more or less the same position as yourself. If you happened to be single and there was no police section house available, you invariably found yourself – as I did – in a succession of lodgings, where the harassed landladies were too busy complaining about the erratic shifts and the disruption it caused to their lives to offer a sympathetic ear, and in the end you ended up having to move on as their patience snapped.

Today police officers have a much more stressful time of it in terms of the risks they run and the level of public hostility they face – largely brought about by misguided policies, which are seen to concentrate on government dicta and political correctness rather than crime prevention and detection. They are also suffocating under mountains of paperwork and mindless bureaucracy, which has drastically reduced the time available to them for basic patrol work. This has resulted in a bruising loss of status as they find themselves steadily replaced on the streets of our towns and villages by cheaper, less qualified police community support officers.

Having said that, a probationary constable has access to greater practical support from the organisation than was once the case. In response to the demands of a much more complex and violent society, there are experienced tutor constables and professional counsellors to talk to when things go wrong and senior ranks are far more approachable than they were. Furthermore, most police stations boast a whole fleet of smart police cars and the patrolling officer is wired to a twenty-four hour control room at the very least. Back-up can therefore be summoned at the flick of a switch and support is provided by a legion of specialist services, including traffic cars, firearms teams, computerised criminal intelligence and police support units equipped with full riot control gear.

Yet some things never change and the biggest problem the probationer will always have to face is his or her own basic lack of confidence – and in this respect good old Joe Public doesn't help to make life any easier.

The rowdy teenage element greeted my beat debut with open hostility – not out of any sense of personal dislike, but because to start with, I represented authority and secondly, it was the thing for so-called hard men to do. The older generation on the other hand just smiled in that patronising way of theirs as if they were humouring a child strutting about in a new cowboy suit.

I found both attitudes equally infuriating. It was bad enough being green in the first place without others making it so obvious. 'You don't look old enough to be a policeman.' 'Fancy sending a boy to do a man's job.' For the next two years I had to put up with all sorts of tactless comments from members of the local community, but I learned to swallow my pride and pretend I had not heard them.

The taunts of the 'yob' fraternity were a different matter though. They really got to me. It was all I could do to keep myself in check and bite my tongue, and what made things worse, they knew it. 'Hey, copper, did your mother know who your father was?' 'What's it like being in the Gestapo?' Only now did I understand what our training centre instructor had meant when he said: 'If you can't take it here, you'll never take it outside on the street'. But for that harrowing experience, those young tearaways might well have been treated to a display of retaliation that would have simply brought me down to their level and achieved nothing.

As it was, I just gritted my teeth, focused my gaze on a distant object and pretended they did not exist. After a while this tactic seemed to work too. Nothing has a more dampening effect on the enthusiasm of the mickey-taker than apparent indifference on the part of the recipient. Eventually the youths lost interest in the novelty of a new copper. This took time, of course, but that was one commodity I had plenty of – all thirty years of it.

Didcot itself was a bit of a letdown really. It was a small one-horse town that lacked only the customary hitching rail. Its sole claim to notoriety lay in the presence of a big power station under construction on the outskirts, which had swelled the population almost overnight with the influx of a huge workforce of foreign labour billeted in a shanty town of huts and caravans on the site. Didcot had not been designed to accommodate such a demanding army. There was only one cinema, a café where the local motor cyclists met and a modest assortment of public houses and private clubs. In short, entertainment was in very limited supply and the police had their work cut out dealing with the trouble that was the inevitable consequence.

Very often the patrolling bobby attended a pub incident on his own or at the most, with a colleague from a neighbouring beat, and the experience was nothing to relish. Few places can become as violent as a bar when someone gets liquored up and starts throwing glasses about. More than enough police officers have been injured by a man wielding a broken bottle and when the call to attend a pub fight comes through, only a fool rushes headlong into the thing.

A common saying amongst the older members of the service during my formative years was 'Run to a fire, walk to a fight' and that philosophy made a lot of sense. A fire conjures up a vision of lives at immediate risk and property being damaged or destroyed on a major scale. Everything is to be gained by speed and dignity is of little consequence. Of course, a fight can be serious too and naturally the bobby gets to the scene as quickly as possible, but at this sort of incident demeanour is the all-important factor. A police officer who rushes to a disturbance and arrives gasping for breath, tie askew and helmet over his eyes, is hardly likely to command the respect needed to deal with the situation. A cool detached approach is crucial if the combatants are to be brought to their senses.

To be fair, this strategy does not always work. When people have a few drinks inside them, they are not that easy to reason with and I found this out to my cost just a few weeks after my arrival at Didcot.

The telephone call came from the licensee of a public house not far from the police station and I went off on my bicycle to see what the trouble was, unaware that I was about to receive a sharp lesson in practical policing. The bar was virtually empty as I propped my bicycle against the wall and stepped inside. The licensee was trying to close. He nodded towards the corner as I entered and my spirits took a nose dive. There were two of them there and a right pair they were as well. I knew them both and they were not just the usual youthful tearaways. These were older men in their thirties and they were always pure aggravation.

I glanced back at the licensee, but, like a character in a Wild West film, he just stayed put behind the bar, polishing the pattern off one of his glasses. I felt a bit like Wyatt Earp as I compressed my lips and strolled over to where the two were seated. Then a strange thing happened. To my astonishment they simply got up, threw me a swift sidelong glance and left. I tried to control my deep sigh of relief, but it was short-lived. I heard the loud crash from the direction of the street a moment later and, dashing outside, saw one of the men blatantly engaged in smashing up my bicycle. The other man had apparently gone.

I was so angry that I grabbed the vandal on the spot, but that was as far as I got. Strong hands seized me from behind and my arms were pinned to my sides in a bear hug. The second character had not gone at all, but must have been lurking in the shadows nearby. With a sadistic leer the first man now turned on me and put the boot in hard. I tried to break free, but it was useless. Out of the corner of my eye I saw the licensee emerge from the doorway and shout at the pair to leave me alone, but apart from waving a broom ineffectually, that was about all he did do.

It was at this point that the grip on me relaxed and I went down under another well-aimed kick, my helmet rolling in the gutter. Then the boots came in at every angle and though I tried to get up, I only managed to reach my knees before I went down again. This is it, I thought, as a black void started to open up in front of me, my first trip to the local hospital.

In fact, I am quite certain that that is how the affair would have ended had it not been for the timely arrival of two hefty colleagues in the Didcot police van. My assailants were whisked away so fast that their feet hardly touched the ground, leaving me to retrieve my helmet and dust myself down, bruised and shaken, but otherwise not seriously injured. Fortunately, it was my pride that took the biggest knock on that occasion, but as I was to find out in later years, other colleagues were not so lucky. The price of law enforcement is seldom cheap, especially for those who have to do the enforcing.

To be fair, it would be wrong to imply that all public houses at that time were hotbeds of violence (anymore than they are today), for nothing could be further from the truth. The majority of hostelries rarely experienced problems of this sort and some establishments had never had cause to dial 999 since opening their doors. Nevertheless, the fact that a particular premises managed to keep a low profile did not mean that the police never set foot there at all, for the local force also had a responsibility to prevent and detect abuses of the liquor licensing laws, especially with regard to under-age drinking.

Nowadays there seems to be much less supervision of licensed premises – especially since the government's radical (and in my opinion short-sighted) relaxation of pub hours – but in my early years on the beat pub checks were an important feature of patrol work. It was definitely not a popular duty, however, either with the publicans and their customers who tended to resent the intrusion or with the police officers themselves who felt self-conscious strolling through a crowded bar in full regalia.

As a new boy, I particularly detested the job. I felt awkward enough in the public eye without this added aggravation to put up with and my attitude towards this onerous duty was not improved when, close on the heels of my previous experience, I suffered an even worse humiliation. I was on a day turn (10am to 6pm) at the time and the sergeant collared me as I was about to head out on my beat after a couple of hours covering the police station office. 'I think we'll check a few boozers this afternoon, me lad,' he growled. Inwardly, I groaned, but there was no escape, so I followed him out to the A55 van with an air of resignation.

The first few hostelries we visited were practically empty, but as the morning progressed, each place we came to was a little bit busier than the last, until around lunchtime we entered the bar of a pub just outside the town and found quite a lively gathering inside.

Most of the customers were locals and they all knew the sergeant by his first name. He endured all the usual inane comments – including the inevitable: 'Hello, hello, hello' – with a good-natured grin and a cheerful wave, but I found the jibes irritating and it must have shown on my face. When the sergeant went up to the bar for the usual chat with the licensee, I came in for some real stick. The younger element obviously recognised a rookie constable when they saw one and, sensing my uneasiness, thought they would have some sport – with the result that the catcalls came fast and furious. The annoying thing was that the sergeant seemed oblivious to what was happening a few yards away and as the mickey-taking went on and on, I just had to stand there and hope that my misery was not too obvious.

I stuck it out quite well until a young woman decided to join in on the baiting session. She was about twenty-five, with a doll-like face and the sort of provocative neckline that plunges to below the navel. When she came over to me, practically thrust her ample bosom up my nostrils and then asked innocently if I liked her blouse, it all became too much to bear. The night air seemed to beckon and, turning on my heel, I walked out of the bar with as much dignity as I could muster – and straight into the broom cupboard!

For a moment I simply stood there in the darkness, feeling thoroughly sick. It was difficult to see how I could possibly have mistaken a broom cupboard for the way out, but it had put paid to any ideas I might have had of a dignified exit, especially as I had actually closed the door behind me.

What made things even worse was the fact that it was not the first time I had mistaken a cupboard for an exit. Only a few weeks before, whilst staying temporarily with a detective constable and his wife due to a shortage of lodgings, I had walked into their pantry on my way to report for night duty. Then only the bobby's wife had been present to witness my *faux pas* – and that had been bad enough as she had gone into hysterics – but this time I could not have picked a bigger audience if I had stage-managed the whole thing myself.

I felt like the doomed Christian slave about to enter the Roman arena when I finally pushed the door open and stepped out into the bar once more – to be greeted by cheers, wolf-whistles and the party piece of one wag who sang at the top of his voice: 'If you want to know the way, ask a p'liceman'.

Loss of dignity is a big thing to someone in a position of authority, particularly at twenty when image is the all-important factor, and in those early days I certainly got my fair share of knocks in this respect. Walking into the occasional cupboard was not the worst of them either. That came during a perfectly routine patrol duty.

He stood at around 6' 3" in his dark green wellington boots and battered brown trilby, a mountain of solid muscle bursting out of a mud-stained donkey jacket. Jimmy O'Reilly, as I shall call him, was the sort of thing that happens to most young coppers sooner or later – a walking incident looking for a place to happen – and he happened to me one Saturday evening.

What strange whim had prompted his rubber-shod size elevens to stagger out into the street from the sanctity of the nearby public house was a mystery known only to God and St Patrick, for Jimmy himself was too far gone to know anything about anything.

Yet whatever the reason, his drinking habits had suddenly become *my* business and that was definitely nothing to want. Not that he was doing anything actually criminal. It was just that the spectacle the Irishman presented as he tried to engage a 'no waiting' sign in conversation was causing something of a stir and a small crowd had gathered.

With a lump in my throat, I advanced to within a few inches of him and coughed discreetly. Abruptly Jimmy's conversation with himself ceased and a pair of bleary eyes focused on me with great difficulty. 'You're drunk,' I said in my most authoritative voice, 'and if you don't move along, you'll be arrested.'

To my astonishment the ruined face split into an enormous good-natured grin and a paw fashioned like a mechanical grapple took my arm in a vice-like grip. 'Right-oh, superintendent, I'm arrested,' he announced happily. 'Take me away.'

For a moment I tried pulling myself free, but it was useless and only made my predicament more obvious. Choking on my humiliation, I was forced quite literally to go along with his ridiculous charade as he set off along the Broadway in the direction of the police station at an unsteady shambling gait, leaving the crowd tittering in our wake.

This was it, I thought, the ultimate humiliation. I could already picture the laughing faces of my colleagues at the nick when Jimmy rolled up with yours truly in tow. But I was in for another surprise. Only yards from our apparent objective, the hold on my arm relaxed and Jimmy turned off down a narrow side street, doffing his hat as he went. 'G'night, superintendent,' he called as his huge shape disappeared into the now gathering dusk. 'See you again.'

'Not if I can help it,' I muttered, rubbing the circulation back into my arm.

As it transpired, however, Jimmy O'Reilly was to cross my path – or more accurately, lie across it – time and time again. Before long it got to the stage when I inwardly cringed if I caught sight of a large object lying on the pavement or a grass verge, waiting for it to stagger upright with the words: 'Hi there, superintendent.'

Yet for all his size, Jimmy was never violent towards the police. He was simply a big affable nuisance and on the last occasion I saw him he did me a service I will always remember. I had made a point one evening at a telephone kiosk outside the local café where all the young tearaways seemed to congregate. It was not long before the mickey-taking started, but I ignored it until someone made a grab for my helmet. I caught the youth by the collar and in seconds I was surrounded by a whole bunch of youngsters just looking for trouble. Things were beginning to look ugly when an enormous figure appeared in the midst of the crowd, scattering it in all directions, and a voice boomed out cheerily: 'Hi there, superintendent, d'ye want a wee bit of a hand?'

CHAPTER 3

PEPPERMINTS AND STIFFS

'Peppermints, lad,' my sergeant said gravely. 'That's what you need, lots of peppermints.'

His sidekick, a senior constable named Phil, nodded in solemn agreement. 'Take away the smell,' he added helpfully.

I shuddered. Until that morning I had never even seen a dead body before and the prospect of attending a post mortem did not exactly fill me with relish.

'All part of the training, lad,' the sergeant declared, his rear end scorching on the fireguard, while he rolled a Woodbine. 'Why, I remember...'

I grabbed my helmet in hasty retreat as the lurid reminiscences started. Even the rain outside was infinitely preferable to the morbid discussion now taking place in the police station general office.

It is funny really, but at twenty years of age you don't really think about death. It is something you hear or read about that happens to other people; an unpleasant event that never actually touches you personally. When you are suddenly faced with the stark reality of the thing, it comes as quite a shock and, as a police officer, you have to face up to this kind of reality all too often.

I was on early turn that morning, which meant up at 4.30am in order to get to work by 6.45, and I hadn't had time for any breakfast. The call came from a local doctor who was not prepared to issue the usual death certificate as he hadn't seen the deceased for some months. Phil took me round with him. 'You might as well deal with a sudden death now as later,' he said with a grin. 'All good experience.' I was to get used to that last phrase after a while. It always seemed to precede a rotten job.

The old man had died peacefully in his sleep, but it was creepy in the small stuffy bedroom with the curtains still drawn. I remember the oppressive silence, broken only by the ticking of the bedside clock and the soft sobbing of the little old lady downstairs. We made her a cup of tea later and got a neighbour to sit with her while Phil, in a quiet soothing voice I would never have dreamed he possessed, asked one or two questions 'just for the record'. Somehow it seemed so callous and yet it had to be done. I could hardly wait for the undertaker's battered wagon to arrive, but when it did, I felt like a heel walking out the door and leaving the old lady helpless and alone. Jim smiled grimly. 'You'll get used to it,' he growled. 'All part of the job.'

The post mortem was set for 3.00pm on the Thursday. The sergeant, who was on a day turn, drove me over in the police van, probably to make sure I got there. The building was a grim brick place in the grounds of a local hospital, discreetly hidden by gloomy cypress trees. I remember cramming almost half a packet of mints in my mouth as I followed the sergeant through the door. I suppose I must have resembled some unfortunate wretch suffering from a double abscess and the pathologist regarded me with icy amusement over the top of his spectacles.

My gaze took in the tiled floor, the Belfast sink in one corner and the huge refrigerators at the far end, then riveted on the object covered by a sheet lying on the table in the centre. 'Come on, lad,' the sergeant muttered, pushing me forward. 'Mustn't let the side down.'

I was to learn that letting the side down was one of the biggest sins a copper could commit. Aside from the more obvious commission of a criminal offence, it also included the display of any perfectly ordinary human emotion, such as anger, sorrow or revulsion that spoiled the carefully projected image of absolute integrity and physical and mental toughness that had made the British bobby the envy of the world.

I suppose the examination lasted about half an hour, but to me it seemed more like a whole afternoon. By the end of it the pathologist had managed to remove and dissect practically every essential organ that there was, commenting as he went on the condition of such unmentionables as arteries, liver and heart and insisting that we took a closer look at some 'interesting feature'. The advice to invest in a packet of peppermints turned out to be sound enough – their sharp sting did much to impair my sense of smell – but unfortunately when the supply in my mouth finally dissolved, I found to my horror that replenishment was virtually impossible without first removing my trousers.

Police uniform at that time was vastly superior to the average civilian suit in that it was equipped with a large number of useful pockets, some visible, some hidden. One of these pockets was located within the right trouser leg and was designed to accommodate the fourteen inch long wooden truncheon, which today has been replaced by the much more formidable telescopic baton holstered externally. On the occasion of my post mortem debut I had left my truncheon behind and my packet of mints now reposed at the bottom of this pocket, just above the right knee. The aperture was not wide enough to allow the insertion of my hand. I could therefore do nothing except try to pull up the pocket lining with two fingers in the hope of recovering the peppermints. But it was a long tedious job and it created an utterly false impression as to what my hand was doing in my trousers. The rather quizzical expression on the face of the pathologist and the sergeant's hastily whispered 'Leave yourself alone' finally convinced me that my antics were causing some degree of consternation and I reluctantly withdrew my hand.

Without the peppermints, I had to content myself with shallow breathing, fixing my eyes on a point two to three inches above the sink unit on the far side of the mortuary. The look on my face must have struck a chord of sympathy in the pathologist, however, for in the midst of his grisly dissections he suggested in his best sepulchral voice that 'the young man should get some air'.

I should have felt relieved, but I didn't. Instead, I was utterly ashamed of myself. I had certainly let the side down on this occasion, I thought. I was surprised therefore when the sergeant followed me outside with a grin on his battered face and clapped me heartily on the shoulder. 'Wasn't so bad, David, was it?' he commented. 'You wait until you get a real messy one.'

In fact, that experience was not long in coming and it didn't actually happen during duty time, but when I was on my day off. I got the telephone call from my sergeant, ordering me to report for duty, just as I was about to go out shopping and his tone was grim. There had evidently been a serious rail crash and all available emergency service units were converging on a section of the railway line about a mile from Didcot railway station. Even as I changed, I could hear the sirens blasting from all points of the compass.

Initially I felt very excited. My first major incident. I could hardly wait to get there. But when I arrived it was a totally different story. The accident had happened not far from a narrow road bridge. Two carriages lay on their sides and another two were tilted over at an acute angle. The whole track was littered with wreckage and personal belongings. The injured had already been taken away by a fleet of ambulances, but there were still plenty of people about – police officers, firemen, labourers from Didcot power station who had helped with the rescue and, of course, the ubiquitous newspaper journalists eager for a story.

Death was here too and one of the labourers pointed out the object on the side of the track as I arrived. With other officers, I went over to the body, pulling on rubber gloves as I went. Like a man in a daze, I bent down and helped load the dismembered remains of what had once been a pretty girl on to a stretcher someone had brought up. It was a filthy business, made a lot worse by the spectators cramming the road bridge, and when we had finished and were carting the pieces away, I stared up at the bridge in a cold fury.

Following that day, I attended many major tragedies of all types and I grew accustomed to the army of ghouls that materialised in a remarkably short time just to have a look – like the so-called 'rubberneckers' on our motorways who cause mayhem when they slow up alongside accidents to try to catch a glimpse of some gore or the souvenir hunters who, given the opportunity, will actually take belongings or bits of wreckage from the scenes of some fatal accidents. But on this occasion it shook me to see those savours of horror cashing in on the hideous misfortune that had befallen innocent people. I suppose it takes all types to make a world and I was rapidly learning about some of them.

I learned a lot in my first two years about death too. It is a strange fact that in the police service every bobby seems to get more than his fair share of one particular type of incident. There's the lucky officer who is always in the right place at the right time and collars the criminals. Then there's the not so lucky one who gets lumbered with every traffic accident that comes along or who is for ever being sent to family or neighbour disputes. For my part, I got what my colleagues colloquially called the 'stiffs'.

Whether death was from natural causes or the result of crime, accident or suicide – by fire, drowning, tablet overdose or gas poisoning – yours truly usually ended up with it. Sunday seemed to be the worst day. Elderly people were always passing away on the Sabbath, often after a heavy lunch, and even where death was from natural causes, the police had a responsibility to attend if the doctor was unwilling to issue a death certificate. Attending involved a lot more than just viewing the body too. Clothing and personal effects had to be removed and safeguarded, the corpse accompanied to the mortuary with the undertaker and properly identified, with a label tied to a toe, and on occasions where it was necessary, actually washed down before being placed in the refrigerator to await the obligatory post mortem. Through some obscure and quite unsavoury arrangement, the officer dealing with the incident received ten shillings from the coroner's office at Abingdon if the corpse was in a reasonable state or a pound if it was a messy one. I shall always remember one officer who had a habit of volunteering to deal with any sudden deaths that occurred – even when he was off duty – so that he could claim the fee. That might in itself sound pretty mercenary, but when you think that a bobby at that time earned in the region of ten pounds a week while people in minor clerical or manual positions were earning three and four pounds on top of that, the temptation to try and make just that little bit extra was understandable.

As far as I was concerned, my colleague was very welcome to any sudden deaths that came my way *and* the money that went with them, for it was probably this aspect of policing that I detested the most. The best I could do was to cultivate a sort of detached approach and above all never get emotionally involved in the situations in which I found myself. Phil once advised that the only way to stop the job getting on top of you was to laugh at it. 'If you don't,' he growled, 'you'll end up going round the bend.'

It is perhaps true to say that after a few years as a police officer, you do get hardened to the more gruesome side of life and even develop an unusual sense of humour, which some people would call warped. As a result, you tend to see the funny side of things in all sorts of unfunny situations. Death is no exception and the circumstances of a particular event can sometimes lend a kind of black humour to the business that makes it much easier to cope with.

The death of an unfortunate Irish labourer from the power station was one such a case. Staggering home after a mammoth drinking session in the local pubs, he decided to take a short cut along the railway track and was pulverised by an express train. When his remains were taken to the mortuary and placed on the slab, it was noted with some mirth that he had an eye tattooed on each buttock. During the subsequent post mortem the pathologist – who was not known for his sense of humour – was heard to remark dryly: 'They obviously didn't help him to see the train coming!'

The local railway line provided the police pathologists with quite a number of mutilated corpses during my time at Didcot, either due to accident or suicide, and even if you escaped the trauma of dealing with the actual incident, you could sometimes find yourself involved in the aftermath. Recovery of a victim's 'parts' was not always achieved in one go; bits could easily be missed and one afternoon, on a visit to the railway station for the customary cuppa, I was just congratulating myself on my good fortune that the accidental death of a railway worker the previous day had not occurred during my shift, when I was approached by one of the staff to say that part of a severed leg had been found in the middle of the track and would I collect it.

Equipped with just a cardboard box, I clambered down on to the line from the platform under the gaze of a dozen curious passengers and followed the railwayman to the spot. Picking the gruesome object up was not easy as it was surprisingly weighty, but I accomplished the task in the end, carrying it back along the platform in my cardboard box to the waiting police van so that it could be whisked away to the mortuary to be married up with the rest of the corpse. Not the nicest of jobs, but there again, as one of my cynical colleagues pointed out to me afterwards: 'If you can't stand a joke, you shouldn't have joined!'

Dealing with death is never pleasant, but there are occasions when the circumstances of the business – like the time and place it occurs – can accentuate the horror of the situation – and one grisly suicide I attended was very much in that category. I had been sent to deal with the death of a local farmer who had blasted himself with a shotgun, plastering most of his brains over the walls and roof of a farmyard barn. It was late in the evening and after the usual investigation, I found myself alone in the dark outbuilding with just a corpse for company. To make matters worse, the hearse was late and a storm was brewing. The scene was perfect for a *Hammer House of Horror* film production, but I was in no mood to appreciate the artistic merits of the situation. When the undertaker did arrive in his battered Daimler, the storm finally broke.

We headed through the blackest night I had ever seen at a record rate of knots, rain lashing against the windscreen and forked lightning chasing our tail. Our route to the mortuary lay over a series of humpbacked bridges and we were in the process of negotiating the second of these when a pair of headlights blazed in our faces and we ground to a halt only inches from a Mini car, which had belted over the bridge from the opposite direction. Confronted by such an austere sight as a great black hearse, the Mini edged back out of the way. I shall always remember the horrified white faces in that little car as we crawled past and the undertaker's solemn voice calling to them through his open window: 'Do you want *me*?'

CHAPTER 4

COFFEE AND COLLARS

For most police officers, arresting criminals (or 'feeling collars', to use the service vernacular) will always be the number one priority on their list of things to do, regardless of what weird and wonderful policies, rules and targets are imposed on them by those in high places. In this respect, although modern criminals tend to operate as much during the day now as they do at night, when I stepped out on to the street for the very first time the hours of darkness were seen as the period during which the villain was at his most active. Nights were therefore regarded as the best shift for feeling a collar or two if the eyes and ears were kept open.

I felt a tremendous sense of excitement pounding the empty streets after dark with only the echoes of my footsteps and the distant screech of a train whistle for company, but to be honest I was also scared half to death. It was all right for the first part of the shift when the sergeant was about and usually one of the lads as well, working a 6pm to 2am shift, but thereafter the night man was more often than not on his own and that meant the new boy as well.

The first part of every night tour was spent shaking door handles (checking the fronts and backs of shops and factories), with a ten minute point somewhere at 11pm. Then it was back to the station for a quick cuppa at midnight before doing the rounds again by torch and cycle light.

Whether it was because I was new or simply that it happened to be on his way home I don't know, but the sergeant usually met me at my 1am point if he finished duty about that time. Then, with a cheery wave, he would become a slowly receding red tail-light, leaving me alone, listening to the faint hum of the telephone kiosk and the fading clank of his chain-guard.

Certain property always gave me the jitters. One such a place was a small tobacconists near the railway line. It was often getting broken into and you never knew quite what to expect when you went there. On one particular night, whilst carrying out a routine check on the premises, I got a very nasty shock. It was bitterly cold and there was a low wind abroad as I forced myself down to the railway line at about 3am and parked my bicycle against the rotten wooden fence. I heard the suspicious sound the moment I shone my torch on the windows and abruptly stiffened. It came from the back of the place, so I drew my truncheon and crept round to have a look, pausing as a train thundered past, shaking the wooden building to its foundations.

With the fading of the express, I heard the sound again – a definite thud – but on reaching the back of the shop, I found there was nothing there. I ventured a short distance into some scrub, my torch flashing wildly everywhere, then suddenly froze. Something had reached out of the darkness behind me and tapped me firmly on the shoulder.

My eyes must have resembled miniature golf balls as I turned very slowly. There was something there all right – a wooden beam that had obviously once formed part of another building extending horizontally towards me. As I stood there feeling downright stupid, another gust of wind caught the beam and slammed it back against the building with a familiar thud.

False alarms are plentiful at night, to such an extent that patrol duties for the young inexperienced bobby are a constant boost to the old adrenalin. It is easy to laugh after the event, but in the darkness of an empty street sounds can become so distorted that it is difficult for a new recruit to decide exactly what it is he or she can hear.

The groan of a garage sign, the rattle of a letterbox caught in a draught, the whirr of the town clock as it reaches the hour or the blood-curdling cry of a marauding cat – anything can sound sinister when the street lights have gone out. Each town has its own peculiar variety of noises too and it takes an experienced bobby to know the difference between the common and the not so common. Even someone with a lot of service can get caught out on occasions and I know of one senior constable who spent a substantial part of his night shift searching an industrial estate for a suspect prowler, only to discover in the end that the author of the furtive noises he had heard was nothing more than a foraging hedgehog.

Despite the high incidence of false alarms, however, most bobbies will get lucky sooner or later and a criminal break-in one night after a week of total boredom provided me with just the stimulus I needed.

I was on duty with a slightly more senior constable named Graham at the time and we were alerted by a telephone alarm to the police station switchboard. The voice of the recording machine at the other end told us that one of the site offices at the power station had received an unauthorised visitor. We didn't bother with bicycles, but scrambled into the station's A55 van and headed for the site with Graham driving at breakneck speed.

There was someone in the place all right, or at least there had been, but as we parked up and approached the darkened building on foot, I saw that we had an unusual problem on our hands. The intruder had opened every single window he could find as a sort of escape insurance, which meant that if we went in one side he would simply nip smartly out the other.

There was little we could do until assistance arrived, so we called up for a police dog on the van's VHF radio and sat tight at opposite ends of the building, watching for the slightest movement. But even that was not a hundred per cent effective. There were still blind spots and we could not cover them all at the same time. What we needed was an edge and we got that when Graham came up with his idea. Maybe if the intruder thought there already *was* a police dog on hand he would obligingly stay put until one actually did arrive – assuming, of course, that he had not sprinted away across the fields long ago.

It was worth a try and so for the next fifteen minutes the pair of us stomped about in the darkness, issuing a succession of stern commands punctuated by our best dog impressions. We got pretty good at it too, but it was a bit tough on the larynx and we were relieved when we saw the lights of the dog van bumping along the unmade track towards us.

The particular brute that headquarters had sent us – and I mean the dog, not the handler – was not actually the barking kind. He excelled in another way – as we found out when we finally decided to search the building following the arrival of another mobile. We got in through one of the windows and beyond we found a long passageway with doors opening off on both sides, all of which proved to be unlocked – all, that is, bar one.

It took us quite a few minutes to break that door in and when we did we found a tiny room containing just a desk and a cupboard. But there was no intruder. Then we noticed something else. The fanlight in the ceiling was wide open. It was only natural that we should assume our man had escaped across the roof. After all, that was what he had intended us to think. But smart as he was, he had reckoned without an even smarter Alsatian. As we turned quickly for the door, shouting a warning to our other recently arrived colleague who was keeping watch outside, the dog poked its nose in the kneehole of the desk and came out with a leg that had a man on the end of it.

There was no fight in the intruder after that and he spent the rest of the night in a cell at the police station, cursing clever animals and counting the teeth marks in his calf.

Burglaries are always a major problem for the police, especially in the larger towns and cities, and some of them really do take the biscuit for sheer barefaced effrontery. In one cheeky incident the crime was not discovered until the early hours of the morning and I was on duty in the station enquiry office at Didcot when the irate householder telephoned. 'Send someone immediately,' he snapped. 'I've been done.' I was perfectly all right until he gave his name and address and then I simply curled up – which was hardly surprising under the circumstances, for the complainant was one of our own CID officers.

There are actually few places that a determined thief will not risk having a go at if he thinks the pickings are worthwhile, for risk is all part of the game as far as he is concerned. Sometimes, however, he can come badly unstuck. This happened to a villain who decided to break into a factory warehouse not far from Didcot's railway station. His entry was via a roof skylight, but he triggered a burglar alarm seconds before he slipped and plunged over thirty feet to the solid concrete floor. Luckily for him, the fall was not a fatal one, but he didn't exactly bounce. When we arrived and began a cautious search of the premises, we became aware of someone feebly whistling. We followed the sound and discovered one very uncomfortable burglar with smashed legs, waiting to be taken to hospital.

The effectiveness of the police in their fight against crime does not depend solely on a beat officer's vigilance or speed of response, of course. Sometimes follow-up action through a laborious process of investigation and evidence gathering has to be taken well after a crime has actually been committed and this can require not only focus, tenacity and attention to the most minute detail, but also unlimited patience from the team involved.

Patience is a particular requirement where observation duty is concerned. Like surveillance, which usually involves shadowing specific criminal targets, 'Obo', as most coppers liked to call it then, is a waiting game demanding patience, self-discipline and a phenomenal capacity for strong coffee. It is possible to spend hours, days – even weeks – on the same job, maybe concealed in a draughty shed or parked up in an unmarked car, watching and listening. Frequently there is nothing to show for it at the end except red-rimmed eyes, a dose of 'flu and a total aversion to coffee.

My first experience of an observation duty was rather like being buried alive. The man-made tunnel in which I crouched stretched away on either side as far as my straining eyes could see, lit at regular intervals by naked bulbs, which marked the intersections. 'Don't move from here to have a look around,' the sergeant had warned, 'or you'll lose yourself.' But he need not have worried. I nursed no secret desire whatsoever to explore this nightmare labyrinth under Didcot power station; I fully intended staying put. But it was an unnerving experience waiting in that semi-darkness, listening to the regular dripping of moisture from the roof of the tunnel and the occasional scurrying of a rat, especially as I had no means of communication with the world above.

The job had seemed simple enough at the start, but that was before the others had left. Alone, the task was enough to make an experienced copper have second thoughts and I was not by any stretch of the imagination an experienced copper. Sometimes I felt that my enthusiasm outstripped my common sense. Fancy actually volunteering to spend several hours buried under tons of earth and concrete in one of the tunnels through which the massive pipes carrying water to the power station cooling towers would eventually run. I must have been mad. I recalled yet again the advice that had been given to me by Rowdy all that time ago at the police training centre: 'The mouth is designed for breathing and eating. At all other times it should be kept shut.' I couldn't help thinking how right he was.

I stared at the low wall enclosing the mouth of the shaft. They said it was part of a natural well and that they hadn't been able to locate the bottom. Whether that was true or just something said to scare me witless was irrelevant, for it nevertheless gave me the shivers just to think about it. Yet that gaping hole held the bait that was expected to trap a thief. The contractors on the power station site above were always losing equipment – it was an occupational hazard – but this time one item, an expensive industrial drill, had turned up hidden on a ledge inside the shaft. In theory, all we had to do

– or rather, all *I* had to do – was wait until the villain returned to retrieve his ill-gotten gains and then pounce. Dramatic stuff.

The problem was how to accomplish the job on my own. I had no illusions about the sort of criminal I would have to tackle. He would almost certainly be a tough labouring type not given to bowing graciously with the words: 'It's a fair cop, gov.' I would have a fight on my hands and that thought left me with a definite feeling of unease.

An hour passed in silence. I was well wrapped up, but even so I was beginning to feel the cold. Cramp had set in too and what made it worse, any sort of movement was risky as the slightest sound magnified itself a hundred times in the form of an echo along the tunnel. So I kept my crouched position and tried to forget the discomfort. After another hour had dragged by, however, I decided enough was enough and I was on the point of risking all by stretching my legs when I heard the sound of approaching footsteps. I froze, pressing myself into a narrow recess behind me. This was it; my man was coming.

The footsteps grew louder and louder, and a grotesque shadow mushroomed up over the curved walls and roof of the tunnel, looking a bit like *Frankenstein's monster*. My heart seemed to be hammering against my ribcage as I tensed my body and waited for the footsteps to pause by the shaft. At the crucial moment I was actually about to launch myself on to the back of the shadowy figure when the man turned towards me and I caught the glint of a tin badge, stopping me dead in my tracks. 'And what did you think you were going to do with that, eh?' my sergeant commented dryly, eying the stick in my hand. 'Pick your nose?' Somehow I hadn't the nerve to say.

We never did catch the villain that time. The inspector had got cold feet about leaving me down there on my own; too risky, he'd reckoned. Knowing what I know now, I suspect his decision also had something to do with the resource implications, for there was no telling when – if at all – the person responsible for stealing the drill would return to pick it up. So we simply packed it in and I returned to normal patrol duties. Pity really, but at least the stolen property had been recovered, even if I had not managed to cover myself in glory with the arrest of the century.

Observations don't always end in failure though. Sometimes they actually pay off and just that odd success makes up for all the other non-events. The saga of the 'knicker snatcher' was like that.

As I have already said, it takes all types to make a world and, like the indecency merchant or so-called 'flasher', the purloiner of female underwear is perhaps one of the more peculiar varieties. He gets his kicks out of raiding washing lines after dark and making off with whatever exotic lingerie he can lay his hands on. What he does with the stuff afterwards does not bear thinking about, but he can become quite a headache in a small community.

The character who inflicted himself on a Didcot housing estate made himself a real nuisance in this respect and panties and other items of female underwear began disappearing after dark at such an alarming rate that it was decided to set a trap for him before the entire female population of the town was rendered knickerless. As a result, one evening I found myself installed in a small prefabricated garage, eyes glued to a heavily laden washing line through the small side window, waiting for the offender to show his hand.

I must admit that I was not over optimistic about the job.

After all, it was a million to one chance that he would select this particular house on this particular night and I reckoned I had about as much chance of catching him as avoiding a dose of the piles from the concrete floor. But I was wrong on both counts; first, because I didn't end up with piles and second, because the offender did put in an appearance.

It happened without a single preliminary warning. No footsteps on the gravel path, no heavy breathing – just a violent jerk on the line that set all the frilly garments dancing merrily. I realised with a sense of shock that the fish had actually taken a bite. The thief was in the process of disappearing down a nearby footpath when I burst from the garage and I must have broken all records in the chase that followed. I did feel his collar in the end, but only after a mini marathon, which left me exhausted at the finishing post and only able to croak 'You're nicked' as I pulled a pair of panties from his coat pocket and waved them triumphantly aloft.

The offender admitted a lot of other similar offences later on and when the bedroom at his home was searched, a whole drawer full of ladies underwear was discovered, indicating that he had committed far more crimes than had actually been reported. For me this was a revelation in itself, but what I found even more astonishing was the fact that our villain of the peace was not some kinky misfit in a dirty raincoat, but a fresh-faced young lad who was just fourteen years old!

The surprise element is ever present in police work and a rookie bobby quickly learns always to expect the unexpected. This is particularly true of night duty and it pays to keep your wits about you.

Between two and four in the morning life tends to be at its lowest ebb and the patrolling bobby can get to the stage where keeping the eyes open becomes a real physical effort.

On such occasions things can assume an unreal almost surreal quality – and nothing could have seemed more surreal to a certain colleague of mine than the situation he faced one particular night.

Over halfway through his shift and looking forward to the end of a long tour of duty, he was on his way to make a point outside the post office in Didcot's Broadway when he came face to face with a horrible apparition that had suddenly emerged from the gloom in front of him – an apparition that looked remarkably like a cow.

In fact, it wasn't *a* cow, but several cows – all of which had just embarked on a walk-about from a farm on the outskirts of town – and it was at this point that the whole lot decided to combine in unholy chorus.

It was time to take steps – preferably great big ones in the opposite direction before the choral evensong awakened half of Didcot – but for all his faults, our intrepid bobby was no quitter; he had a more novel idea. I was sitting in the police station enquiry office when the herd went past. Racing to the window, I had this vision of a score of frantic cattle disappearing into the darkness towards the village of East Hagbourne and there at the back was a uniformed bobby on a bicycle, waving his truncheon in the air and shouting 'Yip...yip...yip!'

CHAPTER 5

MAYHEM AND MURDER

A six foot high hedge was the cause of the trouble and when I arrived on the scene the argument between the two neighbours was already well advanced. In fact, the pensioners were squaring up to each other like a couple of adolescents and even the sight of my uniform did not immediately have any effect.

The hedge separated the back gardens of the two semi-detached houses and had apparently been a source of aggravation for some time, with one neighbour wanting the top pruned because he said it cut out his light and the other determined to ensure it was left untouched.

It wasn't until I threatened both of them with arrest for conduct likely to cause a breach of the peace that sanity returned and they both backed down, but it was touch and go for a while and no one was more relieved than myself when they agreed to settle their differences through their respective solicitors first thing in the morning. It would have proven a bit difficult running them in when the only transport I had to hand was my bicycle.

Attending disagreements between neighbours is a pretty routine job for the beat bobby and, like my hedge incident, they can erupt over the most simple irritations. Noise is an increasingly common complaint, usually in the summer months when windows have to be thrown open at night and someone decides to hold a party in their back garden – complete with loud music and drunken revellers. Then there are the complaints about youngsters skateboarding or playing football in the street, cars parked outside other people's houses – even dogs barking incessantly.

In such situations tempers can easily become frayed and the most sensible law-abiding people will soon resort to violence if something isn't done to cool things down. But arguments between neighbours usually pale into insignificance when compared to disputes within the family home, for then the police have very limited powers and their intervention pleases nobody.

The aptly named domestic usually starts off as an innocuous family argument, but it can soon degenerate into a vicious free-for-all where literally anything goes. Ironically, as with sudden deaths, the Sabbath is always a good day for domestics, maybe because that is the one day in the week when the potential warring factions in the house are together long enough to have a go at each other.

A typical incident gets underway when the so-called head of the house staggers home from his local halfway through the afternoon, with empty pockets and double vision – only to find a cremated lunch and a female version of Attila the Hun waiting for him. A pitched battle follows and the ubiquitous frightened neighbour rushes to the telephone to dial 999.

Inevitably, the police attend to restore order, but in such cases the officers are in a dodgy position. One wrong word in the right place can have the same effect as a lighted match being dropped into a petrol tank. Neither party really welcomes their intervention and at first they are merely tolerated as possible allies. Then, when it becomes apparent that they are determined to remain impartial, they are regarded as interfering busybodies and end up under fire from both sides. A cool head and an abundance of tact and diplomacy are therefore vital in such situations if peace is to be restored – In the words of Rudyard Kipling: 'If you can keep your head when all about you are losing theirs and blaming it on you…, you'll be a man, my son.'[*]

This kind of philosophy is all right in theory, but it is very difficult trying to keep your head when someone is doing their level best to qualify you for admission to the local hospital's intensive care unit. You never stop learning either – no matter how much service you have under your belt – and this fact was brought home to me rather forcibly at another station a few years later when I was sent to a so-called routine domestic with another officer, called Alan, and we found ourselves in the middle of a virtual war zone.

The inebriated husband had shown his disapproval of his wife by reducing the interior of their caravan to debris, but he hadn't got away with it unscathed and when he appeared in the doorway with his head covered in blood and the unmistakable imprint of a steak hammer in the middle of his forehead, he was not in a listening mood. Alan and I had attended the incident with the intention of restoring the peace by the employment of tact, patience and understanding – the three key qualities that the police training school had assured us would defuse even the most tricky situation. Instead, we finished up in a violent bloody struggle with a madman who was arrested only when he was too exhausted to fight anymore.

_____

[*] 'If' by Rudyard Kipling, first published in 'Brother Square Toes' 1910

There was an almost comic twist to the incident too. When the offender appeared in court and was fined for his misbehaviour, far from bearing any malice towards the police, he left the dock, crossed the room to where I was sitting and grabbed my hand in a vice-like grip. Then, to my acute embarrassment, he grinned from ear to ear and in a loud voice declared: 'That was a bloody good scrap, wasn't it?' I shudder to think what the crowded court must have thought of that one.

Fortunately, on the plus side, no one was seriously injured as a result of that violent fracas, but not all domestics end like that – as I discovered to my cost one night just months into my probation.

I had met up with my colleague, Phil, on a local factory estate not that far from Didcot power station when we were alerted by the sound of a disturbance coming from the direction of the main road. Mounting our bicycles, we went to investigate and found two distressed women – a mother and her daughter – on a front doorstep. It turned out that the younger woman had walked out on her partner after relationship problems and sought refuge with her mother. But her other half had found her and had only just left after a blazing row.

Both women were very frightened that the daughter's partner would return and cause more trouble, so before resuming our patrol, we spent some time reassuring them that we would give an eye to the house throughout the night, just in case. This we did, but nothing else happened, so we went off duty, confident that the incident was just another domestic tiff that would probably resolve itself through the courts in due course.

In fact, court action did follow later, but it was as a result of something a lot more serious than a matrimonial dispute, for the man who had caused all the trouble subsequently returned to the scene and carried out a frenzied attack on both women with a long-bladed knife. He was later arrested, but that was of no benefit to his partner who died as a result of her injuries – becoming just another tragic statistic in the police crime book.

That poor woman's death came as a terrific shock to me and at the time I remember feeling I had personally failed her in some way, despite the fact that I had not been on duty when the fatal stabbing had occurred. Sadly, however, only someone blessed with the gift of hindsight could have foreseen that a simple domestic like this would have such a horrific outcome.

In a lot of domestics it is the children who suffer most when mum and dad fall out – making an already bad situation even worse – and, like most police officers, I still retain some particularly unpleasant memories in this respect. You often saw the youngsters when you first entered the house, crouched under a table or behind a chair; little waifs with pinched white faces and big frightened eyes. Your heart went out to them, but you simply could not allow yourself to get personally involved. In fact, in the absence of any evidence of a criminal offence, the only real action you could take in those early days was to have a word with social services afterwards, warning them about the problem and desperately hoping that someone would do something about it before a more serious incident occurred.

Even the whole raft of legislation and child protection practices that have been introduced in the last few years to safeguard children, have in no way become a panacea for the prevention of child abuse and the tragic litany of horrific cases, including those of Victoria Climbié in February 2000, Alisha Allen in January 2007 and Baby P in August 2007, provide a grim illustration of this.

There *are*, of course, occasions when children may be physically removed to a place of safety by police if they are seen as in need of immediate care and protection, but this is a sensitive issue and not quite as easy as it sounds and I shall never forget the day I took this action myself in what I regarded as a clear case of neglect and ended up in some very hot water.

Ironically, it didn't happen during my formative years at Didcot, but much later in my service when I should have been a lot more wary. I had been sent to a house on the edge of a busy industrial estate after a call from a worried neighbour to say that two small children had been left in the house on their own by their parents so they could go out socialising. I found two tots – one about eighteen months old and the other about three – sitting on the living room floor with two large dogs for company. The dogs were passive enough, but the carpet was covered in their excrement. In addition, the electricity had been cut off, the room was cold and the children were dressed in just T shirts and nappies. I didn't hesitate, but grabbed both of them and took them back to the police station where they were given a wash and a solid dinner of fish and chips in the police canteen while social services were alerted. The youngsters were sitting watching the television when their parents turned up at the station and to say they were unhappy would be an under-statement. To my astonishment, I was accused of kidnapping the children and instead of being supported by those above me, I received a stern rebuke from the chief inspector who advised me that I had no power to take the children from the house and should have left the matter for social services to deal with. As for the children, they were returned to their parents, leaving me struggling to come to terms with the fact that I had been dubbed the villain of the peace for doing what was morally right.

As a police officer, you quickly learn that there can be a vast divide between morality and the law. When you are dealing with any kind of domestic issue it is as well to tread very warily indeed and not to allow your own personal feelings to get in the way of things. So when you crunch your way up the hallway through the broken crockery and patiently try to make the grown-ups see sense (resisting the temptation to bang their heads together instead), you make an effort to ignore the children in the background. When peace is finally restored, however, you leave the house with a feeling of angry frustration. From bitter experience you know that this new reconciliation is only a fragile, temporary thing. The couple will be at each other's throats again before too long. The trouble is, there is absolutely nothing you can do about it. Your part in the affair is officially over and the sergeant will have warned you enough times already not to get personally involved. That is all very well, but he hasn't suggested how you should erase the memory of those kids' haunted white faces from your mind.

Still, time is allegedly a great healer and after a few years of domestics, sudden deaths and fatal accidents, there are so many tragic faces jostling for a place in your memory that it is almost impossible to remember a single one clearly. In fact, you tend to develop a protective shell after a while – an invisible suit of armour – which grows on you whether you want it to or not. Like a chrysalis, the hard armoured exterior conceals a soft inside.

Phil, my unofficial mentor at Didcot, had perhaps the thickest suit of armour going, but then his years of service had given him plenty of time to cultivate it. He was apt to shelter behind a perfect mask of indifference. Only once did I see that mask slip and then it was such a momentary thing that if I had blinked, I would have missed it altogether. The cause was not some horrific incident or major tragedy either, but something quite simple and it had me laughing for a long time afterwards.

I was on night duty with him again and had returned from patrol around midnight for the customary cuppa to find Phil standing as usual with his back to the open fire, apparently quite oblivious to the significant scorching smell that pervaded the little office. I had never known him to actually burst into flames, but he had come close to it on occasions and on this particular night a certain telephone call must have only narrowly averted disaster.

'Kettle's on, David,' he announced in the manner of one who had just climbed Everest. I scowled, for I had never known him to make the tea either, just drink it.

Tossing my helmet on to the table, I headed for the kitchen. The telephone buzzer went as I was filling the pot and I returned to the office with two steaming mugs to find Phil already donning his uniform cape. 'You can forget that, lad,' he growled. 'We've got a domestic round on the caravan site.' Sticking his pipe in his mouth with an air of finality, he headed for the door. 'Fit then?'

We shut up shop and cycled off into a black moonless night. There was the smell of rain about and a biting wind cut straight through my raincoat as if it were made of cardboard. I realised now why Phil always favoured his woollen cape on night duty. Maybe it looked old fashioned, but it did the job a lot better than anything else. Next time, I vowed, I would put comfort before appearance.

The caravan site was only a short distance down the road and, predictably, it was dead to the world. There were few lights on and in the absence of the moon I followed the fierce red tail-light of Phil's bicycle as closely as I dared.

We found the caravan easily enough. It was the only one lit up like a Christmas tree. But there was no hint of a disturbance and, as we afterwards learned, there never had been one. Instead, the female tenant had a complaint about prowlers and when she came to the door in answer to Phil's knock I suddenly understood why.

I suppose the lady was about thirty and physically very well-endowed. You couldn't help noticing her endowment either, for she was dressed in just a thin nightdress through which the caravan's interior light blazed scornfully, rendering the material transparent and leaving absolutely nothing to the imagination.

I stood there literally gaping and my normally poker-faced colleague was not entirely unaffected by this vision in nylon either. Out of the corner of my eye I saw that his eyebrows had arched dramatically and his pipe was now clenched tightly between bared teeth. For the first time Phil's suit of armour had developed a crack.

'I didn't bother to dress boys,' the vision explained with a provocative smile. 'I expect you have seen it all before.'

There was a gurgling sucking noise from Phil's pipe and slowly – and with a sort of calm dignity – he withdrew it from his mouth. 'Yes madam,' he said politely and without a trace of further emotion, 'but never in such profusion!'

CHAPTER 6

WHEELS AND WEDDING BELLS

It was certainly no Rolls Royce. The speedometer boasted 60,000 miles, the interior was worn and rust had already begun its insidious erosion of the bodywork. Compared to modern police vehicles, its equipment was pretty basic as well; just a VHF radio on the dashboard and a single blue light on the roof. Nevertheless, that grey stand-up-and-beg Austin A55 van was the pride of the station – it had to be, for apart from a smaller A35 van used by the two resident CID officers, it was the only vehicle Didcot possessed.

Like most new recruits before me, I could hardly wait to get behind the wheel of that A55, but it took almost two years and a stiff police authorisation course, in addition to the standard Ministry driving test, before I was permitted to fulfil my ambition and take to the road. Even then, I only got the opportunity on those very rare occasions when the vehicle was not being used by someone else. As a rule, the job was no more glamorous than taking the odd stray dog to the kennels, picking up a prisoner's meal from the local café or collecting the station's monthly petrol allocation in two gallon cans from the headquarters petrol store and driving back to Didcot with the windows open to avoid being asphyxiated by the fumes – an onerous duty which was abruptly halted when one of my more militant colleagues discovered that it was actually illegal to transport petrol in this way.

But whatever the duty, driving a police vehicle was – and still is – regarded as a serious business and it has often been said that criticising a bobby's method of car control is like questioning their virility. When I first gained my authorisation I was left in no doubt that an accident involving an official vehicle was seen as a smear on the integrity of the force concerned, whether the police driver was to blame or not, and any transgressor would face immediate suspension from driving police vehicles until the case had been thoroughly investigated. In short, a prang was classed as virtually a hanging offence – which was why I thought the world was about to end when I actually suffered a mishap in Didcot's A55 van just days after qualifying at the police driving school.

I had been sent out on to the Blewbury Downs with a Scottish colleague named Sam to search for a seventy year old man who had embarked on a cross-country walk several hours before and had not been seen since. The autumn light was fading and the air was bitterly cold. We were both acutely conscious of the fact that if the elderly man had injured himself and was left to the mercy of approaching night his chances of survival were pretty slim. So we worked quickly, making sweep after sweep of the high undulating country, fingers crossed, but with little real faith in providence.

As it turned out, our missing person was eventually found safe and sound, but not by us. All we found was trouble. The little grassy track had appeared firm enough, despite recent rain. Sam had thought so too, but our combined assessment of the situation proved to be badly flawed. After only a few yards we became hopelessly bogged down and all my efforts to free the back wheels met with failure. Finally, Sam, in his infinite wisdom (or lack of it), suggested we tried reverse. That was the biggest mistake of all. I did manage to reverse out of the mud all right, but then slithered across the track diagonally and into the recently ploughed field.

I felt sick to the stomach when I clambered out of the driving seat, for the van was straddling the edge of the track with the offside wheels on the grass verge and the nearside wheels buried in the field. I could see what was going to happen like a vision in slow motion. As the vehicle's nearside wheels sank deeper and deeper, it would eventually tilt at such a severe angle that it would overturn completely and there seemed nothing the pair of us could do to prevent the disaster either.

Then, to cap it all, we got a call on our radio to say that the superintendent was on his way out and would meet us at a given location only yards from the point where the track joined the main road. Sam burst into a roar of laughter. Nothing seemed to bother him. 'It's no your day, David, is it?' he said. 'I'm glad I was'na driving.'

I closed my eyes tightly, praying for divine deliverance. The superintendent, of all people. The inspector would have been bad enough, but to a rookie constable the superintendent was only one step removed from God Himself. I could well imagine his reaction when he saw what had become of one of his divisional vehicles. Talk about fire and brimstone... At which point, the van gave a weary groan and settled further into the mud, bringing the front offside wheels up off the grass track altogether.

'D'ye want to commit hara-kiri afore he comes?' Sam suggested helpfully. 'There's an auld screwdriver in the back.' I glared at him. Very funny, I thought, but before I could think of a suitable reply he set off along the track towards a distant farm, shouting about getting some help as he went. After fifteen minutes he was back, followed by the most wonderful sight in the world – a great big tractor.

The farmer was a typical country character with a ready grin and an arsenal of caustic comments. Right now his grin practically split his face in half and the funnies just kept on coming. But I didn't care. At least we now had a chance and my humiliation was a small price to pay for salvation.

With the aid of a strong chain our deliverer in dungarees did the job in record time too, towing us back to the main road itself. We made our rendezvous comfortably and parked the van with its nearside as close as possible to the adjacent hedge so that the mud smothering the wheels and lower wings remained hidden from view. The superintendent didn't even notice, but the state of the vehicle did not escape the eagle eye of the sergeant when we returned to Didcot. He nearly had a fit. 'Where the hell have you been in that?' he exclaimed. 'Across a ploughed field?' Sam smirked behind his back, but I felt it best to say nothing.

I wasn't the only one who had problems with police vehicles though. The sergeant himself was inclined to be somewhat accident-prone, though in a rather more unconventional way, and he had one classic mishap that gained him notoriety overnight and put my little *faux pas* well and truly in the shade.

It was the practice at that time to take the police station fire extinguisher to the local fire station at regular intervals to have it checked out. On one fateful morning the skipper decided to do the job himself, mainly because he knew that there was always the odd drop of ale to be had at the fire station club.

He got the job done all right and headed back to the police station in the A55 van, but halfway home things went seriously awry. Unfortunately he had evidently hung the fire extinguisher on a hook in the back of the vehicle and suddenly the string holding it in place snapped. As ill-luck would have it, the thing bounced on the floor and the firing button struck a projection with considerable force.

Of course, the sergeant stopped the vehicle at once and tried his best to shut the extinguisher off, but it is no easy task grappling with a heavy pressurised cylinder that is leaping about like a live thing in the close confines of an Austin van, pumping foam in all directions. Suffice to say that when the van eventually kangarooed into the police station yard and he staggered out into the light of day, he was most definitely not a pretty sight.

This venerable campaigner seemed permanently fated where vehicles were concerned too, sometimes through no fault of his own either. One incident occurred actually in the precincts of the police station yard.

It was fairly common practice in those days for local bobbies fortunate enough to own their own cars to use the garage and the concrete apron in front of it to clean and service their vehicles when they were off duty, provided the inspector was not around when they did it. On the day in question one of my colleagues had taken advantage of the garage inspection pit to carry out some essential repairs to his car while the inspector was out on a run with our sergeant in the station's A55 van.

The young constable made sure he was long gone by the time they returned, but he was in such a hurry to finish his repairs and get away without being spotted that he neglected to leave things entirely as he had found them – and that was a big mistake. When the inspector and sergeant returned to the station and parked the van nose first in the open side of the garage, there was nothing to suggest that anything was wrong and assuming the inspector was right behind him, the skipper ambled into the police station via the back door with a beaming smile and an imperious call for me to 'put the kettle on'. But his smile quickly disappeared when the back door suddenly crashed open after him and a dishevelled oily figure staggered into the front office, his face set into a malevolent mask. For a second the inspector just stood there glaring at us, one hand clutching his knee and the other trying to wipe his face with a large handkerchief. 'Right,' he said in a carefully controlled voice, 'what I want to know is the name of the clown who left the woods off the inspection pit?'

Owning your own vehicle is something that is taken for granted by most bobbies today, but in the mid sixties it was actually not that common, especially for probationary constables who could barely afford to buy a bicycle let alone a motor car. My weekly salary rarely exceeded ten pounds and although, like most of my colleagues, I worked quite a bit of overtime, payment for the excess hours was not an option. Instead, reimbursement was usually through some weird and wonderful arrangement called EDP (or Extra Duty Performed). This meant being given time off in lieu of the hours worked, provided there was sufficient shift coverage on the day it was requested – which was usually never. As a result, you often ended up being told when you could take the hours owed and if your sergeant was not in a particularly good mood that could be the day after you had finished a week's night duty, which meant you slept through half of it.

Trying to earn a bit extra to pay for life's little luxuries – like a beaten up old van, for example – was therefore almost impossible. Generally you could obtain permission to do some fruit picking at the apple orchards of neighbouring Harwell and beating for pheasants was also allowed during the game shooting season, but otherwise moonlighting was strictly forbidden and it could result in dismissal if you were caught.

Forced to wash out any idea of four-wheeled transport, I took a massive risk and signed a hire purchase agreement for a 250cc BSA motor cycle, which was on sale at the local motor cycle dealers for the princely sum of £210. I well remember my euphoria when I passed my driving test first time and roared up outside the police station to check on my duties for the following day.

My moment of glory was short-lived, however. When I stomped into the office in my black leathers, jackboots and red and white crash helmet, I failed to consider the effect my appearance was likely to have on my staid conservative colleagues. Astonishment and disapproval was written all over their faces and although none of the three bobbies present actually made a comment, the sergeant warming his backside in front of the open fire was not so reticent. Studying me for a few moments with cynical amusement, he shook his head slowly. 'You know, lads,' he said, carefully rolling a Woodbine, 'this must be the only nick in the country with its own built-in yobo!'

Though said partially in fun, the message was unmistakable and it brought home to me with even greater force that, as a police officer, you no longer owned your private life. You were expected to comply with set of standards of behaviour – to conform to the long established template of what a police officer *should* be like – and there was no room at all in the organisation for individualists.

Nevertheless, despite my vulnerability as a probationer, I

didn't sell my motor cycle because of the sergeant's remarks – I got rid of the machine to please a much higher authority – my wife!

Her name was Elizabeth and she hailed from Northern Ireland. We actually met for the first time on holiday on the honeymoon island of Guernsey and within fifteen months we had both said 'I do' in a little church just outside Belfast. The date was 9 September 1967 and little did we know that in two short years the province would be trembling on the brink of civil war.

The lads at Didcot affectionately nicknamed Elizabeth 'Spud', because of the almost legendary love of the Irish for potatoes, and her cooking immediately won them over – not that they could get away from it, for the rent-free house we had been allocated was right next door to the police station.

The smell of homemade scones, fruit cake and apple tart would regularly bring the other bobbies to our back door on some pretext or other and the comment 'that smells good, Elizabeth,' would invariably guarantee them a taste. I didn't mind them having a *taste*, but very often I would return home from my shift to find only the smell was left; my so-called colleagues had devoured the lot.

I have some very happy memories of those days, but there were problems too and the house itself was certainly not ideal. It was an old draughty place with huge, rattling transom windows that did not shut properly and yet refused to be wedged. The drop on the landing window was so colossal that we couldn't afford to curtain it and had to make do with nets pinned to the window frame, one under the other. Going to the loo at night was particularly difficult, because it meant trying to get from one end of the upstairs corridor to the other in our nightclothes without being spotted by anyone in the large caravan site that adjoined our back garden.

There was no central heating either and we had to make do with inadequate coal fires and electric heaters that gobbled up our meagre income a lot quicker than they did the draughts, despite Elizabeth's pay as a wages clerk at a local food wholesalers, which actually bettered my own salary as a bobby by around three pounds a week.

Living right on top of the job had its disadvantages too, mainly because privacy was virtually non-existent. We were one of a terrace of three with the police station in the middle. I only had to open an internal connecting door in my hallway to be at work and our main bedroom was situated over the station's front office. We could hear practically every sound through our floorboards, from the buzz of the mini switchboard to the raucous laughter of some of the lads after a particularly crude joke. This worked two ways as well and to my intense embarrassment my skipper would often claim he could hear our bedsprings twanging at night. 'You newly weds,' he said one day, grinning from ear to ear. 'I don't reckon your bed will stand the pace.' That did it. We moved into our second bedroom the night afterwards.

Yet we did have the last laugh. In an effort to make the bare scuffed floorboards of the upstairs corridor more presentable as we couldn't afford to carpet it, we decided to use a powerful wood stain instead. The acrid smell it created, however, was so strong that we had no option but to open all the windows and desert the house for the rest of the day to give it time to dry. Unfortunately, we didn't take into account the effect it was likely to have on the police station next door and I was greeted with open hostility when I returned to work the following morning. 'Whatever were you doing in there yesterday?' the sergeant said venomously. 'That stink was so bad that I had to eat my sandwiches in the bloody toilet?'

Living next door to an operational police station certainly did not make for domestic bliss and there was a lot more to put up with than hostility from our neighbours. The police station forecourt extended right the way along the front of all three properties and every single caller seemed to park his or her vehicle up against our living room windows. One afternoon, when we wanted to go shopping, we had to leave by the back door, because some clot had blocked the front door with the rear end of a large furniture van and we couldn't get out. There were also the people who mistook our front door for the entrance to the police station and if we forgot to lock it we had all sorts – from lost motorists to drunks – bursting in on us.

Elizabeth had a very nasty experience in this respect too. I was on late turn, manning the station front office when it happened. It was just getting dark and I was waiting for my relief to arrive so that I could go for my meal break when I heard Elizabeth scream. I ran out of the station and found a mentally retarded youngster peering in through the living room windows. Apparently Elizabeth had gone into the room to pull the curtains when she heard someone rattling the front door, which fortunately was locked. She chose to look through the window at the very same moment as this simple lad decided to press his face up against it. He wasn't particularly good-looking at the best of times and, with his face horribly distorted through contact with the glass, he must have presented quite a frightening sight. Already nervous, it took Elizabeth quite a while to get over that experience.

Unexpected callers were not the only aggravation either. On the opposite side of the house to the station was the police garage and yard with all the official comings and goings to put up with at all hours of the day and night. The stray dog kennels and petrol store were situated at the bottom of our small garden and a narrow path leading from the rear door of the police station to the yard ran past our kitchen windows. Elizabeth couldn't even go into the pantry on occasions without having to endure a string of obscenities from certain prisoners who happened to be detained in the single cell opposite.

We were, of course, very grateful to be given free accommodation and as it was our first home together we were happy enough to try and make the best of it until something better came along. But the stresses and strains of living on the job soon took their toll on both of us and we started to feel increasingly as if we were under siege. Within just a few months I began submitting regular applications to the inspector for a move to another vacant police house on the sub-division, but I got nowhere – firstly, because vacant police houses were snapped up by new arrivals almost before the previous tenants had left and secondly, because no one in their right mind wanted to live next door to Didcot nick.

But even as we tried to face up to the dismal prospect of long-term residence at 27A Hagbourne Road, help was on its way. My frequent requests for a move had evidently stirred things up in the headquarters personnel department and as the force teetered on the edge of amalgamation with four other neighbouring forces, a piece of paper was already winging my way to pack me off into the country.

CHAPTER 7

PEDALS AND POACHERS

Job satisfaction counts for a lot in any career and where the police service is concerned, probably one of the most satisfying jobs of all is that of the country bobby.

I got my first taste of the rural life in the May of 1968 – just a month after the Berkshire County Constabulary amalgamated with the forces of Buckinghamshire, Oxfordshire, Oxford City and Reading Borough to form what later became known as Thames Valley Police. The posting to the little Oxfordshire village of Kencot came through whilst Elizabeth and I were on holiday in Cornwall and my inspector dropped me a line to let me know. We could hardly wait to get back to check it out and when we did it took our breath away.

The house, with its own police office, stood alone at the end of the village, a yellow stone place backing on to a sea of rippling corn. Quaint slate-roofed cottages, their walls weathered grey by time, smiled sadly among a blaze of spring flowers and on the other side of the road the parish church thrust above a line of trees at the far end of a sun-dappled meadow. It was all like a sequence from some marvellous dream.

We moved in about a month later and it was then that we discovered the only real drawback to living in Kencot. We were just seconds from the main runway of RAF Brize

Norton with its squadron of VC10 jet aircraft, which regularly screamed over us at almost rooftop height. So low were they that my predecessor had evidently been complimented by a pilot on one occasion regarding the colour of his pyjamas. 'Why,' the astonished bobby is alleged to have exclaimed, 'fancy you being able to see what's on my clothes line from up there.' The pilot is said to have grinned. 'I didn't see them on your clothes line, Jim,' he retorted. 'They were on your bed!'

Like the locals, we soon learned to live with the noise of the jets and when our first daughter Caroline was born twelve months later, she managed to sleep through the racket without so much as a twitch. The effect on the unwary visitor could be quite dramatic, however, and when Elizabeth's parents first came to stay with us for a holiday, I neglected to pass on a warning about the aircraft to her nervous mother – with dramatic results.

We were all sitting down to tea one evening, staring out of the French windows across the field at the back of the house, when a pair of blazing headlamps appeared in the sky, rising above a line of trees on the far side, which bordered the aerodrome. It was a ghostly sight, for at first there was no sound at all, just those two great yellow eyes lifting silently into the heavens. For a moment or two we simply sat there as if mesmerised. Then quite suddenly there came the customary thunderclap that shook the house to its very foundations, followed by the shriek of jets as the aircraft seemed to level out and head straight for the house. As I knew from past experience, the plane was still climbing, but even so, I realised that this was going to be an exceptionally low take-off and I braced myself accordingly.

I had not considered the probable effect on my mother-in-law though. She was already suffering from bad nerves and the colossal din, coupled with the sight of those giant headlights, was just too much for her. As her cup and saucer went one way, she went the other in a wild dive for the door and I am quite sure that if we had not gone after her, she would not have stopped running until she had reached the next village.

Aircraft noise was a small price to pay for independence though and I had plenty of that all right – mile after mile of it. No one interfered with the way I managed my beat and supervision was kept to a minimum. I rarely saw my sergeant who was based at neighbouring Burford and when he did pay me a call, it was more of a courtesy visit than anything else. In fact, I patrolled my 'manor' entirely at will, even arranging my own hours of duty myself within certain limits, most of the time working four hours in the morning and four in the evening.

Because of the discretion factor, some of my fellow police officers working the urban areas on tightly organised shifts believed that the job of a country bobby was a cushy number, but nothing could have been further from the truth.

On top of this, I discovered that, as far as my parishioners were concerned, I was never off duty, but available at any time. I often had found property handed in or driving documents produced for inspection on behalf of another station when I was digging my garden or doing some decorating, and on one occasion I even dealt with a road accident as Elizabeth and I were about to leave the house to go on holiday.

As the wife of 'the constable', Elizabeth had her own unofficial unpaid duties to carry out too and she soon found that a great deal was expected of her. Our telephone and doorbell rarely stopped ringing some days and when I was out Elizabeth often ended up with writer's cramp as she took down the messages that came in. If a job sounded urgent she would give me a ring on one of my telephone kiosk points, but when I could not be contacted at all she had to use her own common sense and take some sort of positive action herself. At times this presented her with some very awkward moments.

One of these involved a mentally retarded boy who had been found wandering the streets and was quite literally dumped in her lap. He was a big lad, around twelve years of age, but with a mental age of about five, and he had bitten his fingernails down to the quick so that they were raw and bleeding. I wasn't around, so Elizabeth had to sit with him on her lap, trying to provide him with the right sort of reassurance as she telephoned the police divisional control room for assistance. I don't think she was ever more relieved than when the staff of the hospital from which he had absconded arrived to collect him.

On another occasion she answered a knock on the door at 7am while I was in bed, sleeping off a long night shift, and found herself face to face with a dishevelled couple. To her astonishment, the man confessed to having abducted the young woman at gunpoint as she was driving home from college in her van and said he wanted to give himself up. Elizabeth kept her cool and did the only thing possible under the circumstances – she invited them both into the police office and made them a cup of tea until she could rouse me to deal with the job.

The young man's tale turned out to be true too. The woman had been reported missing a couple of days before and the gun – a starting pistol – was later found in a ditch a mile away. The ironic part about it all was the fact that the kidnapper had only decided to turn himself in because his captive's van had run out of petrol right outside the police house and what he hadn't known at the time was that there was a real firearm belonging to her brother lying under some rugs in the back. Heaven knows what might have happened if he had found it.

Getting around on the Kencot beat proved to be a strenuous task from a patrol point of view, for unlike some rural officers who were issued with a van or a lightweight motor cycle, I was forced to rely on pedal power. This made life very difficult at times, because I had twelve villages and hamlets under my jurisdiction (one of the biggest rural beats in the force) and as these were in some cases miles apart, it was only possible to visit two or three a day at the most, especially if there were official enquiries to be carried out. Traditionally, rural policemen are seen as heavy-set rubicund country boys riding old-fashioned bicycles at a snail's pace, but I was just the opposite and I certainly raised a few eyebrows. I regularly hurtled along the country lanes at such a phenomenal speed that it must have seemed to the locals that my bicycle was fitted with fuel injection. 'Blink once,' they used to say, 'and you'll miss him altogether.'

One particular morning my speed of travel was actually my undoing and I came a proper cropper. It was the practice then for the rural beat officer to book on by telephone with the divisional headquarters at Witney at the start of each tour of duty and to pass over a list of telephone kiosk points he would be making during the course of his tour. These points were usually arranged at two hourly intervals instead of every hour and in a different village each time so that the bobby could cover as much ground as possible during his tour of duty.

On the day in question I had underestimated the time in hand while visiting my parishioners in Broadwell and, glancing at my watch, I suddenly realised that I was going to be late for my Clanfield point if I didn't get a move on. In order to shorten the distance involved, I decided to head across country via a narrow gated road – and that was a real error of judgement.

Much of the route to my destination was uphill, but about two-thirds of the way along the lane the ground fell away in a fairly steep slope, before climbing at an equally steep angle again. I knew from experience that if I could gain enough speed going down, I would be able to reach the top of the hill on the other side without having to resort to pedal power. There was one small problem. Nestling in the dip was a five-barred gate, which was hidden from view until you had actually commenced your descent, but I wasn't unduly worried about it as the gate was always left open and I had no reason to believe today would be any different.

It is amazing how quickly confidence can evaporate and mine died in a frozen lump in my throat when I caught my first glimpse of the gate, for some clot had shut it! I braked of course, but the impact was none the less severe and I left my saddle in truly spectacular fashion, landing a few feet away on the hard rutted track. Though bruised and shaken, it was only my pride that was really hurt that day, but I never did make my Clanfield point and when the chief inspector – who had apparently waited there for a good twenty minutes – asked me for an explanation later on, I hardly said a word.

Unless you are a masochist, patrolling a large beat on a bicycle is not something to be savoured and I lost my liking for pedal power very soon after my posting to Kencot. Struggling along an exposed road, head down into a miniature hurricane in the winter or trying to pedal up a one in ten hill on a scorching summer's day are not experiences that exactly endear you to cycling. I had been used to a bicycle at Didcot, but not all the time and never over such long distances.

It was even worse at night as you couldn't see where you were going unless the moon chose to show and consequently every pothole was a potential disaster area. Luckily I did not do too many night duties, but I was expected to perform one or two here and there just to introduce a little bit of uncertainty into the life of the local criminal.

It was a creepy old number though negotiating those winding country lanes at 2am. In the town you could expect to come across the occasional passer-by. Even if it was only a railwayman going to work or a courting couple heading home after a late night party, the sight and sound of another human being broke up the monotony. In the country, however, there was a sense of total isolation. You got the feeling that the whole world had been stricken down with some kind of fatal plague and you were the only one left alive.

The road from Kencot to the village of Shilton was a particularly lonely ride – a long poorly maintained tarmac strip that snaked its way between dry-stone walls across the undulating countryside and offering very little cover from the elements. There were no houses along its route, only outlying farm buildings and a sizeable refuse tip. You could actually smell that tip from Kencot itself and on warm still days a kind of haze hung over the acres of decomposing rubbish as the refuse wagons churned in and out.

In anybody's language the tip was a blot on the landscape, but at night it took on a distinctly sinister aspect too. Big brown rats infested the place and as they scampered along the tunnels they had created under the mountains of rubbish, the fires that had been lit by the workmen during the day and which had become dormant were re-kindled by the sudden rush of air. The effect was indescribably eerie and enough to give any lone traveller a start on a dark night.

I must admit, however, that during the summer months working nights had one compensation as far as I was concerned. At least the cooler air enabled me to breathe more easily. The trouble was that I suffered from acute hay-fever and when the pollen count was at its highest, the rural life became a real trial for me.

In my condition, accepting a posting to the country was, I suppose, sheer stupidity – almost as bad as someone suffering from vertigo applying for a job as a steeplejack – but there are occasions when you have to try and put up with your own particular problems and carry on as best you can. Nevertheless, there were moments as I pedalled along between tall scented hedgerows – careering about in the road with every sneeze, nose streaming and eyes so inflamed and itching that I wanted quite literally to tear them out – when it did cross my mind that maybe, just maybe, I didn't have all my marbles.

Fortunately the summers were not too long, but the winters at Kencot presented their own peculiar difficulties for patrol work. The wind that whipped across the fields was almost enough to cut you in half some days, stripping trees and hedgerows bare and plucking the slates off the roof of many a cottage with frenzied fingers. When Mother Nature sent rain she really put on a show, turning roads into rivers and flooding great tracts of open country, especially around the isolated village of Kelmscott as the river itself burst its banks.

The area got more than its fair share of snow as well, in

company with the rest of the Cotswolds at that time, and this made patrol work next to impossible. A high wind you can endure, floods you can usually find a way round, but snow is a different matter altogether, particularly when it is piled up in drifts several feet thick, often completely smothering roads to the height of the dry-stone walls.

Our first winter was a very white one indeed and it came as quite a shock when we got up one morning after a night-long blizzard to find ourselves actually snowed in. The most spectacular drift not only blocked our gateway, but rose above it in a long point like the horn of some dinosaur trying to force its way in. I was so amazed that I took a photograph of the thing and later I even went to the trouble of measuring it. The dimensions of that drift may not have been sufficient for a mention in the *Guiness Book of Records*, but at twelve feet long, nine feet wide and five feet high, they were certainly enough for me. I was almost sorry when the snow plough finally managed to get through and began demolishing that beautiful natural work of art.

During very heavy snowfalls there was nothing for it but to abandon the bicycle altogether and resort to shank's pony as a means of travel. I still had a job to do and it was no good sitting indoors waiting for a thaw. At such times the white world had an attractive almost fairytale quality and I was often reminded of the stories of *Hans Christian Anderson* and *The Brothers Grimm* as I crunched my way on foot along the lanes past partially buried cottages and barns.

This romantic impression was obviously not shared by the farmers scouring the bleak countryside for missing livestock or the local doctor called out to a patient several miles away. To them snow meant aggravation and misery; there was nothing romantic about it. The novelty soon wore off for me too. It was an exhausting business plodding from village to village and by the time I got home my legs felt like jelly and my face was chapped raw. The thought of the hot bath and drop of scotch that awaited me was all that kept me going.

But if getting about was a problem, overcoming my own basic ignorance of all things country was even worse. I managed to get into quite a few scrapes through my lack of knowledge, one classic instance being my first encounter with suspected poachers.

The rural bobby can get a lot of aggravation from these characters, but the popular image of a poacher as a rough country yokel dressed in a cap and smock sneaking across moonlit fields with his shotgun or rabbit snares is nothing more than a myth. The modern poacher more often than not hails from suburbia, drives a powerful 4x4 and makes his forays into the country at weekends and in broad daylight, blasting away at anything that moves. A lot of suburban poachers at that time were young thugs operating in gangs and I regularly heard about their unsavoury exploits in the area. For this reason, when on patrol I kept my eyes peeled for strange cars parked on lonely roads and my ears tuned for the crack of a twelve-bore or four-ten.

Late one afternoon, while on my way home after a ten minute point at the village of Clanfield (which I managed to make on time on this occasion), I came across a suspicious looking Ford Cortina parked at a peculiar angle in a gateway. The engine was still warm, but there was no one about, so I decided to have a look around in the immediate vicinity. It was then that I stiffened to the sound of a gunshot, apparently originating from the far side of an adjacent field.

I peered over the hedge and waited patiently. Sure enough there was another sharp crack shortly afterwards. I could see no one, but there was a small wood to one side of the field, so I guessed the character with the gun was among the trees.

Swinging my leg carefully over the gate, I started across the first field, intending to make a rapid diagonal approach. But there was nothing rapid about it, for I immediately sank up to my ankles in juicy mud. It had been raining on and off for several days and the soft recently tilled ground had turned into a morass.

Cursing through clenched teeth, I was therefore reduced to plopping one foot after the other in a sort of frantic shambling lurch towards the wood and in no time at all my boots were brown/grey glutinous blocks that spat mud and slime up both trouser legs and over the hem of my raincoat. My disillusionment was complete when I staggered on to firmer ground on the fringes of the wood just as an almighty bang erupted only yards from where I stood and, peering over the hedge, I closed my eyes in resignation. Some sort of crop – I never did find out what – was growing in the next field and right in the middle of it was a peculiar looking mechanical contraption that exploded at regular intervals with a sound like a gunshot. I had nearly arrested my first bird-scarer.

The trudge back to the main road was not as bad as the outward journey. After all, I was already covered in mud and I reasoned that a bit more would make little difference to my miserable state. But as I climbed back over the gate to where I had left my bicycle, I saw that the Ford Cortina had gone and standing there in the middle of the road was a local farm labourer with a look of utter astonishment on his face. 'Whatever yo' been doin', constable?' he queried at length. Before I could think of a suitable reply that infernal bird-scarer exploded again and a slow grin of understanding spread over the man's weathered features. 'Poacher get away then, did he?'

he chuckled. 'Now fancy that.' With a sinking feeling in the pit of my stomach I suddenly realised that I was destined to become a topic of conversation in the local hostelries for a long time to come. But such is the price of experience.

That was not to be my last humiliation in relation to poaching either. There was an even worse one to come and this was much closer to home.

It happened during the very fortnight that my mother and father-in-law chose to spend with us at Kencot. The old man loved the countryside and he was out one day on what I imagined to be a healthy ramble when there was a thunderous knocking on the police office door. I opened up to admit a very influential and irate local landowner dressed in cloth cap and tweeds. 'Hodges,' he barked, 'you will have to do something about these damned poachers.'

Thinking of my disastrous encounter with the bird-scarer, I smiled ruefully. 'Doing my best, sir,' I said lamely.

'Well, 'tain't good enough,' he snorted. 'Only just finished re-stocking my river with trout and this morning what do I find? Damned tramp in a dirty old raincoat and cap actually fishing in it.'

'I will look into it, sir,' I soothed as I ushered him gently out through the door. 'You can rely on me.'

I watched him climb into his Land Rover and pull away and was on the point of turning to go back into the office when I happened to look back up the lane. At once I cringed in my boots. A familiar figure, dressed in a shabby raincoat and cloth cap, was slowly approaching the house from the direction of Broadwell. It was my father-in-law and he was carrying a fishing rod over one shoulder. 'Hey boy,' he shouted with a cheerful wave, 'there's some great fish in yonder stream!'

CHAPTER 8

CRITTERS AND CHARACTERS

It was a bit like a scene from a satirical remake of that classic Wild West film, *High Noon*. Clanfield's dusty main street was deserted in the heat of the midday sun, but behind the windows of the stone cottages there was timid movement and I could sense the many pairs of eyes fixed on me expectantly.

I felt distinctly uneasy. What was going on? The rush for cover had begun suddenly. One minute there had been the usual bustle of a vibrant rural community going about its everyday business and the next the street had emptied as if by magic. What surprised me even more was the fact that the faces now pressed against the window panes did not exactly reflect the anxiety of a community under threat of some impending calamity; those that I could see wore broad grins of amusement.

It was as I shielded my eyes against the glare of the sun and studied the street in front of me that I caught sight of something at the far end, something that pranced into full view, then stopped dead with legs wide apart and head rigidly held high. I could hardly believe my eyes. The thing was nothing more than a mangy goat. Surely this was not the cause of the mass panic? It was too ridiculous for words.

They say ignorance is bliss and at that precise moment I was blissfully ignorant as to the aggressive nature of the average male goat – especially this particular goat, which was evidently notorious. However, as it turned out, enlightenment was only a few trots away.

The first charge caught me completely unawares and raised the first real doubts in my mind as to my ability to cope with the situation. But I didn't get long to ponder the issue, for after backing off a reasonable distance, the creature went for me again, cannoning into my leg and practically knocking me off balance. This time I managed to get my own back, hitting it up the rear end with the back wheel of my bicycle. But my satisfaction was short-lived as this retaliatory action served only to enrage the animal further. A third charge followed, to be met by another swing from my bicycle, then a fourth and a fifth...

My helmet had slipped forward over one eye and perspiration streamed down my face. I knew that I was fighting a losing battle. The most I could do was to put my bicycle in between myself and my horned adversary as every new charge commenced – each time from a different quarter – and hope that the animal would eventually get bored and trot away. But 'Belligerent Billie' displayed no such inclinations and continued the erosion of my shins with renewed vigour, much to the delight of the locals, some of whom leaned out of their windows with howls of laughter punctuated by one witty shout of 'Olé!'

In the end it began to look as though flight was the only option open to me and I had actually started to retreat towards the sanctuary of a nearby garden gate with as much dignity as I could muster when suddenly help arrived in the form of a grinning youth with a length of cord. Seizing the scraggy ruminant with a kind of practised ease, he led it away as casually as one might lead a dog, leaving me wondering who looked the bigger goat, the animal or me.

Goats were the least of my problems during my time at Kencot, however. As the months went by farm animals became the bane of my life and I seemed to be permanently fated to be on the receiving end of anything that had horns or teeth.

The very first day I visited a particular farm in the hamlet of Grafton, for instance, I fell foul of the resident collie dog. I had set out with the best of intentions to introduce myself and check the farm stock records – an onerous task that was, thankfully taken over by Ministry inspectors some months later. It was a fine sunny day and there was the sweet smell of spring in the air as I cycled along the winding country lanes, totally at peace with the world and quite unaware of what awaited me.

I rode up the short unmade drive, propped my bicycle against the wall of the farmhouse and ducked into the porch. The front door was wide open, but there was no sign of life anywhere, so I announced my arrival with a cheery call and stepped back on to the driveway. I saw the black and white collie curled up in the long grass a few yards away at the same moment, but as he merely yawned and gave me the once over with apparent disinterest I took no notice of him. That was my first mistake. Turning my back was the second.

His teeth caught me on the right ankle the moment I took my eyes off him. But before I could retaliate he had withdrawn to a safer distance and simply sat there watching me with a stupid lopsided grin on his face. Fortunately the wound was not serious, though some skin had been broken and my sock was torn, but inspecting my ankle was my third mistake. This time the collie went for the other leg and after a quick nip retired once again to a point well out of range.

In a sudden fury, I grabbed a large stone from the ground

and hurled it at the empty space where the animal had been crouching, then whirled round instinctively as I caught sight of blurred movement out of the corner of my eye. He missed me that time and vanished back into the long grass, but even as I turned to look for him he was leaving cover on the far side of the undergrowth, coming in for another try.

On this occasion he kept right on past me and disappeared behind the farmhouse, but I wasn't convinced and turned first one way and then another, positive he was sneaking up behind me for a third mouthful. To the farmer who, unbeknown to me, had just at that moment appeared in the doorway, I must have presented a rather extraordinary sight, leaping about in his driveway like someone demented, and his loud cough brought me to an abrupt standstill. As I turned to face him, I could feel the hot flush creeping up my neck. 'Your dog...' I blurted angrily.

He grinned. 'Had you as well, has he?' he queried.

I showed him my ankles. 'Twice,' I snarled.

He nodded sympathetically. 'Had the postman too,' he declared with a chuckle, apparently not in the least bit intimidated by my uniform, 'and the binman.'

I stared at him incredulously. He actually sounded proud of the fact. 'He can't go around biting people,' I exclaimed.

His grin broadened. 'You tell him that,' he retorted without the slightest hint of contrition. 'He thinks he can!'

Hostile animals came in all shapes and sizes at Kencot, but by far my worst experience was with a beast I had never actually considered to be any sort of a threat before. When I first made its acquaintance, however, I came close to suffering a lot more than a nipped ankle. The encounter itself occurred on another farm at Grafton and this time the villain of the peace was nothing more remarkable than a large mud-spattered sow.

Unfortunately, my knowledge of the porcine species did not extend much beyond the breakfast table. Pigs, I had long ago decided, were rather stupid inoffensive creatures that lurked in mud wallows and suffered from acute nasal congestion. That they could be capable of aggression was not something that had ever really occurred to me. It was hardly surprising therefore that when I eventually took it into my head to pay a call on the farm, I was not deterred by the fact that the approach to the house lay along a rutted unfenced track through a huge field liberally scattered with chubby porkers. Again, ignorance was my undoing.

Ordinarily, of course, my appearance would have aroused little interest among the occupants of the field, but spring had been sprung and the big sows had suddenly found themselves with hordes of squealing youngsters. Consequently, they were not only short tempered, but over protective and suspicious of anything that moved.

I was about a third of my way across the field when a lady appeared behind the fence enclosing the house and began waving a long stick furiously in my direction, urging me to 'go back'. At first I was a bit put out by her behaviour; after all, I was only calling to say 'hello'. Then for some reason I happened to glance sideways and my feet froze momentarily on the pedals. Around two-hundredweight of belligerent porker was hurtling towards me like a runaway express train and there was no mistaking its intentions.

I didn't waste much time looking though, but went for the world speed cycling record with a fervour that would have put a professional to shame. Even so, the old sow did manage to get within striking distance and her powerful jaws closed only inches from my left ankle. Then with her hot breath burning a hole in my trouser leg, I headed for the gate of the farmyard at a little under the speed of sound.

The farmer's wife got the gate open just in time and I had barely flashed through before it slammed shut again. I dismounted shakily and did a quick inventory. I wouldn't have been a bit surprised to have found something missing, but with a sense of relief I was able to confirm that all my parts were still there. The sow was still there too, her long snout thrust through the slats of the gate and those little beady eyes fastened on me balefully. 'They's a mite touchy just now,' the lady commented gravely. 'But I did try to warn you.'

A mite touchy, I thought? More likely homicidal. Maybe pigs in this part of the world needed educating that human beings normally ate them, not the other way about. One thing was certain as far as I was concerned. Nothing would induce me to go anywhere near one of them again unless it was cut up into neat little rashers first.

A country bobby is not usually called upon to move as fast as I did that day and one of the nicer things about a rural beat is that community life generally proceeds at a much slower pace than elsewhere. This in turn enables folk to have the time to be themselves and to preserve a quaint kind of individualism. The Kencot beat was no exception. The locals all seemed to be characters of one sort or another and in many cases they were so typical that they might just have been the products of a caricaturist's pen.

The village of Filkins even had its own built-in hobo who wandered the woods and lanes at will, living off the residents' back kitchens. I first came across him about lunchtime one day and it was a meeting to be remembered for all the wrong reasons.

I had only just entered the winding main street on my bicycle when I was brought to an abrupt halt by what can best be described as an approaching cacophony of metallic clankings, accompanied by a raucous voice raised in song. The next instant a bent figure dressed in an old fawn coat and floppy hat, with a sack over one shoulder and an array of pots and pans dangling from his belt, hove into view round a bend and stopped dead a foot or so away. A wrinkled and very red face thrust up towards mine and a pair of bloodshot eyes studied me critically for a few seconds. 'And who might you be?' I said.

But that was as far as I got, for without any warning the old tramp deliberately barged into me, knocking me off my bicycle into the middle of the road. Then he simply trudged off along the road, singing away as if nothing had happened.

He had to come in for that, of course. You can't have people going around knocking unsuspecting policemen off bicycles. But the tramp had the last laugh. When he was collected by a police van and taken to the cells at Witney Police Station, still singing at the top of his voice, quite an army of little friends went with him – the kind that either hop or crawl – and the heat of the police station soon encouraged them to desert their benevolent host for a while to have a look around. To be perfectly frank, I was not the most popular man on the division after that day's work.

Few of the characters I encountered on my travels were actually a source of aggravation. But they were characters nevertheless and almost icons in their own communities – Like old Tom, the village postman from Filkins, who often brought me over a cabbage or two from his allotment on the handlebars of his ancient bicycle, and Harry, one of Broadwell's most ardent churchgoers, who would stand in the pews singing at the top of his voice, despite the fact that he was tone deaf, and who will always be remembered for unwisely chasing a cow off the small bowling green, which resulted in hoof marks in the sacred turf the size of mortar craters. Then there was Bill, the manager of a supermarket in Witney and a local church warden, who lived in a lovely cottage in Kencot itself with his wife Mavis. Like a number of other volunteers on my beat, Bill provided regular unpaid service as a special constable – once actually turning out to direct traffic at a local incident in his tennis whites, wielding his racket – and I shall always remember his indignation when children from a local problem family, who had been shoplifting all over Witney, had the temerity to complain to him that someone had stolen their ill-gotten gains after they had left them outside his shop while they embarked on a shoplifting spree inside!

Another particularly larger than life 'local' was not actually an Oxfordshire man at all, but a well respected 'import' from the north of England, named Joe, who lived with his wife, Elsie, and their two children in the village of Clanfield, and drove the local dustcart. Only about 5'5" in height he was not the type to stand out in a crowd, but that hadn't stopped him from also becoming a special constable. On the physical side he was one of the toughest men I have ever met and he still carried lumps of shrapnel in his body to remind him of his very active army service during the second world war when he had parachuted into enemy territory. Yet there was no aggression in his personality at all and he would do anything for anyone. He had a tremendous sense of humour too. The wide craggy face nearly always wore a cheerful grin and his vibrant personality revealed a truly amazing zest for life and a 'can do' philosophy that enabled him to overcome virtually any obstacle.

One such obstacle was finding suitable uniform for his special constable duties. Joe's muscular build was the root of the problem as only the largest of shirts would fit him. Unfortunately the bigger the collar and chest size, the longer the shirt tail and he ended up with something that looked more like an old-fashioned nightshirt than anything else. According to Elsie, the sight of him wandering round the house clad in his monster shirt looking for his trousers was enough to send an undertaker into hysterics and there was one occasion when he managed just such a walkabout – in the garden of all places.

The incident took place on a cold wet night shortly after he had enjoyed a hot bath and was in the process of getting dressed to go on duty. He had donned his shirt and tie, but before he could get hold of his trousers he was interrupted by a yell from Elsie who had gone into the bathroom after him. 'Here,' he heard her exclaim, 'who's that peeping?'

Joe didn't wait to hear any more, but in his bare feet and with his shirt tail flapping around him, he left the house like a bullet, eager to get to grips with the fiend who had dared to peep at his Elsie in the bath. Two circuits of the bungalow in thick oozing mud convinced him that the intruder had gone and feeling somewhat cheated, he staggered back indoors. 'Hey, Elsie,' he shouted through the bathroom door, 'there's no one out there peeping.'

'No, lad,' came back a trifle impatiently, 'not peeping – *beeping* his horn!'

Despite all the wonderful characters I came across during my time at Kencot, I suppose the one that really typified that idyllic country beat for me though was a retired farmer from Filkins, named Jack. Around ninety years of age when I first met him, with snow white hair and a matching neatly trimmed moustache, Jack was every child's idea of the perfect grandfather – and he carried an ancient timepiece in his waistcoat pocket to prove it. He lived with his unmarried daughter, Laura, in a rambling house full of horse brasses and ticking clocks near the centre of the village, spending most of his time tending his large vegetable garden, which in spite of his age he dug by hand.

I often dropped by the place for a chat and a cuppa both on and off duty, for Jack, though deaf, was in full possession of all his other faculties and the tales he used to tell of his youth were well worth hearing. He was a special favourite with children and when my first daughter, Caroline, was born, she took an immediate liking to him and to the big watch he carried in his pocket. From the beginning the old man had a habit of pressing the timepiece against her ear so that she could hear it ticking and it was perhaps inevitable that an association of ideas should develop in her young mind between Jack and his watch – so much so, that as soon as she learned to talk she christened him affectionately 'Mr Tick Tock'. The name stuck too and when my second daughter, Suzanne, came into the world she followed her sister's example. No matter what anyone chose to call him, so far as these two little citizens were concerned it was 'Tick Tock' and nothing would induce them to change their minds.

Like poor old Joe, Bill and Mavis and most of the other characters I knew, Jack is gone now. He passed away just short of his hundredth birthday – but one of the fondest memories I have of the Kencot beat is that of two little red-haired girls sitting on a garden seat beside a kindly old man, listening to the tick of his ancient pocket watch.

For me Kencot symbolised policing as it was always meant to be – visible, local and personal – but if I was honest, I'd known from the very first day of my posting that it was a concept that was on the way out. Massive change was already in the wind and the flavour of the decade was centralisation. Two short years after force amalgamation Kencot, like so many other stations of its kind, became a casualty of the new police commitment to mechanised response. Almost overnight I exchanged my bicycle for a Morris 1000 Traveller and found myself back on shifts, patrolling not one but several different beats that had been lumped together under the control of the modern police station at nearby Carterton.

The new system made it impossible to provide the local community with the level of service it had been accustomed to for so long and to make matters worse, the police hierarchy was encouraged to regard rural policing as a wasted and hitherto untapped resource, which could be plundered at will whenever shortages occurred in the urban areas or extra personnel were needed to police major events. As a result, many rural beats across the force were frequently left with only minimal coverage when officers were borrowed for other 'more important' things and this led not only to bitter resentment among the local people, but a significant loss of morale among the bobbies themselves who could no longer see any real purpose in the new bits and pieces role they were being required to perform.

I felt very much the same way and though I continued to live in the Kencot police house with my family for a while, it didn't feel the same. I was no longer 'the constable' – master of all I surveyed. Policing had become an anonymous 'fire brigade' service, as the critics of amalgamation had predicted, and I didn't like it one little bit.

In the end I decided that if I too was going to become just a face behind a windscreen, then I might just as well go the whole hog and do a town beat again. Furthermore, having now passed my sergeant's examination after a year of intense study, there was a real need for me to gain more experience if I wanted to advance my future promotion prospects. When the force's deputy chief constable made a plea at a divisional meeting for rural officers to apply for postings to the busier urban areas, which were short of personnel, I slapped in a report and the gods at force headquarters practically bit my hand off. In a matter of weeks I was posted to the other side of the Thames Valley and the bustling Berkshire town of Maidenhead.

CHAPTER 9

CLIPBOARDS AND PANDAS

Despite the fact that I had made myself author of my own destiny, I left Kencot with a heavy heart, feeling a little bit like *Rip Van Winkle* awakening from his enforced snooze. During my sojourn in the country time, it seemed, had passed me by and I arrived in Maidenhead blinking in the sunlight of the new policing era.

I found that the helmeted bobby on a bicycle had been largely supplanted by a so-called unit beat officer in a peaked cap driving a panda car and that the old telephone points system had disappeared altogether. Instead, in addition to the VHF radios with which most marked police vehicles were equipped, all local patrol officers – whether on foot or driving a police car – could now talk to a mini control room in their own police station by means of a radio pack-set. Sophistication had become the order of the day, but this in turn had brought about other more fundamental changes.

The old style discipline with all its military flavour was on the way out. Parading for duty had become a much more informal affair, while the practice of saluting senior officers was rapidly heading for the history books. A less severe image was also being cultivated by the senior ranks. Sergeants had ceased to be the tyrants of my early service (though one or two did try to keep up a token pretence), inspectors were now two a penny and superintendents had at long last lost the divine status attributed to them under the old regime. As for standards of dress, constables were actually permitted to wear light shoes instead of the old-style army boots, could revert to shirtsleeve order in hot weather without waiting for a directive from headquarters and could grow their hair longer than the old short back and sides with which I was so familiar.

The development of sexual equality within the service was rapidly gaining momentum too and the role of women officers was becoming much more on a par with that of their male colleagues – so much so, that in just a few short years I was to see Elizabeth herself joining the special constabulary as a constable and carrying out voluntary unpaid duty in the town when I was off duty and could do the necessary babysitting.

The parochial attitude of the county force had in theory been swept away by amalgamation and we were now – or so we were told – part of a bigger, more efficient organisation. It was certainly true to say we were bigger, but there was a remoteness about it all, a loss of personal contact both inside and outside the job that I didn't much care for. Sadly, the cosy image of the approachable local bobby was over and the replacement article, complete with flat cap, clipboard and snazzy blue and white patrol car, took some getting used to.

After rural Kencot, Maidenhead with its housing estates, factories, supermarkets and traffic jams, was a massive culture shock too and it took both Elizabeth and myself a while to acclimatise ourselves to our new urban life. Elizabeth was especially upset by the move. We had left a beautiful new detached house surrounded by open country for a drab red-brick semi on the edge of a large development known locally as 'the Bomber Estate', because most of the roads were named after aircraft.

What made things worse was the knowledge that I had actually applied for such a posting, which meant that I could hardly complain about it now. But as Elizabeth and I sat in the echoing hallway of our new home waiting for the removal team to arrive with our furniture, I remember glancing at her pale tear-stained face and wondering if I had made the right decision.

One thing was clear anyway, it was too late for regrets now. Whether we liked Maidenhead or not, we would have to get used to the place, for it was likely to be our home for some considerable time to come. So Elizabeth got on with the business of settling in while I buckled down to my new job as a so-called panda driver.

The town was divided up into four panda car areas, each operating continuously over a twenty-four hour period by means of the three shift system (6am–2pm, 2pm–10pm, and 10pm – 6am) I found the work a novel experience and it was nice to be under cover for a change when the rain lashed down. But there were drawbacks to the job too.

The idea of unit beat policing was simply increased police mobility and response. The panda car had never been intended for use as a permanent patrol vehicle. Instead, it was seen as a means of getting from A to B more quickly to enable a wider area to be covered by each individual officer. The bobby was expected to park up as often as possible and to get out and about on foot to meet the public in much the same way as the rural beat officer had done.

The idea may have worked all right in theory, but reality was a completely different thing. Because of the hard sell tactics of the police public relations machine, the ordinary man or woman in the street had been encouraged to expect an immediate police response to each and every telephone call –

and that included the trivial calls as well. To be perfectly honest, even now I wonder whether police mechanisation was a direct response to mounting public demands, as was claimed by some in high places, or whether those demands actually increased, because mechanisation itself led the public to expect much more of the service than could be provided.

Whatever the truth was, it is no exaggeration to say that as a unit beat officer the job could sometimes be an absolute nightmare. You rarely got the chance to park up and walk as you were required to do, let alone chat to the public on your area. You were on the go from the moment you started duty to the moment you handed your car over to your colleague on the following shift. Burglaries, traffic accidents and fights, coupled with domestic disputes, missing person enquiries – even calls from distraught people who had locked themselves out of their homes or cars – kept you always on the move. You were often late for your meal break, sometimes didn't get one at all, and each new incident resulted in book entries and reams and reams of paperwork, which you had little opportunity to complete without incurring overtime.

'I wish I had a nice car to ride around in all day.' 'What took you so long to get here?' 'You want to try working for a living.' The familiar caustic comments came thick and fast from different sections of the community, each complainant so preoccupied with their own problem that they were unable to appreciate the fact that there were others in far greater need of help than themselves.

In return, you simply nodded your head patiently, swallowing the remark that was building on the tip of your tongue, and dealt with each job as calmly as possible – even if your stomach was aching for the cremated dinner you were unlikely to see this side of the rubbish bin and your head was bursting with all the things that had to be done before you could go off duty.

To someone like myself who was new to this type of policing, the work took some digesting and I quickly decided that my number one priority had to be to get to know my area. Local knowledge is of vital importance to every police officer, whether they happen to be driving a patrol car, riding a bicycle or pounding the beat on foot, and I knew from past experience that until I managed to familiarise myself with my patch and its own special problems, I would find it impossible to do my job properly.

As the new boy, I took to carrying a map around with me, which at first I had to consult every time I received a call to go anywhere. This usually kept me out of trouble and I rarely got lost for very long, but on one occasion I forgot to put it in my pocket and I got myself into a very embarrassing situation – ironically on the very housing development where I lived.

The Bomber Estate was a regular problem patch. We had numerous calls to attend domestics and other nuisances in that area. The difficulty from my point of view was that the area was a maze of alleyways leading to the backs of houses and lock-up garages, some of which looked identical, and when one reasonably quiet evening I decided to put the theory of unit beat policing into practice and actually get out and about on foot, I didn't realise what I was letting myself in for.

I parked my panda car in one of several small car parks, locked up and went for a stroll. It was a cold autumn evening and darkness had already fallen. For this reason the streets were almost deserted and I must have walked for close on half an hour without seeing hardly anyone. In the end I decided it was time to get back before I wandered too far from the car. But as I tried to retrace my steps, I found that this was easier said than done. The trouble was, I had not made a note of where I had parked the thing and I had by now made so many right and left turns, crossed and re-crossed so many streets and alleyways, that I hadn't a clue where I was in relation to the vehicle.

Anyway I made a start, heading back along the alleyway I had been following until I came to an intersection. Somehow I couldn't remember whether I needed to turn off here or later, so I took a chance and kept straight on, bearing left at the next intersection instead. Eventually, by a devious route, I found my way out into a brilliantly lit street and there, a few yards up on the same side of the road, was a car park. Breathing a sigh of relief I made my way to the entrance, but then stopped dead. There was no sign of the panda car. My heart was racing and I had broken out in a cold sweat. Either this was the wrong car park or (perish the thought) the car had been stolen.

At this point my personal radio crackled and the lad in the control room detailed me to attend a job on the other side of town. Frantically I raced back along the alleyway I had just left and took the first intersection I came to. It brought me out behind some houses, but there was no sign of a car park there. I tried another alleyway with the same result. By now I was panic-stricken. How on earth was I going to explain to my sergeant that I had lost my panda car? I would be hung out to dry.

For nearly twenty minutes I searched that estate practically from end to end, but every car park I checked looked the same (probably was) and there was no sign whatsoever of any police vehicle. I suspected that it must after all have been stolen and was probably on its way to Slough or somewhere with a couple of tearaways on board. I was on the point of calling in on the radio to tell control what had happened when they somewhat testily called me, querying why I had not yet attended the commitment I had been given and advising me that the complainant had telephoned the station a second time to chase things up. I closed my eyes in resignation and started to answer, intending to reveal all, when the alleyway I was following suddenly ended in a car park and there, tucked away in the far corner, I spotted one blue and white panda car. Somehow life was worth living again.

One of the advantages of the new unit beat policing system was the team spirit it engendered among those on the ground. Whenever you were on patrol there was always a colleague in another panda car on a neighbouring beat who could be called upon to provide assistance if required. Backing up fellow officers or being backed up by them was a pretty common practice too and when I first started at Maidenhead I have to say that knowing support was always available gave me a lot of reassurance. Nevertheless, I saw it as rather ironic that just a few months before, when police resources had been so limited, a single bobby on a bicycle would have been expected to deal with incidents that, since centralisation and the explosion of technology within the service, suddenly required the attendance of at least a couple of patrol cars.

At first sight the new policing system seemed hard to justify, especially as it often resulted in overkill with more units being sent to some incidents than was strictly necessary, but on the other hand, the increased resources and speed of response it provided meant that patrol officers had a definite edge when it came to feeling collars.

This was demonstrated one afternoon during a late turn (2pm – 10pm) duty when I was detailed to attend an automatic alarm at premises in the town centre with back-up provided by the sergeant and another unit. We were all some distance from the scene when the radio call came through, but even so, we managed to get there in record time and while my colleague in the other panda car positioned himself at the front of the place, the sergeant and I raced round the back. At once we discovered that one of the downstairs windows was wide open and, pausing to listen for a moment, we heard stealthy noises coming from inside the building. We were on the point of scrambling through the window when there was a loud thud and the offender practically dropped into our arms from a skylight above a small square hallway inside.

I don't know who was more surprised, him or us, but he was pretty gutted. The alarm system guarding the building incorporated a built-in delay to audible activation to give the police sufficient time to attend before the bell went off. This meant that although the break-in had registered with police control, the bell itself had not been triggered and it only actually screamed into life after we had made our arrest. Our burglar had been wandering round the building completely oblivious to the fact that his entry had been detected and the police were already racing to the scene. He really had to be one of the unluckiest villains around that day.

Crime calls were not the only commitments where speed of response paid dividends, however, and a fire I attended with another colleague on a local housing estate was one such a situation.

It had been a case of everyone for themselves when the tea towel left near the cooker caught fire and as the kitchen of the small council semi filled with smoke, the first thing in the minds of the residents was to get out as quickly as possible. By the time we arrived on the scene – to find that no one had actually thought to telephone the fire service – smoke was already billowing through the open front door and a small knot of spectators had gathered outside. Radioing for the fire service to be called, we turned to the distraught tenants for more information, only to learn that, incredibly, one of their children was unaccounted for and had probably been left behind in the kitchen.

There was no time to pontificate. With handkerchiefs over our mouths the pair of us managed to crawl through the smoke to the partially blazing kitchen at the back of the house and haul the terrified youngster to safety, but it wasn't an experience I would want to repeat. Apart from the hazard presented by the smoke, polystyrene type tiles attached to the ceiling had begun to disintegrate with the heat, turning into a gooey substance that was dripping everywhere and would have caused nasty burns had it come in contact with the skin. Luckily no one was injured as a result of the incident and, once called, the fire service were on the scene to put out the fire within minutes. But acute discomfort from smoke inhalation was an inevitable consequence for a while and I never did entirely rid my uniform of that bonfire-like odour.

Without a doubt our ability to respond so quickly to the fire call that day had prevented a real tragedy from hitting the headlines afterwards, but for me the key message that came out of that particular incident was the importance of radio communications. All the much publicised potential for rapid response would have been of no value whatsoever, but for that first emergency call from Maidenhead control. The whole policing operation was therefore totally dependent on the quality of our radio communication system and if that system went down, everything would be thrown into chaos.

That is exactly what happened one memorable evening,

shortly after a major power cut blacked out the whole of Maidenhead and the entire police personal radio system with it.

I was parked up in a lay-by near the river bridge, making some notes in my pocket book, when the lights went out. It was really weird sitting there in the darkness without hearing the comforting voice of the control room operator on the pack-set allocating commitments as they came in and I felt strangely isolated – a feeling I had not experienced since leaving Kencot. Maybe, like the rest of my colleagues, I was already becoming dependent on an electronic lifeline.

I saw the bus pull up on the other side of the road, but took little notice until the conductor got out and appeared at the window of my car. 'I've got trouble on board,' he said. 'Can you come please?'

He had trouble all right, in the shape of a six foot yobo who was refusing to pay his fare. Inwardly I groaned. I certainly managed to pick them, didn't I? The character stood in the gangway, gripping the vertical handrail and obstinately refusing to get off the bus. He had two mates with him as well, but they didn't really want to know and seemed to have remained with him only out of a sense of loyalty. The bus itself was packed and it struck me as faintly amusing the way all those passengers just sat there silently staring out of their windows into total blackness, trying hard to pretend they were somewhere else. I would get no help from them, that was for sure.

I tried to reason with the man first, but it was a waste of time. He just stood there defying me to try and move him. In the end I realised I would have to do exactly that. I took hold of his arm, but he simply laughed and held on to the rail more tightly. 'Well, copper?' he sneered. 'Go on, shift me if you can.'

I felt my temper start to rise, but controlled myself with

an effort. 'Aren't you going to get him off my bus?' the conductor broke in impatiently. I gritted my teeth. Yet another character who thought I was *Superman*.

'Look, mate,' I said to the problem passenger. 'If you don't leave the bus you will be arrested, so be sensible.'

He shrugged. 'Okay, then arrest me.'

So he had called my bluff and I knew there was nothing I could do about it. Alone, it is next to impossible to shift someone in this sort of situation and resorting to a more physical approach, such as the use of my rather pathetic fourteen inch long truncheon to break his grip, was out of the question.

I stared around the bus. The passengers, many of them able-bodied young men, would not look at me, but stirred uneasily in their seats. As for the bus crew, both were getting on in years and obviously not too keen on having a go. The conductor fidgeted nervously in the background while the driver stood in the road by the doors undecided. Who could blame them really? No one in their right mind wants a good hiding if they can avoid it and if all three of us tried to remove the troublemaker by force, a fracas was certain to develop, probably with the yobo's two friends joining in. Anyway, having got him off the bus, what would I do next? I couldn't take all three youths down the station single-handed.

'Well, copper? Lose your bottle?' The subject of my deliberations was off again. He was obviously really enjoying this; it was the highlight of his miserable existence. Then I happened to glance down and saw the personal radio still clipped to my tunic. An idea suddenly occurred to me. So the thing didn't work at the moment, but the yobo was not to know that, was he?

'Have it your own way,' I said tersely and spoke quickly into the dead transmitter, requesting immediate assistance.

The trick worked one hundred percent. The bus driver saw the move from the doors and came on to the platform, the conductor stepped closer and 'Mr Big' started to look around him for the first time a little uncertainly.

'Come on, Bill,' one of his friends said and tapped him on the arm. 'We don't want no trouble with the law.' Bill still looked undecided, but his two sidekicks led him off the bus all the same. Suddenly he wasn't so brave anymore.

Neither was I when I finally stepped down into the street, for the bus driver returned to his cab and the big double-decker pulled away with a shuddering whine, leaving me on the kerbside with three discomforted reprobates for company. Bill now got nasty. 'I could fix you easy,' he said close to my face. 'I ain't scared of the uniform.' His two mates tried to pull him away, but he shook them off. Any second, I thought, he would blow completely.

'Maybe you could,' I retorted, trying to keep my voice level. 'But then you would end up in the nick for a pretty long time.'

'Leave it, Bill,' one of his friends exclaimed. 'The other coppers will be here in a minute.'

For a moment it was touch and go. Then the headlights of a car with an illuminated roof sign appeared from the direction of the town centre. That settled it and Bill allowed himself to be hauled away, still yelling abuse over his shoulder. He need not have worried though, for the approaching vehicle was not a police car at all. I have to admit though, I have never been more pleased to see a taxi before.

CHAPTER 10

STOP-CHECKS AND BROWNIE POINTS

Police officers are constantly faced with criticism from the public that they spend far too much time chasing 'innocent' motorists instead of catching criminals. What the critics conveniently overlook, however, is that the police have a road safety enforcement role as well as one of trying to prevent and detect crime. Ironically, a surprising number of motorists pulled over by patrols turn out to be anything but innocent and it is not uncommon for a bobby following up a relatively minor traffic infringement to stumble upon something a lot more serious.

I found myself in this situation early one morning at about 4am, very soon after my customary visit to an isolated petrol filling station on the outskirts of Maidenhead. The garage itself was a regular port of call for patrolling officers at night, firstly, because it was a twenty-four hour station and therefore vulnerable to robbery and secondly, because the bobby could always count on a cup of tea from the attendant, who welcomed any company he could get during his long night duty.

I had actually finished my tea and was in the process of leaving when the solo motor cycle went past. There were two youths on the machine and it was not displaying a rear light. That made it my business.

I pulled the motor cycle over about a mile further on and

went up to the pair with the intention of giving them a lecture on road safety. As I did so, my hand came in contact with the petrol tank and I noticed at once that it was tacky, as if recently painted. Curious, I examined the rest of the machine and found it to be in the same condition.

'Doing it up,' the youth on the front grunted in explanation, but I saw the quick glance he exchanged with his pillion passenger and my suspicions were instantly aroused. I was even more suspicious when I took a look at the rear number plate, for it was very much a do-it-yourself job. A quick vehicle check over the radio produced the final confirmation I wanted – the index number was bogus.

The magic words 'I am arresting you' were greeted with howls of protest from both youths, but it did them no good and with the arrival of the big police van, they and their motor cycle were quickly whisked away to Maidenhead Police Station.

Enquiries later revealed that the motor cycle had actually been stolen several days earlier and concealed in a lock-up garage while it was given a new identity. But the temptation to go for a spin had proved too much to resist and it was ironic that in the end the joyriders had found themselves in custody all because of a defective rear light.

As with my motor cycle thieves, there is an element of luck in most successful stop-checks, but intuition can play an important part too and many a good arrest has been made by a bobby acting on nothing more definite than a hunch. It is the law of averages, of course, that some hunches will turn out to be unfounded, but every one is worth following up and once that nagging gut feeling has been aroused, it is very unwise to assume anything – I did a few days later and came close to making a very career limiting mistake.

I was cruising along the main A4 Bath Road, which cut the town in two, when I saw the small dark man in the floral patterned trousers ambling along on the other side of the road. Something about him and the way he threw me a swift sidelong glance as I passed slowly by aroused my suspicions, so I turned round at a suitable opportunity and drew up beside him. 'Just a routine check, mate,' I said pleasantly and asked him the usual questions. What was his name and date of birth? Where did he live? Where was he going? Where had he just come from?

I expected some sort of hostile reaction from him, since from past experience I knew that a lot of people tended to object to being stopped and were prone to start screaming 'harassment' and 'police state' when it happened. To my surprise, however, this individual did not object at all, but told me everything I wanted to know without any hesitation whatsoever. As a result, I let him go on his way, concluding that such a nice cooperative character could never be a member of the criminal fraternity – which just goes to show how dangerous it is to accept anyone at face value.

I had turned the car round again and was in the process of driving away when I was struck by a nagging doubt. Whether it was some sort of sixth sense I don't know, but suddenly I felt that my obliging little man was not all he seemed to be. Snatching up my personal radio transmitter, I passed the details he had given me to the control room and a few minutes later back came the answer. 'Is he still with you?'

I evaded the question. 'Is he known then?' I queried incredulously, for it isn't often that someone with a record provides a passing copper with his proper details.

'Known?' There was a short laugh. 'He is wanted on suspicion of at least four burglaries. You seem to have struck oil, David.'

Struck oil? I felt sick as my eyes flicked to my rear view mirror. The road behind me was empty. My cooperative roadside check had vanished – which was hardly surprising under the circumstances. Now what? My sergeant would crucify me when he found out about this. But what chance did I have of locating the wanted man again? There were dozens of minor streets in the vicinity. He could have gone anywhere. Still, I had to try.

Sticking to the main road, I cruised slowly back towards the town centre, my eyes searching the mouth of every intersection. Nothing. I was about to give up and admit to my *faux pas* when Fate suddenly smiled on me. I caught just a glimpse of a floral patterned trouser leg disappearing through the side door of a garage. With a sigh of relief I spun the wheel and turned into the entranceway.

The door led to a male toilet and my quarry was combing his hair inside when I found him. His eyes met mine in the mirror and he slipped his comb back into his pocket. 'You're wanted for burglary,' I snapped.

He smiled. 'I thought you'd be back,' he replied simply and, preceding me outside, he got into my car without any argument, as if he were nothing more than a hitchhiker accepting a lift into town. When I got back to the station I was congratulated by the inspector on 'a very good arrest' and I hadn't the courage to tell my superior what had really happened. Luckily for me, the man in the floral patterned trousers didn't tell him either, but at the same time I never did find out why he had revealed his true identity when he was stopped and not the first bogus name and address he could think of.

That particular incident taught me a salutary lesson and I never made that sort of mistake again – which was just as well, for I faced a very similar situation just weeks later.

I had been sent to deal with a complaint of illegal parking near the local hospital and I wasn't feeling all that happy about the commitment as it was already 9.30pm and I was supposed to be off duty in half an hour. I drew up outside the house where the complainant lived and then stiffened. About 40 yards away a beaten-up old Bedford van had stopped in the act of pulling out into the road from another side-street. I formed the impression that he had been about to turn towards me, but was uncertain after seeing the police car. What was he up to, I wondered? The Bedford was the sort of vehicle I would have stopped and checked automatically anyway and I felt certain this one was well worth a pull.

I thought quickly. If I showed the least bit of interest he was likely to turn the other way and I would have a chase on my hands. I therefore got out of my car, went to the boot and started unloading some portable 'no waiting' signs. Still the Bedford hesitated, so I began placing the signs out along the kerbside, which should have aroused his suspicions as there were double yellow lines there already. But he didn't tumble to my ruse, for the next moment the Bedford pulled out and turned in my direction.

My heart was racing as I sprang across the road and flagged it down with my torch. There were two gypsies inside, but unusually for a traveller's vehicle, there was nothing at all in the back; it was completely clean. Far from satisfied, I asked the driver what he was doing in the area. He made a face and nodded towards his companion who was holding his right wrist with his other hand and rocking backwards and forwards in the seat. 'Taking him to the hospital, sir,' the driver explained. 'Burned his hand in the fire.' I shone my torch on the passenger and even in the poor light could see that his wrist was badly injured. The hospital was directly opposite so I quickly sent the man on his way to get himself some treatment and concentrated on the driver, asking him for his details. As in the previous case, I got them without any difficulty, but he seemed tense and anxious to get things over and done with as quickly as possible, which only served to heighten my suspicions.

The result of my radio check came back much sooner than I had expected and my stomach lurched when the control room operator issued a standard coded message indicating that she had some confidential information to impart. Instructing my man to remain in his seat, I moved to the rear of the vehicle, secure in the knowledge that the Bedford could not go anywhere anyway as I had already removed the ignition keys.

'Are you single-crewed?' the operator queried after I had informed her that I was out of my stop-check's earshot. When I replied to the affirmative, there was silence for a moment before the voice continued briskly. 'Check subject has a 'v' shaped scar to right shin. If so, could be (LP) who is wanted for numerous burglaries. But exercise extreme caution. Has convictions for serious assault and is known to carry firearms.'

I swallowed hard and my skin prickled unpleasantly. I glanced sideways at the sliding door of the van, but the gypsy was still sitting behind the wheel; I could see his leg sticking out. 'Request back-up,' I advised control, trying to keep my voice steady.

'Negative,' the cold clinical voice replied. 'All units fully committed.'

In the darkness of that deserted street I did some rapid thinking. So I was on my own. It gave me a funny feeling.

Well I was committed now. I would just have to be careful that was all – damned careful.

I reached under my tunic and pulled my truncheon up a couple of inches in the long pocket of my right trouser leg – ready for a quick draw, I thought grimly – then returned to the front of the van.

'Would you mind rolling up your right trouser leg?' I said.

The man did so without a murmur, his dark eyes fixed on my face. I shone my torch on his leg and felt my heart skip a beat. The 'v' shaped scar was clearly visible. 'I am arresting you on suspicion of burglary,' I said, conscious that my own right leg was quivering slightly.

'There must be some mistake, sir,' he said quietly, his eyes studying me with an unwavering intensity.

'No mistake,' I replied. 'Now will you step out of the vehicle please?'

Just for a moment he hesitated and I felt myself tense, waiting for him to produce a weapon of some sort or jump on top of me. But to my astonishment he simply shrugged and, climbing out of the vehicle, ambled past me to the police car, commenting dryly over one shoulder: 'I hope this doesn't take long. I haven't had my dinner yet.'

Actually my man got his dinner a lot quicker than he had anticipated, plus free en suite accommodation courtesy of Maidenhead Police Station. It is most unlikely that he was happy with the services provided, but he was nevertheless made a very welcome guest by my colleagues on CID and subsequently admitted eleven burglaries countrywide. To this day though I still wonder why a professional villain with such a history of violence would choose to throw in the towel the way he had when he could just as easily have driven off, leaving me lying in the gutter in a pool of blood instead.

There is no doubt that the ever present risk of being stopped and checked by police makes the criminal's life that much more difficult – whatever the so-called civil liberties lobby might choose to say – and during my time at Maidenhead planned stop-check operations, involving two or more officers, were set up during the early hours on a regular basis. These produced some very good collars too, but there was also the odd hiccup just to make life that little bit more interesting and one particular operation had a very unexpected and embarrassing outcome.

I had arranged to meet up with another unit beat officer to carry out random stop-checks on vehicles travelling out of Maidenhead on the A4 Bath Road and we had agreed to rendezvous at Maidenhead's Thicket Roundabout just after 1am. This had always proven to be a good time and location for catching villains heading home from a job under cover of darkness and we were reasonably optimistic that we would turn up something in the two hours we had allocated. We managed to do that all right, but what we ended up with certainly didn't earn us any brownie points.

I spotted David's panda car even before I reached the rendezvous point. It was parked in a long lay-by a hundred yards or so on the far side of the roundabout with its lights out. Pulling in behind it, I switched off, expecting my colleague to throw open his door and join me when he spotted me in his rear view mirror. But he failed to appear and it was only then that I realised he was not actually in the vehicle at all. There was no sign of him anywhere else either and I began to feel uneasy as I climbed slowly out of my car to look around, conscious of the door hinges cracking like pistol shots in the still air. I stood there for a moment, listening and studying the lamplit road, but strangely, there was not another sound apart from the ticking of my car's hot engine and the distant murmur of traffic on the M4 motorway.

The main road was deserted – a straight black ribbon glittering with stone chippings under the cold light of the lamp standards as it cut through the Thicket's wooded acres towards Reading. I turned and followed it with my eyes back to the roundabout itself and the point where it joined the then A423 Henley road on one side and the A423 (M) link to the M4 motorway on the other. The roundabout was empty too.

I moved off the pavement on to the grass verge and stared into the woods just below me. The remnants of ancient forest, which made up Maidenhead Thicket, were said to have once been the haunt of the legendary outlaw Robin Hood and infamous highwaymen like Dick Turpin, but in recent times they had become the stomping ground of far more unsavoury criminals and some serious offences had been committed within those leafy acres. If David had decided to poke his nose in there on his own, I thought, he wanted his head examined.

Then suddenly I stiffened, the hairs on the back of my neck doing a good imitation of a hedgehog's spines. From the depths of the woodland had come a hideous spine-chilling wail. I stood perfectly still and listened for movement among the trees. There was none, but the awful cry was repeated once again. Then there was a crashing sound and David appeared from the undergrowth directly in front of me, carrying a flashlight. He obviously *did* need his head examined. 'Hear it?' he queried excitedly, staring back at the trees. 'It's the fourth time too. It seems to be moving from right to left – towards the A423 (M). Could be a vixen of course.'

I shook my head firmly. 'Didn't sound like a vixen to me,' I replied, calling on my rural experience.

'In which case someone could be in serious trouble in there,' he added. 'We had better call for back-up.'

Conscious of previous reports of sexual assaults that had taken place in the same area and nursing lurid thoughts of some unfortunate woman staggering, battered and bleeding through the undergrowth, I went to my car for my flashlight as he got on the radio to Maidenhead control.

Help arrived within minutes in the form of the other two panda cars, plus the chief inspector – a dry old stick with a caustic wit and an irritating habit of tilting his head on one side when he was listening to people. He did it now as David explained the situation.

In fact, my colleague was actually in the midst of his dramatic account of events when abruptly everybody turned round to stare incredulously at the roundabout. An articulated lorry had just appeared off the A423 (M) and was lumbering towards us in the direction of Reading. A familiar enough sight certainly and not one that would ordinarily have attracted the sort of attention it was getting now. But there were obvious reasons for this. The driver of the lorry was no doubt surprised to see so many police cars parked beside the road and had reacted instinctively by applying his brakes. As the speed of the HGV was dramatically reduced to a crawl, a familiar spine-chilling wail was produced from somewhere within the vehicle's braking system...

CHAPTER 11

PRANGS AND PERVERTS

From a career point of view, one of the biggest advantages of policing a busy urban area over that of a rural backwater is the fact that it is a much more high-profile job. This enables individual officers to demonstrate their potential far more effectively to the people who really matter. My move to Maidenhead was initially like that and a string of good (or maybe lucky) arrests gave my reputation a very welcome boost, earning me a nice quota of brownie points.

On top of this, following my earlier success in the sergeant's promotion examination, I sat and passed the qualifying examination to inspector – the last academic obstacle to future promotion. Then, completely out of the blue, a sealed envelope came my way, bearing news that put my name up in lights at force headquarters itself.

A keen freelance writer, I had submitted an entry for the Home Office inspired Queen's Police Gold Medal Essay Competition on the subject of *The Role of Police in the Prosecution of offenders*. It was a heavily subscribed competition, with entries coming from police forces throughout the United Kingdom and the Commonwealth, so I had not expected to get very far with my offering and had forgotten all about it. I was therefore both astonished and delighted to learn that I had actually gained second place in the competition and would receive a nice cash prize and the award of a certificate signed by the Secretary of State. The chief constable was rather pleased too and the letter of congratulation I received from the 'big house' really made my day.

But if I had expected my run of luck to last, I was disappointed. Every bubble bursts eventually and it wasn't long before things took a sudden turn for the worst and I found myself heading for the rocks again.

I was on night duty when I had my prang and the annoying part about it all was that if I had simply gone straight back for my meal break as I had originally intended, it would never have happened in the first place. But the sight of someone creeping furtively across the cinema forecourt in the early hours of the morning aroused my suspicions, so I did a quick about-turn to investigate.

The character in question had disappeared by the time I got there and I was left with no option but to drive slowly round the car park in a circle with my headlights full on, trying to pick him out. A few seconds later I spotted a shadow climbing over one of the perimeter chains that enclosed the acre of tarmac and, slamming the accelerator pedal to the floor, I raced after him. I didn't see the patch of oil or grease in front of me, but I soon found it was there when I braked and just kept on going – straight under the perimeter chain. The chain whipped up over the roof and there was a horrible splintering crash as the blue light cone flew off into the darkness.

I am not normally an abusive person, but as I sat there in the darkness I think I must have covered pretty well every four-letter word in existence. Then I picked up the bits and headed back to the police station, suspecting that I would be walking from now on.

I was right too. Within twenty-four hours of reporting my crunch, or POLAC (police accident) as it is called in the service, I was back on foot patrol while the incident was investigated. It was another in a long list of humiliating career experiences I had suffered in around seven years of police service, for by then I had gained a bit of seniority in the force and the younger members of the station took great delight in pulling my leg about my accident. On top of this, the superintendent refused to accept that the damage had occurred in the manner described in my report. If I had simply told lies and claimed that vandals had smashed the light cone while I was away from the vehicle, he would no doubt have believed me, but he found it impossible to accept that one of his officers had actually managed to skid under a cinema forecourt chain. In telling the truth, I had made a rod for my own back.

The only thing in my favour was the fact that when my sergeant visited the scene with me to carry out his investigation, he fell flat on his face on the forecourt as he was climbing out of the car's front passenger seat. This at least served to add credibility to my story, because I was able to say that even my supervisor had slipped on the offending patch of oil. Both he and I knew this wasn't quite accurate, for he had actually caught his foot in the trailing seat belt – something this particularly accident-prone skipper was always doing – but he wasn't about to admit to anything so stupid and simply went along with my story to save face. Despite his grudging support, however, I knew it would be several weeks before I was allowed behind the wheel of a police car again and that was a bitter pill to swallow.

The trouble was that being relegated to foot patrol in the town centre meant I was presented with far fewer opportunities to maintain my hard-earned arrest record and that was a severe blow to my aspirations for a transfer from uniform to CID, particularly since I had already been recommended for the appropriate selection interview. In an effort to overcome the problem, I paid a visit to the collator (or local intelligence officer) to find out what crime information he had on his files and to see whether any of it could be followed up in the town centre area. Almost immediately I spotted exactly what I was looking for – a note on one of his bulletins to the effect that children making their way home from a local youth club in the evenings were being accosted and propositioned by local perverts loitering in the vicinity of nearby public toilets. Suddenly I knew I was back in business.

The following night I exchanged my uniform for plain-clothes and positioned myself in the shadows between the toilet block and a patch of dense shrubbery. It was a cold clear night and, apart from groups of noisy youngsters heading for the youth club, there were not that many people about. Once an old tramp went by muttering to himself, closely followed by half a dozen leather-jacketed youths who gave me a hostile once-over as they slouched past. But for over an hour nothing untoward occurred and I began to feel I had picked myself a loser this time.

Then quite suddenly I spotted a scruffy Asian man, aged about sixty, walking towards me from the direction of the town centre. I glanced away from him as he entered the toilet and was surprised when he re-emerged within a matter of seconds, waited a moment or two and then went back into the toilet again. Instinctively, I knew that this was one of my offenders. I was proven right too, but in a way I had certainly not envisaged. After making several trips into the toilet and back out again, the man approached me with a big smile on his face and indecently exposed himself, asking if I wanted 'a jig-a-jig'. Stunned for a moment by his directness, I just stared at him, realising that I was actually being propositioned.

There was worse to come though. Before I could recover from the shock, the unpleasant character not only repeated himself, but put his suggestion into practice – indecently assaulting me.

He had to come in for that of course, but the shame of it. Even as I arrested him and radioed for a police car, I wondered how on earth I was going to tell the sergeant what had happened. I had expected to nail someone accosting a passer-by, not end up as the victim myself.

In fact, the sergeant was quite understanding about it – so were all the other officers who crowded into the charge office for a look. 'Hey, Dave,' one chortled, 'who's your little friend?' And a young policewoman winked at me and whispered huskily 'Fancy you not telling us.'

Now bitterly regretting bringing my man in at all, I tried a damage limitation approach, suggesting to the sergeant that we should forget what was after all a very minor indecent assault and just go for the lesser propositioning charge. But he wouldn't hear of it, pointing out that indecent assault on a male person was a very serious offence and had to be pursued – especially as it also meant a nice little red entry (or detection) in the crime complaint book. Then with a wink to my colleagues he added that it was a pity I hadn't allowed the offender to go the whole way with his amorous intentions, as then we would have had better corroborative evidence! Not surprisingly, I didn't find the joke particularly funny under the circumstances, even though everyone else laughed.

My man subsequently appeared in court and was heavily fined for the offence, but I carried on paying the penalty for his arrest for a long time afterwards. Naturally the news spread round the division like a smallpox epidemic and life became a real pain until the novelty of it all wore off. Everyone seemed to want to get in on the act and I was ribbed incessantly – so much so, that on night duty I used to quit the station as soon after briefing as possible to lose myself in the dark streets. The fact that my arrest and the resultant publicity had no doubt deterred other indecency merchants from accosting innocent passers-by was disregarded; I had been indecently assaulted and that was all that interested the wags.

Even the chief inspector who actually prosecuted the case came up to me to take the mickey when I was off duty. I was out shopping with my wife at the time and he spotted me as I left a local supermarket. 'Hello there, Jig-a-jig,' he said with a broad grin and sidled up to me winking suggestively. Since he was in plainclothes at the time, Elizabeth did not at first appreciate that he was a policeman and as he walked away again, she raised her eyebrows and fixed me with a quizzical stare that said: 'Is there something you haven't told me?' But her reaction was as nothing compared with the looks I got from a couple of passing shoppers. Talk about a ruined reputation.

I made sure I kept well clear of public toilets after that experience, but my determination to maintain my arrest record was not diminished in any way.

Unfortunately desperation can be a dangerous motivator and in my efforts to keep up the good work I made an error of judgement on another night shift that very nearly turned out to be my last.

It was regular practice then for town centre night patrols to check any derelict properties that lay on their patch to see who was sleeping rough. Although the likelihood was that most of those 'in residence' would prove to be local down-and-outs or winos, sleeping off a heavy day's drinking, sometimes a simple routine check would throw up someone a lot more interesting, like a missing person or a villain on the run, and that was enough of an incentive in itself.

Turning over these abandoned properties, however, could be a dangerous unnerving experience. The buildings themselves were often on the verge of collapse and one unwary step could send you crashing to the basement in an avalanche of rotten floorboards. Then there were the sinister shadows that played hide-and-seek with you as you crunched your way from room to room; most of them social outcasts of one sort or another who had sunk to the lowest depths of human existence and would delight in plunging a sharp instrument in your back if the opportunity presented itself.

Caution was therefore the watchword and it was established practice to seek back-up prior to carrying out a check on a derelict or at the very least to advise the control room of the intention to do the check before venturing into the premises on your own. Foolishly, on this particular night I did neither and the derelict of derelicts was just waiting for me.

The ramshackle building itself stood in a side-street just off the High Street and was regarded as in such a dangerous state that patrols were actually forbidden to enter it without strict authority. This instruction was conveniently forgotten, however, when I saw the two men slip through the entrance gates in the early hours of the morning, carrying something bulky between them that seemed to be wrapped in a length of carpet. I went after them without a second's thought.

The building was like something out of an old Alfred Hitchcock film and on this particular night a moderate wind had breathed temporary life into the place. Shutters swung backwards and forwards on wailing hinges, doors banged and tin cans clattered across the cobbled yard. It was difficult to hear anything above the resultant din, but I reasoned that at least it allowed me to walk about freely without fear of being heard by the pair I was tailing. Had I had any sense at all, I would have appreciated the fact that this worked both ways – I couldn't hear them either – but you don't think of such things when the adrenalin is surging through your veins.

Looking back on the incident now, I think it highly likely that the two men were actually more aware of me than I was of them, having probably left the building by another exit even as I had entered it and although I went over the place pretty thoroughly, I found not the slightest trace of either of them.

Nevertheless, I continued my search and eventually stumbling upon a large basement area, I flashed my torch round the walls until something caught my eye. It was some sort of strongroom with its door wide open. Curious, in spite of the main reason for my search, I wandered inside. There were one or two ancient looking ledgers on the shelves lining the walls and I was in the process of leafing through one of these in the light of my torch when I sensed furtive movement close by. I spun round and was just in time to see the heavy door slowly closing behind me.

For a moment I froze, hardly able to credit what was happening, but the next instant I was seized by sudden panic and this undoubtedly saved me from a nasty suffocating end. Hurling myself across the room with a yell, I slammed into the door a split second before the lock could be engaged. At first I felt some resistance from the other side and forced myself into the gap to prevent it narrowing any further. Then abruptly the opposing pressure relaxed and I shot forward into the basement as the door lurched back on its hinges with a reverberating crash. My wildly arcing torch beam revealed that there was no one there, but I sensed movement in the blackness beyond its reach and even above the muted voice of the wind I fancied I could hear the sound of someone or something scurrying off into the depths of the rambling old building.

To this day I cannot say for certain what caused that door to swing to. Maybe a sudden gust of wind down the open stairway was responsible, though that seems hardly likely considering the weight of the strongroom door and the resistance I encountered when I tried to push it open. Then again, perhaps someone *had* been there, someone who didn't like policemen very much and thought he'd even an old score. One thing I do know, however; I left that derelict a whole lot quicker than I had entered it and for a long time afterwards I could still taste the staleness of a small airless room that could easily have become my tomb.

I never actually told a soul about that incident. I thought it best to keep my own counsel, rather than risk official castigation for disobeying a local instruction. This was probably just as well too, for very shortly afterwards I landed a key role in an important local operation.

The job itself was to maintain several weeks surveillance on a local restaurant, which was suspected of illegal nightly gambling sessions and said to be attracting the patronage of the professional criminal fraternity. The object of the operation was to secure enough evidence by noting all comings and goings, including car numbers and the identities of any known villains, to justify the issue of a warrant for a raid. It seemed a simple enough task, but it turned out to be anything but.

The main problem was that there were few places I could conceal myself within a satisfactory distance of the target premises, so I had to dodge about the car park, recording the comings and goings of the punters in my notebook as best I could. Initially I was not too worried about being spotted, because I was dressed in civilian clothes and felt sure that no one would suspect I was a policeman. Unfortunately, being in civvies also had its downside, as I quickly discovered on the second week when a tough looking character caught me standing in the shadows behind his car. He must have thought I was up to a bit of thievery and we spent the next twenty minutes playing hide-and-seek among the other vehicles, before I was able to slip away unnoticed.

After that I decided to opt for a safer static observation point, even if it did mean that I was further away from the restaurant than I wanted to be. Eventually I selected a small outhouse with a slatted door and settled among a litter of orange boxes and dustbins to await developments. Through gaps in the slats I could still see the rear door of the premises and could watch arrivals and departures without changing position, so at first I thought it was ideal.

But while the outhouse ensured I remained hidden from view, it had one important disadvantage; I was virtually a prisoner in my own hideaway. This fact was brought home to me just before twelve one night when two leather-jacketed figures materialised from the shadows soon after I had settled in. They were of the biker fraternity – a youth and a girl – and to my annoyance they chose a spot right in front of the outhouse for a heavy petting session, completely blotting out my view of the restaurant. I could hardly show myself and ask them politely to move on, so I was forced to sit there and put up with it, praying that the lad, who was facing the outhouse door, would not peer through the slats and see me sitting there on my orange boxes.

Thankfully, he didn't and after about twenty minutes the two of them slipped away again. But my problems were far from over for the night and the next incident I had to contend with a couple of hours later nearly torpedoed the whole thing. This was bad enough in itself, but what made it a lot worse was that one of my own colleagues was responsible. Why? Because no one had thought to tell him what was going on. He was a casualty of what the cynics in the police service like to call 'The Mushroom Policy' (kept in the dark and fed on bullshit).

The whole essence of the waiting game is secrecy. Many a good job has been blown because someone spoke out of turn and the general consensus of opinion in police circles is that the fewer people who know about a particular operation the better, and that includes other police officers. But although this practice is generally sound, it can sometimes lead to complications, with the left hand being totally ignorant of what the right hand is up to – which is what happened in this case.

When the young town centre beat man strolled into the car park at the back of the restaurant and shone his flashlight through the slats of the outhouse, the last thing he expected to see was a pair of eyeballs staring back at him. He recovered pretty quickly though and to his credit he did not shrink from doing his duty. 'Okay, mister,' he snapped. 'Out you come!'

I toyed with the idea of ignoring him, but realised that this would only result in a scene and I could see that he was already attracting enough attention from a group of people in the car park. So I just pushed the door open and sat there, blinking in the glare of his flashlight. There was an immediate intake of breath. 'Dave?' he exclaimed. 'What the hell are you doing in there?'

I sighed wearily. 'Trying to remain unobtrusive,' I retorted dryly. 'I happen to be on observation duty.'

That should have been enough for anyone, but my young colleague was the curious type. 'Observation on what?' he queried in a lot less than a conspiratorial whisper.

I just stared at him in disbelief. 'If you like,' I said acidly, 'you can ask the superintendent in the morning. Now clutter off!'

That registered all right. He quickly re-closed the door with a bang and turned sharply on his heel. My relief at his departure was short-lived, however, for even as I relaxed on my makeshift seat of orange boxes, his voice floated back to me across the car park in full hearing of people arriving. 'See you then, Dave,' he called cheerfully. 'Have a good night!'

Not surprisingly, I was tempted to pack the whole thing in there and then, feeling sure now that my cover must have been completely blown, but I need not have worried. A few weeks later the raid took place as planned and the unhappy gamblers were caught well and truly with their chips down. But the sequel was not quite so brilliant. When the case finally went to court, it was actually thrown out by the magistrates and the defendants were acquitted. For a while I felt totally disillusioned. All my hard work seemed to have been wasted. But there was a plus side. At least we had managed to put paid to the illegal gambling sessions and despite all the problems I had encountered on the ground, my side of the operation had been successfully completed. That had to count for something, surely?

Whether it did or not was not immediately obvious, for

apart from the standard 'job well done' comment from those on high, no real feedback was given as to whether my efforts had actually earned me forgiveness from my sins as a wrecker of police cars. But my luck was about to change for the better. Close on the heels of the surveillance operation came another job that put me back in the frame for a double quota of brownie points.

Acting on a tip-off that a youth wanted for offences of violence was known to have been lodging at a house on the 'Bomber Estate', another officer and myself armed with a newly acquired warrant, descended on the place one sunny afternoon to carry out a search. We didn't expect to find the youth himself, just something to indicate his whereabouts, such as a letter or piece of paper with an address or telephone number on it. Instead we made a shock discovery that subsequently resulted in our being summonsed to give evidence in a serious criminal trial at the Old Bailey in London.

The bedroom he had been occupying was only small, taking hardly any time at all to go through, but instead of letters or bits of paper carrying addresses or telephone numbers, we were presented with a whole assortment of wicked looking knives and other weapons that made our flesh crawl. But there was worse to come. Checking under the bed we discovered a heavy object wrapped up in several layers of paper like some nondescript parcel waiting to be posted and, tearing the thing open on the coverlet, we found ourselves in possession of a fully operative sawn-off shotgun.

A further search revealed several shotgun cartridges, which had been prised open and the contents emptied out, plus a small bottle containing a sinister greasy looking substance, which defied identification.

After some deliberation, we decided to take all the stuff

back to the police station, though I had some reservations about the bottle of liquid. It looked like something pretty nasty and as there was evidence of the shotgun cartridges having been tampered with, I got to wondering exactly what activities the previous occupant of the room might have been engaged in.

Fortunately, it later turned out that the substance in the bottle was nothing more dangerous than ordinary lighter fuel and that was just as well under the circumstances, because in my ignorance of things that go *bang*, I had carried the bottle back to the police station on the front passenger seat of the panda car, gripped tightly between my thighs for stability!

CHAPTER 12

POPPERS AND RAVERS

They were encamped on a small wooded hill just outside Royal Windsor and their bonfires crackled and flared among the trees like those of some raggle-taggle army. The smell of wood smoke and burning joss sticks drifted towards us on the still air and the ground trembled to the cacophonous challenge of distorted electronics and pagan drums.

We arrived in a Ford Transit, crammed together like commuters on a London tube, and the moonlight glinted on our polished helmet badges and tunic buttons as we clambered out in twos and threes to relieve the contingent already policing the area.

'You're welcome to it,' one of the latter grunted as he scrambled aboard the Transit. 'Bloody head-cases, they are.'

A few moments later I watched the red tail-lights of the Transit pull out on to the main road and mingle with a stream of others heading for home. I only wished I was going with them. Instead, ahead of me stretched a long twelve hour night duty, prowling around the woods and fields, 'showing the flag' as our governors put it.

Plucked unceremoniously from my unit beat at Maidenhead and sent to Windsor Great Park as part of a huge complement of officers drawn from stations throughout the force area, this was my very first experience of a pop festival. Other years it had been CND with its sit-down demonstrations, 'Ban the Bomb' marches and the folksy image of the so-called 'Flower Children', but I sensed that this was going to be something completely different.

I was absolutely right too and, though I didn't know it at the time, the so-called Windsor Free Festival was to be the forerunner of scores of illegal rave parties destined to hit the countryside in future years. Certainly there was nothing passive or dedicated about many of those who had gathered here. Their music was loud, their mood militant and their message buried in a confusion of immaturity and drugs. They might just as well have come from another planet. Nevertheless, our orders were precise enough. Keep it cool. Be firm, but tolerant and don't be surprised by anything you see. That last piece of advice turned out to be a lot more valid than I realised at the briefing.

I doubled up with a young constable from another division and we ambled casually up the slope towards the campsite. Among the trees I got a closer look at some of the festival-goers. They sat in cross-legged powwow round their campfires, their faces unnaturally gaunt in that ruddy glow.

The men were for the most part bearded and wore their hair shoulder-length. They were largely barefoot and dressed in a variety of unconventional clothing, though extra long overcoats and jeans with an assortment of floppy wide-brimmed hats seemed to predominate.

As for the women (or girls as a lot of them seemed to be), shawls, jeans and the same sort of floppy hats were in evidence, but there were some who wore headbands and had gaudy designs painted on their faces like Red Indians from a nightmare Western. Like the men, their feet were often bare and I couldn't help wondering how they managed to walk over the rough ground without suffering an injury.

The air among the trees was even heavier with the smell of burning joss sticks, but there was also another peculiar sickly scent that had me baffled, until my young colleague sniffed in the manner of a bloodhound and said in a conspiratorial whisper: 'Cannabis'. That certainly doubled my interest in things, but it soon became apparent that it was one thing to smell the stuff and quite another to spot who was actually using it. The only light came from the campfires or the odd butane or paraffin lamp and in the confusion of tents, sleeping bags and undergrowth it was difficult enough to see where you were going, let alone identify someone smoking a reefer. So we just prowled around as best we could, tripping over tent guy ropes or the occasional prostrate figure and hoping that we would strike lucky.

The discordant music we had heard on our arrival came from the centre of the wood where a makeshift stage had been erected, and a few spotlights and naked light bulbs operating off a generator provided the only bright space in the camp. Any proper groups (if there ever had been any) had long since played and gone and now it was amateur night. I winced at the noise they were creating and we retreated discreetly towards the outskirts of the wood for the sake of our eardrums.

I really saw some sights that night, which added to my education. In one part of the wood I became separated from my colleague and came upon a tight little group sitting well away from the main body of the camp. At first I was suspicious and moved quietly towards them from behind, convinced by my feverish imagination that I was about to seize a narcotics haul single-handed. Instead, when I got closer, I suddenly realised what was going on and it had nothing to do with drugs at all; it was something far more basic.

A bright orange tent was pitched about three yards from the group and the occupants had foolishly lit a lamp inside it. I was in time to see two clearly defined silhouettes – one a shapely girl – peeling off their clothing in apparent ignorance of the presence of their moronic giggling audience. I left as something more intimate began to take place, but the group of onlookers stayed where they were, thoroughly enjoying every minute of their moving picture show.

I rejoined my colleague minutes later, but I was in for an even bigger shock. We had stopped to talk to another couple of policemen in the light of a deserted campfire when a girl emerged from a nearby tent. She must have been about twenty and appeared to be reasonably well groomed, wearing trousers and a sweater of some sort. An attractive youngster, I thought, and one who just did not seem to fit in at this type of event. But I was wrong about that, for the next moment in full view of everyone she pulled down her trousers and proceeded to relieve herself on the ground. The four of us stopped talking and stared in disbelief. But 'madam' was quite unconcerned about the attention she was receiving and when she had finished what she was doing she stood up, wriggled unhurriedly back into her trousers and blew us all a kiss before returning to her tent.

This was the first of several outlandish occurrences I was to witness. In fact, after a couple of nights at the festival I became immune to shock and when on the next night I tripped over a couple performing on the ground, I hardly gave them a second glance.

To be fair, not all the festival-goers behaved like this. Some of the youngsters I stopped to talk to were quite respectable and had only come for a weekend of fun and adventure – they got that all right and in a lot more ways than one. I saw families too – mum, dad, the two teenage children and even their pet dog – who were along because the daughters or sons wanted to come and the parents, understandably, didn't like the idea of them doing so on their own. When I saw what these liberated parents had let themselves in for, I couldn't help but marvel at their courage.

There were, however, a hard core of undesirables who looked on the festival as an opportunity to indulge in an orgy of drug-taking and sex. These were the people we were interested in, especially the pushers who made a nice little packet out of trafficking in LSD, heroin and cocaine. A number of arrests were made and special courts set up to deal with the problem, but sadly, a lot of those who ended up in custody for 'using' were actually first-timers and it grieved me to think how many once decent youngsters would this weekend be introduced to drug addiction and set on the path to self-destruction by the ruthless men and women who moved like shadows around the campsite plying their filthy trade.

As a police officer, you soon realise you cannot right all the wrongs of the world on your own, but at the same time you cannot help feeling angry and frustrated to see some fifteen year old being rushed off to hospital by ambulance in a coma. A number of overdoses were reported during the festival and it is frightening to think just how many of those gullible victims of criminal exploitation might have since been found dead on a toilet seat in some backstreet lavatory or have thrown themselves in front of a train or off a high-rise block of flats while on a hallucinogenic trip. A lot of rubbish is said by so-called 'experts' about drug abuse, but when you meet the problem at gutter level you tend to see things differently.

On probation. Author after his appointment as trainee constable (1964).
Photograph: Studio Atlanta, Didcot

Rocker or Copper? Author off duty indulging his passion for motorcycles (1966).

Up the aisle. Author and his wife, Elizabeth, on their wedding day in Northern Ireland (1967). *Photograph: Charles Nelson, Belfast*

Living over the shop. First home. Police house adjoining Didcot Police Station (1967).

Bobby on bicycle. Author heading out on to his country beat at
Kencot in Oxfordshire (1969).

We are now four! Author with his wife and two daughters, Caroline
and Suzanne (1972).

A Special Job. Author's wife, Elizabeth, (on right of picture) on duty at Maidenhead as a Special Constable, with colleague, Dilys Gordon (1977). *Courtesy Maidenhead Advertiser.*

Left: Riding a Shift. Author's cop 'partner' David Foster, with his patrol car during a 'busman's holiday' at Madera, California, USA (1981).

Right: A proud moment. Author receiving Exemplary Police Service and Long Service medal from Chief Constable, Colin Smith QPM (1987).
Courtesy Thames Valley Police

Above: A prize win. Author receiving certificate and gold medal from the then Rt. Hon Douglas Hurd MP, Home Secretary, after winning 1986 Queen's Police Gold Medal Essay Competition (pic 1987).
Courtesy Home Office

Above: Entente Cordiale? Author (far right) with colleagues from the Gendarmerie Nationale on twinning visit to Liffre in Brittany (1991).

Above: Lunch with 'the Master' – Author (on left) with Inspector Morse's Colin Dexter at local hostelry (1994). *Courtesy of Scope Features*

Above: Farewell Thames Valley. Author (on left)) with Deputy Chief Constable, Brian Reynolds OBE at author's retirement clebrations, police HQ (1994). *Courtesy Thames Valley Police*

Drugs were not the only festival headache, however. Petty theft was a persistent aggravation. In the darkness it was simple enough for a villain to make off with virtually anything that caught their eye. Usually the targets were sleeping bags, cooking utensils or expensive personal items, such as watches, cameras or bicycles, but we did have one very unusual incident.

A young lad complained that he had gone to bed late at night in his ridge tent and had woken up in the morning feeling rather cold and trying to work out why he could see the gently waving treetops overhead. There was one very good reason. While he had slept his tent had 'walked off' into the night, courtesy of some very enterprising thief who must have had the lightest touch imaginable in the removal of tent, guy ropes and pegs. I don't think we ever did recover that tent and we certainly never found the culprit.

The festival itself only lasted a couple of days and by the early hours of Monday morning the mass trek back to homes all over the country had begun. Most of the youngsters looked tired, dirty and disillusioned as they humped their sleeping bags and guitars along the empty road through twisting spirals of a cold dawn mist. As I clambered aboard the Transit, which had arrived to collect the night shift, I guessed that a large proportion of these festival-goers would not be attending another one for a very long time.

But this assumption proved to be grossly inaccurate. Other open air festivals followed and it was my misfortune to attend a number of them at Windsor, Reading and elsewhere. When I did, it was to see familiar grubby faces turning up again and again. These persistent masochists were the hard core that kept the spirit of the outdoor music experience alive year after year, much to the disgust of local residents and the frustration of our chief officers who were desperately trying to find ways of balancing their overspent budgets.

It has to be said that pop festivals did tend to vary in quality quite considerably. As well as the so-called 'free festivals' in Windsor Great Park and a number of other venues throughout the country, there were the big commercially run ventures at Reading (and nowadays, Glastonbury in Somerset), complete with perimeter fences, gate security and all the essential amenities, like car parking, toilets and first-aid posts. The latter attracted vast crowds and many big names in the pop music world attended. There was a catch, of course; it cost a lot to get into the arena to see the show. But there again, as is so often said, you only get what you pay for.

If the festivals varied though, so did my duties each time. One of my most boring recollections was that of manning one of the lodges at the entrance to the restricted part of Windsor Great Park, checking vehicles in and out. Another year, at Reading, I found myself patrolling the arena where the show was being held and on a further occasion manning what was referred to as the 'Documentation Centre', where prisoners were brought for processing immediately after arrest.

There is one pop festival duty I will always remember, however, and that was the night I was detailed to drive the police personnel carrier and patrol a restricted, heavily wooded area of Windsor Great Park, in company with a colleague and a civilian park ranger. My job was to prevent trespass by campers from the nearby festival and the tour was completely uneventful until I dropped an enormous clanger in the early hours of the morning.

We had been driving around continuously for quite some time when my police colleague suggested we checked one of the Royal residences. I agreed and so at about 4am we cruised up to a pair of large gates in the middle of the park and switched off our lights. After a couple of minutes a door opened in the small lodge and what looked like a very ancient police constable appeared and approached the gates with a halting step. He opened up when he saw who we were and came over to my door. I cut the engine and a brief chat ensued, in the course of which he invited us into the gatehouse 'if we were quiet'. Unfortunately we were anything but, for as I fumbled for the lights in the darkness, I inadvertently hit another switch and to my horror a pair of powerful two-tone horns abruptly blasted the tranquillity of the estate to shreds.

Naturally, I quickly snapped the offending switch off again, but for some reason the horns had jammed and flick though I might, I just could not put a stop to the awful din, coupled with which I was unable to re-start the engine either. Lights now began to come on in the big house at the end of the long drive and the constable from the lodge seemed to shrink in stature. 'Well, I'll be going now,' he murmured in a quavering voice and promptly disappeared through the gates into the lodge, closing the door carefully behind him.

The house was now lit up like one of the terminal buildings at Heathrow Airport and I could practically hear the 'present arms' of the firing squad at my disciplinary hearing. In the end, it was the ranger who saved the day. Leaping from the vehicle with the agility of an airborne commando, he ripped the wires out of the horns altogether and to the relief of all concerned they died in mid-blast. At the same moment I finally managed to get the personnel carrier going again, but even as the ranger scrambled aboard and I accomplished the fastest reverse of my career, a terse radio message from the police festival control room was demanding the identity of the mobile responsible for the blunder – no doubt as a result of a meltdown call from the Royal residence concerned. For once in my life, however, I decided that honesty was definitely not the best policy and after the two-tone horns had been reconnected, I put as much distance as I could between ourselves and the scene of my *faux pas*. As we vanished back into the woods from whence we had come, however, I felt sure we left behind one very unhappy bobby, sitting in the darkness of his little lodge, thinking about his pension with his hands clasped tightly together in prayer.

CHAPTER 13

GUNS AND GAS

One of the great things about a career in the police service is the variety of opportunities that are on offer to those with the right skills and though in the early days of my service those opportunities were not quite as wide-ranging as they are today, there were still a lot of positions that could be applied for in departments like traffic and CID, dog section, mounted branch or the specialist units of the drug, fraud and crime squads.

For me the attraction was always CID and though I knew that selection for the department was a highly competitive process, I somewhat naively assumed that my crime arrest record in itself would ensure my early success. But it was not to be. When the selection interview finally came round it was a complete disaster. I was badly briefed, ill-prepared and didn't even make the short-list. Bitterly disappointed, my confidence torn to shreds, I was forced to resign myself to the fact that, despite my best efforts, I was not going to make detective in the near future and needed to think very carefully about what I should do next. Unbeknown to me at the time, however, my see-sawing fortunes were in the process of changing yet again and my career was about to take off in an entirely unexpected direction.

I had never really thought about joining the support group until I failed the CID board, but then, on the helpful advice of one of the inspectors at Maidenhead who saw 'the group', as it was called, as an eventual back door into the department, I slapped in an application as soon as vacancies were advertised in *Force Weekly Orders*. After failing my CID board I was not very confident about my chances, but to my astonishment I was not only selected with flying colours, but within a few weeks of my interview was actually posted to the unit.

Like the Metropolitan Police special patrol group, the support group at that time was a hard-nosed highly mobile task force made up of specially selected firearms trained officers with a roving commission that extended force-wide. Its main role was as a go anywhere, do anything unit, backing up overstretched divisions and assisting operational departments like the then regional crime squad, drug squad and CID with serious crime investigations, major incidents and public order situations, especially where the criminal use of firearms was involved.

The unit itself was divided up into teams – or 'parties' as they were called – each one under the control of a sergeant, and the personnel in the parties normally worked in twos as regular partners, each pair using an unmarked police car equipped with an illuminated drop-down 'Police Stop' sign in the rear window.

You got to know your partner pretty well in the period that you worked together and inevitably a strong bond of friendship and trust developed between the two of you. No matter what the odds were, you knew that you could always rely on your team-mate one hundred percent. It had to be so, for tight corners were a regular occupational hazard of this particular unit and often there was no one else around *to* rely on.

Everything was shared, from spells of driving to what coffee was left in a flask. If praise was due for a job well done, both partners received it together; if on the other hand a castigation was handed out, the same rule applied. The group took a special pride in its *esprit de corps* and without a doubt the worst sin a member could commit was to let a colleague down.

I was particularly lucky with my partner, for we hit it off right from the start. Geoff was a fresh-faced youngster with around four years service under his belt. This was not a lot of time in the job compared to the service of some of the other group members – even I had approaching eight years by then – but what Geoff lacked in time he made up for in other ways. In fact, he was a regular live wire, motivated by unbounded enthusiasm, and he had a nose for crime and criminals that produced many a good arrest in the months we were teamed up together.

A high proportion of the work of the unit actually involved proactive patrol duties, either on wheels, stopping and checking suspect persons or vehicles or on foot, policing public events like horse race meetings and football matches. But the big jobs occurred with surprising regularity too.

Very soon after taking up my new duties, my party was sent to assist local officers dealing with the aftermath of a serious disaster at Loddon Bridge near Reading. A section of motorway in the process of construction had collapsed in an avalanche of steel and concrete, taking with it those workmen who had been standing on the bridge at the time. It was a major tragedy that kept us all occupied for several days.

On another occasion we attended the scene of a grisly murder where the corpse had been partially burned and dumped on some wasteland in rural Buckinghamshire. Our job was essentially to keep unauthorised people away, especially the press and the usual army of morbid spectators, and although, despite the gravity of the incident, the work itself was very routine, at least we were spared more gruesome duties. As I watched the scenes of crime officers sifting through the wet sticky soil in search of human remains, I felt no desire whatsoever to change places with them.

Another incident calling for the group's assistance was even more horrific and once again Buckinghamshire was the venue. This time a child had been snatched from its bed in the middle of the night via an open window and a full-scale search was initiated. With other members of the unit, Geoff and I spent many hours in very sombre mood pushing through scrubland and along roadside ditches in the vain hope that we would find the youngster alive. Tragically, our search was all in vain, for the poor little lad was found brutally murdered in a ditch not far from the house itself and a deranged woman not connected with the family was later arrested for the crime – an awful business that deeply affected even the most hard-bitten coppers involved in the search operation.

All sorts of other duties came our way as well, ranging from a raid on a private house being used for illegal gambling in Reading to another full-scale search operation on the Blewbury Downs at Didcot – this time for an armed criminal wanted in connection with a series of ram-raids on shops in the southern area of the force. We worked a lot with local CID officers and a number of times with the drug and regional crime squads, doing both plainclothes and uniformed duty – sometimes even outside our own force area.

The job was varied to say the least and it was not always

popular. Group members were often referred to as the 'heavy mob' by local officers and their presence could quickly arouse resentment – even hostility – among some of those who regularly policed the area in which we were operating at the time. Much of this anti-group feeling stemmed from the fact that we were a headquarters operations unit and seen as having no allegiance to any specific division, coupled with the fact that the tactics we adopted tended to be more confrontational than the traditional policing approach. Such an approach included leaning on local yobs, pulling in suspected criminals for questioning and clamping down hard on the sort of street offences that the local bobby would normally handle with a verbal caution. Many in the 'softly, softly' camp saw us as creating more trouble than we solved and some unkindly suggested that it took weeks to sweep up after we had been working the area.

Thinking back to my time as a rural beat constable, I could understand why some uniformed officers would see us as the enemy rather than welcome back-up, because our styles of policing were so different, but the zero tolerance strategy we pursued did have its value – particularly in the larger busier towns like Reading and Slough where crime and public disorder were much more of a problem. Our reputation so often preceded us that young tearaways who were stopped and checked on the side of the road by one of our plain cars would provide their personal details immediately on request, whereas one of the local area units in the same situation would invariably be met with a mouthful of abuse.

Nevertheless, the hostility we received from our divisional colleagues did rankle at times and what made it worse was the fact that it wasn't confined to the lower ranks. There were those in much higher positions who were equally anti-group, but for an entirely different reason. They regarded us as élitist and a total waste of resources, and they would have liked nothing better than to see the unit disbanded altogether and everyone returned to routine divisional duties.

This backstage polarisation between the pro and anti lobbies introduced a political element into things, which put our own hierarchy into the position of having to constantly justify the group's continued existence. This in turn put every member of the unit under pressure to deliver a result every time we went out on patrol, for our lords and masters made no secret of the fact that a consistent lack of productivity by any group member was likely to mean them being thrown off the unit altogether. This led to intense rivalry between the parties as each one tried to better the other in the unofficial league tables, but it also ensured we were kept motivated and focused all the time and that went down very well with our plainclothes colleagues. CID were always pleased to see us on their manor, for they knew that they were almost guaranteed at least one body (or prisoner) in the cells before the end of our tour of duty. That meant another nice detection in their crime book – something that was always welcome in an environment where statistics was king.

To be fair, arrests weren't that difficult to come by in the larger conurbations and as a group member you could always count on the misbehaviour of the local yobs to help you out when you needed a collar or two. On one routine patrol in Slough Geoff and I had an arrest for criminal damage practically handed to us on a plate, but the gain wasn't without pain and I almost set the soles of my boots on fire in my eagerness to beat a patrolling traffic officer to the same prisoner.

We were driving along the A4 Bath Road with Geoff in the driving seat when we spotted a youth jumping up and down on the roof of a car parked on a car dealer's forecourt. Unfortunately, I was in such a hurry to secure an arrest that I quite forgot the support group car was still in motion and a split second after I had thrown my door wide I found myself clinging to the edge of the door frame as my feet practically hammered holes in the tarmac in a frantic effort to match the rapidly reducing speed of the police vehicle.

As it turned out, I did manage to beat the traffic officer to the prisoner that time, but there was a definite smell of scorched leather as he was marched back to the support group car and, though our man received his just desserts with a heavy fine for his misbehaviour when he subsequently appeared at court, I lost out too, for the incident cost me a new pair of leather soles for my boots! Not that I admitted this to anyone, since as it was Geoff couldn't stop laughing about the job for days afterwards and the last thing I needed was to give him even more ammunition.

Accepting an element of risk to make a good collar was actually all part of the support group philosophy, but it got members of the unit into some quite hairy situations on occasions. The day Geoff and I tried to stop a suspect van on the outskirts of Slough was like that and instead of scorched shoe leather we nearly ended up with smoking tyres and a casseroled engine.

The van attracted our suspicions from the moment we first clapped eyes on it, but as soon as we tried to pull it over the thing took off like a rocket, heading deep into a network of lanes on the approach to the village of Burnham. Geoff, who was again behind the wheel of the support group car, responded to the chase with a lot more enthusiasm than I would have liked and despite my team-mate's undoubted driving skill, by the time we managed to pull the miscreant over I was on the verge of bequeathing my worldly possessions. The collar itself did turn out to be well worth the chase in the end, however. Our man was already wanted in the Metropolitan Police District for a catalogue of offences relating to stolen cars and an appreciative Met assistant commissioner sent a very nice letter to the chief inspector in charge of the group, suggesting we be commended for our work. Sadly though, we were out of luck. Had we been on division we might have ended up with a nice little mention in despatches, but as members of the support group we were seen as only doing what we were supposed to do, so official accolades were considered unnecessary. Still, at least we had achieved a satisfactory result for both our team and our party, and had managed to enliven the day with the sort of adrenalin rush that made the job so worthwhile.

Adrenalin rushes were actually pretty common on the group and nothing was more calculated to set the old pulses racing than incidents in which firearms were involved – especially when you knew that the people carrying them were professional criminals who would not hesitate to use their weapons if they had to. I found myself in this situation the day Geoff and I joined up with several other teams in an armed stake-out operation, though there was little glamour in the job for me this time.

A tip-off had been received that there was to be a wages snatch by an armed gang at a factory in High Wycombe when the money was being counted and support group personnel had been placed in strategic positions all round the place, waiting for the villains to show. The disappointing part about it all from my point of view was that, although I had been included in the operation, I could not be issued with a firearm like my colleagues, because I had not at that time been through the necessary training course. As a result, I had been given what was seen as the next best thing – a wooden pickaxe handle – and relegated to the ground floor gents toilet.

The toilet in which I was closeted had large frosted windows opening directly on to the street. My job – in theory – was to try and prevent any of the gang getting into the place to use it as an escape route, should things go awry when the trap was sprung in the nearby wages office. But to be perfectly honest, although I fell in with the plan, I was not entirely happy with my part in things – and this was principally due to a certain lack of faith in the deterrent value of a pickaxe handle in the event of a confrontation with a professional thug carrying a sawn-off shotgun or a .45 revolver.

Fortunately, the issue was never put to the test, for although after a tense few hours the gang finally did put in an appearance, I never actually saw them. Apparently our governors had decided at the last minute that to try and arrest dangerous criminals in the confines of a wages office as they attempted to carry out an armed robbery was far too risky for both the wages office staff and the police themselves. The trap was therefore sprung outside the factory before the gang had a chance to produce their weapons and they were arrested without a shot being fired, later receiving hefty prison sentences at crown court on conspiracy and firearms charges.

As far as stake-outs go then the Wycombe operation was a great success with no one injured, a vicious gang brought to book and a number of lethal firearms taken off the streets. As things turned out, my toilet vigil had been a rather pointless exercise, but a few wasted hours beats an armed confrontation any day and at least while I was cooped up among the flushing cisterns I was able to make good use of the facilities on hand.

When I first joined the police service in 1964, the number of incidents involving the criminal use of firearms was miniscule compared with the situation today, but evidence of a developing trend towards gun crime had nevertheless become evident as long ago as the early seventies. It was this that prompted many police forces to introduce formalised firearms training for selected officers and in some cases to set up specialist armed teams to deal with the threat.

Although at that time Thames Valley's support group enjoyed a remit that went far beyond that of a specialist firearms team, one of its key functions was nevertheless to respond to any armed incidents that occurred within the force area and for this reason every officer assigned to the group had to be trained and authorised for the purpose.

I was no exception and shortly after joining the unit and experiencing my first armed stake-out at High Wycombe, I found myself nominated to attend a firearms authorisation course at a military base not far from the group's operational headquarters. Since I had never fired as much as a bow and arrow in my life before, I didn't expect the course to be easy, but in fact it was even harder than I had anticipated.

The training was not, as I had imagined, simply a question of learning how to handle a gun and firing the thing accurately; that was just the start. You also had to be fully switched on to the legal and procedural requirements imposed on you when you buckled on that holster, to understand the particular characteristics of individual weapons and ammunition and to appreciate, by means of practical and filmed scenarios, when it was and was not appropriate to pull the trigger. The job demanded the ability to assess a situation and make the right sort of clinical judgement almost at the drop of a hat, taking into account the level of the threat involved, the penetration potential of the ammunition being used and the risk to other members of the public in the vicinity or in adjacent buildings and vehicles. There was no room for hesitation and the right mindset was absolutely vital. Furthermore, it was considered just as important for an armed officer to be prepared to shoot when the situation demanded it as not to do so if the circumstances were inappropriate. The message was hammered home time and time again that the only person who could make the decision to pull that trigger was the person actually holding the gun. For this reason armed officers carried (and still carry) an awesome responsibility that could be shared solely with their own consciences and there is no better illustration of this than the tragic fatal shooting of Jean Charles Menezes at Stockwell tube station in London in 2005 by officers of the Metropolitan Police

With the potentially high stakes that were involved in the issue of a firearm to a police officer, it was hardly surprising that the training was as rigorous as it was. You were subjected to continuous assessment, not only in relation to your practical abilities, but your mental attitude and fitness to carry a firearm in the first place, and no allowances were made for 'bad hair days'. You either passed to the required standard or you failed and that was the end of it. Clearly, it could not have been any other way and that remains the philosophy today.

Hard though the training was, overall I enjoyed the experience immensely, but there was one aspect of it that I did not enjoy at and it had absolutely nothing to do with firearms.

I had heard all about CS gas training even before arriving on the course and had tried to put all the lurid accounts about what it was said to involve out of my mind, hoping that somehow the stories I had heard were all exaggerated. But they weren't and about halfway through the course, a dozen of us clad in blue overalls and gas masks found ourselves crammed into a small underground air raid shelter for what the sergeant had described as 'the best cure for hay fever and blocked sinuses ever'.

As the shelter filled with clouds of dense white smoke we were all instructed to advance towards him one at a time, to remove our gas masks and recite our name, rank and shoulder number. This virtually guaranteed that we got more than a lungful of the stuff, but if there was any doubt about that, he made sure the situation was rectified by asking us for our home address and even our telephone number as well.

It had already been explained to us that the purpose of this part of the course was to familiarise us with the physical effects of CS gas, so that if we were ever called upon to use it we would know exactly what it was like to be on the receiving end. I don't think there was anyone in the tiny underground shelter with me that day who had any illusions about the noxious power of the stuff.

CS gas can affect people in different ways and some suffer to a much greater extent than others. For me, the experience was made a lot worse by the fact that in my panic to get the whole thing over and done with as quickly as possible, I managed to inhale a lot more of the gas than was advisable. As a result, instead of ending up like my colleagues with the unpleasant, choking, gasping fit and itching, smarting eyes that was the typical reaction to the gas, I found myself physically unable to breathe at all as my diaphragm locked up completely and my entire respiratory system closed down. My ordeal could only have lasted a matter of seconds, but it felt like forever and even after my diaphragm had managed to kick-start itself back into life and the worried sergeant was himself able to breathe more easily, it was a good hour before I felt well enough to resume the rest of the day's training.

That frightening experience left me feeling both proud and relieved; proud that, despite my fears, I had forced myself to go through with it and relieved that the spectre of CS gas, which had hung over me for so long, had at last been exorcised. My relief was short-lived, however. By a cruel twist of fate, all my efforts on the course, and in particular my determination to face up to my gas ordeal, came to nothing as a ghost from my unit beat past suddenly manifested itself and dropped a massive spanner in the works. Right out of the blue I received a summons to attend the Old Bailey in London to give evidence in a serious criminal trial, part of which involved my seizure of the sawn-off shotgun and other weapons at the house on Maidenhead's Bomber Estate so many months before. It seemed that I had become a victim of my own success.

Frustrated beyond measure, I packed my bags and departed the course, praying that it would be possible for me to resume the training again when the case was over. But it was not to be. Tied up in London for a lot longer than I had expected, I was so far behind in the programme by the time I got back that it proved impossible for me to catch up and I was left with no option but to do the whole thing again – including the dreaded CS gas training. As it turned out, this didn't happen until a place could be found for me on another course several months later, but at least my hard work paid off the second time around and I got the tick in the right box, authorising me to be issued with an automatic pistol or revolver from the police armoury when required.

The ironic thing was that after all the trauma I had been through to gain that authorisation and, despite my involvement in a number of firearms incidents afterwards, I never actually had to draw a firearm in a live situation. Nevertheless unbeknown to me at the time, both the weapons handling skills and the tactical awareness I had acquired in my training were to be of immense value in the future and I retained a healthy respect for guns and their awful destructive power for the rest of my police service.

CHAPTER 14

LAW AND DISORDER

The rise in gun crime has certainly become a cause for concern, especially over the last decade, but even more worrying is the fact that the problem itself is only a reflection of the sort of society in which we live – a society where standards of behaviour have hit an all time low and terrorism and street violence are now a depressing feature of everyday life.

For the police, the maintenance of that fragile condition once referred to as 'the Queen's Peace' has never been an easy task and at no time is it more fragile than during a protest march or demonstration when feelings are running high and tempers are getting shorter by the minute.

On such occasions it is all too easy for disorder to break out and for the whole thing to degenerate into a full-scale riot situation. This may happen because the protesters themselves get carried away and try to achieve their aims through the use of brute force and the power of the mob or because an opposing group attempts to put a stop to their activities by employing the same sort of tactics. Whichever it is, the police, in their efforts to restore order and to protect lives and property, are likely to have to face both physical and verbal abuse and will invariably end up as the meat in a very unpleasant sandwich.

During my time on the support group, carrying out public

order duties was an all too frequent occurrence and I often found myself in the thick of things when the unit was called upon to back up hard-pressed sub-divisions in the policing of local events, like football matches, demonstrations and pop festivals. At such times it paid to keep your wits about you, for you could easily become a target for missiles when your back was turned, while allowing yourself to become separated from your colleagues was just asking to be hospitalised.

My very first experience of violent disorder was not actually as a member of the support group at all, but during my time on division and it provided a very good grounding for the future. Then the decision by the controversial politician, Enoch Powell, to speak at a special function in Oxford produced public outrage, particularly among the more militant student population, and as the storm clouds gathered, police officers from all over the force area were drafted into the city in an effort to ensure that the protest did not get out of hand.

We all arrived at dusk in uneasy coach loads, not really knowing what to expect, but sensing that this event was going to be a lot different to the more familiar CND protests with their peaceful sit-down demonstrations and 'Ban the Bomb' marches or the running skirmishes between the so-called Mods and Rockers, which had characterised the early sixties.

This feeling was reinforced when, after the initial briefing, we assembled in the then traditional uniform lines, linking arms across the ancient thoroughfare of St Aldates, and got our first real sight of the opposition. What an opposition it was too – a great quivering mass of tightly packed humanity that reminded me of a gigantic tidal wave about to force its way down the street, engulfing everything in its path.

For a while not much happened, apart from a few shouted insults, revolutionary songs and the occasional missile, but when the MP finally arrived and was ushered into an adjacent building all hell broke loose. From the depths of the mass came a menacing unified chant that quickly increased to a roar. Then quite suddenly the tidal wave broke and swept down on us, accompanied by a hail of missiles that included eggs, stones, half-bricks and anything else the protestors could lay their hands on.

I felt the grip of my colleagues on either side of me tightening and a second later my arms were practically wrenched from their sockets as all the breath left my lungs in a long agonised gasp. A bearded face pressed close to mine and to my disgust a young girl began deliberately spitting down my neck. Unidentified hands clawed at my arms, trying to force me to break my grip, and in the line behind me I heard the sergeant's voice yelling above the roar of the crowd: 'Hold 'em, lads. Don't break ranks.' A heavy boot slammed into my shin, but I hardly felt it. My whole body was going numb and coloured lights were flashing in front of my eyes. I needed to breathe out, but the crush prevented my diaphragm from working properly. Then, as my knees started to give way, the awful pressure relaxed. The crowd was falling back on itself. Round one to us.

It was almost as painful trying to breathe as not being able to, but I didn't get long to think about it as the mob slammed into us for a second try. This time I managed to thrust my shoulder forward, twisting round at an angle, which at least enabled me to breathe sufficiently, but there was nothing I or my colleagues could do about the kicking feet or the assortment of missiles that rained down on us in the darkness.

Again and again we held the mob back, though not without cost to ourselves. Several familiar faces were soon missing from our ranks and I learned afterwards that a number of my colleagues had been injured. Despite our determination, however, the mob always returned for more and with each new rush our resistance weakened. Once or twice the thin blue lines actually broke, only to reform with difficulty as the human flood poured into the gap, and before long I began to wonder just how much more we could take. But the thought of what would happen if the mob got through steeled our resolve.

Then abruptly the function which had caused all the bother came to a close, the eminent speaker was whisked away in a big black limousine and it was all over bar the clearing up. Reluctantly the crowd fell back and began to disperse in twos and threes. Behind them they left a street littered with debris like a vacated battlefield and an army of battered, exhausted bobbies who could hardly believe that the demonstrators were not coming back for more.

The Oxford incident caused quite a stir in the local newspapers afterwards. Street violence on such a scale was unheard of at that time – especially in the hallowed precincts of the 'dreaming spires' – and to a lot of people it was a bit like sacrilege. Today, of course, nowhere is sacred. A violent protest is almost as likely to flare up in a quiet Berkshire backwater as it is in the most socially deprived area of Liverpool. Everyone is protesting now and whether the theme is nuclear weapons, globalisation, unemployment or global warming, inevitably the police end up in the middle of it all. This more aggressive climate has brought about a significant re-think on public order tactics. Lines of smiling bobbies with linked arms are no longer sufficient to deter a mob and the specially trained units that have replaced them are now equipped with military style helmets, protective clothing and defensive shields.

Mass violence is not only restricted to demonstrations either. This social cancer has even spread to the sports field and in many cities the prospect of hooliganism on the football terraces and on the soccer trains presents the police with a considerable headache virtually every time there is a home game.

Sometimes even relatively minor fixtures can end in a serious disturbance too – as I found out first-hand when the support group was sent to patrol the streets of Slough in the proximity of the stadium where a football match was being held. There were only a few of us on duty, for the match had been described as a 'friendly', so our presence was seen as more of a gesture than anything else, but were we in for a surprise!

Slough Stadium was situated on a dual carriageway, adjacent to a large roundabout where several main roads converged just outside the town centre. Geoff and myself were detailed to remain with the police patrol car on the roundabout itself to give an eye to the fans when they turned out at the conclusion of the game. 'Show a bit of uniform,' the sergeant had explained, 'just to keep things orderly.' Keep things orderly? As it turned out, it was as much as we could do to protect ourselves, let alone do anything else.

We heard the first mutterings of trouble over the radio at half-time and other officers joined us on the roundabout as a precautionary measure. But though we were prepared for a bit of aggravation when the final whistle blew, we did not anticipate the amount of trouble that did erupt.

Geoff and I had just climbed out of the car when our

radios announced the end of the game. The next instant we stared with a mixture of horror and disbelief as an enormous mob of several hundred supporters poured out through the stadium exits into the car park, fists flying, boots kicking in a gigantic brawl that quickly spread beyond the precincts of the stadium on to the roundabout. Soon figures were running everywhere, bringing cars screeching to a halt with horns blaring and lights flashing, as bovver-booted youngsters dashed in front of them or leapfrogged bonnets in the hysteria of the moment.

Those of us on duty at the scene moved in, of course – we had no choice – but the odds were too great, even for the most confirmed optimist. The crowd simply swallowed us whole. Geoff and I did manage to make a couple of arrests initially, placing the two youths in the back of the police car handcuffed together, but the mob was soon all around us and as we struggled to restore some semblance of order we became separated. Then on my way to help another colleague who had gone down in a mêlée of struggling bodies, I ended up on the ground myself desperately trying to shield my face and vulnerable parts from the lethal boots that slammed into me with evident glee.

Things were beginning to look pretty bad when a local CID man suddenly waded into the fray and did an excellent recovery job on me. Then abruptly it was all over as reinforcements arrived and the yobs scattered, heading for the bus and railway station in cowardly panic. Within half an hour the stadium was virtually empty, the roundabout had returned to normal and the big traffic build-up had begun to clear itself. It was soon difficult to believe that anything had happened there at all and when I went off duty that night the violence of the afternoon seemed more like part of some unpleasant dream.

Under normal circumstances I would have quickly forgotten all about that particular incident. After all, it lacked the scale and significance of the Oxford incident, coupled with which, football hooliganism was fast becoming a fashionable disgrace among some of the younger set, so had ceased to become memorable. The fact that I didn't forget was due firstly, to the skill of one enterprising press photographer who, at the press of a button, managed to capture me at my 'Waterloo' for the next edition of the local newspaper and secondly, the knowledge that the two prisoners Geoff and I had placed in the back of the police car before being diverted elsewhere had been freed by their friends and had disappeared into the crowd, still handcuffed together.

Very soon afterwards, along with several other colleagues who had been on duty at the scene of the incident, we found ourselves under investigation for neglect of duty over the escape of the prisoners. An interview with a senior officer followed and then the inevitable long wait began while enquiries were made into the circumstances of the case. Loss of prisoners is a very serious matter in the police service and the fact that our small group had been hopelessly outnumbered at the time or that I had been receiving a systematic kicking while the pair were actually being sprung, did not seem to count for anything in the eyes of the police hierarchy; we had allowed two prisoners to escape and lost a pair of police issue handcuffs into the bargain and that was all that seemed to matter to them.

Only a police officer who has actually been the subject of a rigorous internal investigation can really appreciate what it is like having the threat of disciplinary action hanging over your head for weeks on end. The whole thing is very traumatic and if the allegation itself is unfounded, the fact that the finger has been pointed in the first place can give rise to a deep sense of injustice and lead to resentment and bitterness.

In my case, the situation was made a lot worse by the fact that I had only just received the best news of my career so far; I had actually passed the sergeant's promotion board and could expect to be offered my first step up the ladder within the next few months. I should have been dancing with joy, but under the circumstances I felt that any show of jubilation could be rather premature. I knew only too well that a black mark on my record at this stage in the game was likely to set me back in the promotion stakes for a long time to come and depending on which way the disciplinary enquiry went, there was a real chance of that now happening. I felt sick to my stomach. To have three stripes almost within your grasp and then to find that there was a possibility of them being snatched away at the very last moment was even worse than being rejected for promotion in the first place.

Then one morning I received a summons to the inner sanctum of the chief inspector in charge of the group. 'You are to see the chief constable tomorrow,' he announced.

I swallowed several times. The news conjured up all sorts of horrible visions. Minions like myself only saw the chief on matters of grave importance. 'Any idea what it's about, sir?' I ventured to ask.

'Well, my son,' he replied with a tight grin, 'you're either going to get done for losing those two prisoners or you are going to get promoted.'

I slept very little that night and I was a bundle of nerves when I arrived at force headquarters the next day. But I need not have stewed myself at all. The appointment had nothing whatsoever to do with the disciplinary enquiry; that result did not come until much later and even then it was a complete vindication of my conduct. Instead, the old man was all smiles as he looked up from his desk. 'Hello, young man,' he said quietly. 'How would you like to be a uniformed sergeant at Reading?' There was only one possible answer to that kind of offer and I didn't hesitate for one moment.

CHAPTER 15

BISCUITS AND BOMBS

There must have been at least twenty pairs of eyes studying me from both sides of the long parade room table and I suddenly became acutely conscious of the newness of the sergeant's chevrons stitched to the upper arms of my neatly pressed uniform jacket. The whole shift, it seemed, had assembled for my first parade briefing – panda car officers, town centre foot patrols, even those on the area or community beats – and despite the presence of both the duty inspector and the shift's own veteran station sergeant, I felt strangely self-conscious and exposed.

Fortunately, in the end, the briefing went well and as the bobbies dispersed about their various duties I received welcoming smiles from several of them, plus an encouraging wink from one of the old sweats who must have seen more sergeants come and go than I had years of service. It was a good start to my time at Reading, but I knew I had a lot of hard work ahead of me before I could even begin to earn the trust and respect of the shift as a whole.

The urban sprawl of Reading was a policing challenge in itself. Once a pleasant market town famous for its brewery and the Huntley & Palmers biscuit factory, the ancient borough was already expanding fast and had the sort of large cosmopolitan population to rival some inner cities – plus the crime to go with it. The police station in Valpy Street, I was told, had once functioned as a dairy of all things and when the constabulary moved into the building, no one had foreseen that it would eventually have to serve the needs of the massive conurbation that was now developing around it. To be fair, a spanking new custom-built nick was eventually established on the other side of town, but for those working out of Valpy Street at that time such a prospect was light years away and they were left with no alternative but to make do with what they had.

Making do was not that easy either. The big austere building had been crammed with so much accommodation that it had become a claustrophobic's nightmare and they had even had to take over other premises opposite to accommodate some of the administrative offices. To make things even worse, the place was grubby and poorly ventilated with so few decent sized windows and so many partition walls that working by artificial light during the day was the norm for a lot of operational staff. This was particularly true of the basement area, which comprised the large parade room, flanked by tiny cubicles provided for interviews and report writing, and the canteen. After a few months you began to feel a bit like a termite emerging from its mound when you signed off at the end of your shift and stepped out into the fresh air.

The closeness of everything brought its own unique problems too. As one of my colleagues remarked at the time, Reading nick had to be one of the few police stations in the country where you could actually sit at the charge office desk with the smell of bacon and eggs wafting up from the canteen in the basement and the stench of a drunken prisoner's recently discharged vomit issuing through the cell gate a few yards away.

For all its abysmal working conditions, however, one good thing could be said of Valpy Street's antiquated police station. Its cramped accommodation and poor facilities engendered a strong sense of camaraderie among those who had to share the limited space – or to put it another way, getting on with your colleagues is never an option when you are practically working out of each others' pockets.

Not that operational personnel actually got the chance to spend much time in the station, for this particular borough generated a massive police workload in comparison with most other urban areas of the Thames Valley and it was often said by the senior ranks that two years service at Reading was equivalent to four years experience anywhere else in the force. This was all very well, but it lost sight of the fact that the majority of the constables working at the sharp end were either rookie probationers trying to earn their spurs or bobbies in their first four years of service whose numbers were hardly dry. There were very few old hands on the core shifts, apart from those assigned to fixed area beats or on permanent station duty, either manning the front counter or the small divisional control room.

This placed a heavy responsibility on the shoulders of the supervisory ranks, particularly the three shift sergeants appointed to each of the operational shifts, many of whom, like me, were new to the job in the first place. No allowances were made, however, and there was no settling in period. When you came off that promotion assembly line you came off as a fully-fledged sergeant – someone who was, in theory, equipped to deal with any situation and to solve any problem. No quarter was given and none expected. The buck stopped at you and you had to get used to the idea. The problems came thick and fast too and very often decisions had to be made on the spot, using nothing more than a combination of experience and that very same policing skill – or gut feeling – acquired over the years as a constable on the beat. Sometimes you got it right and other times your instincts played you false, but that was all part and parcel of the job and the worst sin a skipper could commit in the eyes of his troops was to do nothing at all.

That being so, there were still occasions when, following the resolution of a particular incident, you were left thinking that doing nothing at all would actually have been the wisest option. One very strange affair involving a local council dustcart was just such an occasion for me, even though at the outset the incident had appeared to have all the necessary ingredients of a major crime.

The initial complaint had come from a lady living in one of the backstreet terraced houses off Reading's Oxford Road who had telephoned the police control room to say she had seen what looked like blood oozing through the teeth of a dustcart crusher after a passer-by had thrown a cardboard box into the back of the vehicle. Fearing that some hapless baby's dismembered corpse may have been dumped among the piles of rubbish, I raced to the scene with a young constable, only to find that the dustcart had long since gone – which was hardly surprising under the circumstances, since our witness had left it for over an hour before deciding to telephone the police. Worse still, by the time we got to the local refuse tip a whole fleet of lorries had already disgorged their loads of rubbish and we were faced with an enormous heap of garbage that resembled something out of a science fiction horror film.

Nevertheless, like it or not, I knew that the heap had to be searched for any grisly remains and, summoning reinforcements, I launched the team in a full frontal assault, armed with sticks, crowbars and anything else they could use for the purpose. Meanwhile, house-to-house enquiries were made in the area of the incident and the woman who had thrown the cardboard box on to the dustcart was quickly traced. Her reaction to police questioning was totally unexpected, however, for instead of showing resentment or animosity, she doubled up with shrieks of laughter. It was only after she had calmed down enough to reveal exactly what had been in the cardboard box and the box itself – partially crushed, but still recognisable – had been recovered from among the piles of rubbish that the reason for her mirth became apparent. Then it was all we could do to hide our embarrassment, for our dismembered corpse turned out to be nothing more sinister than a large out of date container of tomato sauce.

I received a lot of ribbing from CID when news of the 'ketchup killer' hit the grapevine, but it was only to be expected under the circumstances and the mickey-taking didn't really bother me, for deep down I knew that no one else in my position would have actually handled the commitment any differently. A police officer can never afford to disregard any information received from the public, however bizarre it might appear to be, for there is always the chance that a dubious report will turn out to be one hundred percent legitimate.

This was very much the case during my time at Reading, for I arrived at the height of the IRA's murderous bombing campaign on mainland Britain and the police control room was often inundated with hoax messages about explosive devices left in buildings and well-intentioned calls from the public concerning suspicious packages and vehicles. Each report had to be treated seriously, even though most led to nothing, and while this invariably meant multiple shift hours lost in the process – especially when building or street evacuations had to be carried out – the ongoing situation did give rise to a number of incidents that got the heart beating a whole lot faster.

In one instance I all but walked into a very nasty situation without the slightest inkling of what was going on. I had decided to take my refreshment break early so that I could go to my bank in the town centre and draw out some money and I was heading out of the sergeant's office with a civilian anorak over my uniform when I was halted by a shout from the inspector's office behind me. It was the duty inspector himself. 'And where do you think you're going?' he queried sharply, grabbing his uniform tunic from the back of his chair. I raised my eyebrows a little, for I was entitled to my meal break like everyone else. 'The bank,' I replied testily. 'I won't be long.' 'Which bank?' he snapped, snatching his uniform cap from his desk. I told him and he gave a short grim laugh. 'No you're not,' he retorted. 'They've got an armed robbery on the go there! Get your kit on.'

I felt a bit shaky as I followed him out of the nick at a run, for I had no illusions as to what might have happened if I had blundered into the bank foyer in part uniform while the hold-up was in progress. Criminals tend to be hyped up in such situations and an itchy finger on the trigger of the sawn-off shotgun I later learned our man had been carrying would have spelled very bad news for me. Fortunately, the gunman had already fled with his ill-gotten gains by the time we joined most of the shift at the scene, but he had left a little present behind – something he'd claimed would shortly go *bang*. A major operation was therefore required to evacuate not only the bank, but every other premises in the vicinity and to seal off the whole street until the bomb squad arrived.

The operation obviously caused major disruption to the town centre and you would have thought that shoppers and traders alike would have understood the need to close the street as a safety precaution, but not a bit of it. Like lemmings on their way to the cliff edge, the good old British public used every trick in the book to try to get through the police cordon. Reason was completely lost on them and excuses ranged from 'I'm expecting a telephone call at the office' to 'I've left my sandwiches on my desk'. The fact that if there had been a real explosive device in the bank they might all have been blown to kingdom come or buried under tons of masonry did not seem to occur to them.

The biggest aggravation I had to face that day, however, did not come from some irate office worker or the familiar 'I know your chief constable' type manager, but from a little old lady who looked as though she might have stepped straight out of a Giles cartoon. I first became aware of her presence when I received a sharp jab in the ribs from a rolled-up umbrella and a voice, which called stridently: 'Young man!' I turned quickly and found myself staring down at around 5'2" of bristling indignation, clad in a heavy black coat and woollen hat. Sharp eyes met mine over the top of bifocal lenses and a Miss Marple stare subjected me to critical scrutiny. 'What's going on here?' the lady snapped.

I started to explain as tactfully as I could that there was a suspect bomb in the bank and the road was therefore closed, but it was a big mistake trying to patronise this elderly citizen and I received another painful jab from her umbrella for my trouble. 'Closed?' she echoed. 'Closed? Rubbish. I have to collect my pension from the post office.'

She made to brush past me, but I barred her way. 'I'm

sorry, my love,' I said firmly. 'I can't let you through just yet.'

'Nonsense,' she persisted. 'I'm not afraid of any bomb. I was in the Blitz, you know.'

Inwardly groaned. I could do without the British Bulldog spirit at that precise moment. 'Look, dear,' I said gently, 'why don't you just go home and make yourself a nice cup of tea?'

The umbrella lunged at me a third time. 'Tea?' she exclaimed. 'Tea? I don't want any bloody tea!'

I stared at her aghast, wondering for a moment if I was hearing things. But I wasn't and before I could recover from my astonishment, she had ducked under the tape cordoning off the road and was scurrying along the street like a long dog. Short of bringing her down with a rugby tackle – which was hardly the appropriate thing to do under the circumstances and would have raised more than a few eyebrows – I had no option but to let her go.

Whether she actually got to the post office before all the staff were evacuated I never did find out, but as it transpired, she was not in any danger anyway, for the so-called bomb turned out to be a hoax – a ruse employed by the armed robber to tie-up police resources long enough for him to effect his escape. But it could so easily have been otherwise and I couldn't help wondering at the time if the then RUC in Northern Ireland were presented with little old ladies wielding rolled-up umbrellas at the scenes of such incidents. If they were, then they deserved every sympathy, for I was quite sure in my own mind that there was never a more formidable antagonist.

Little old ladies aside though, the police containment that day was actually quite successful despite the escape of the gunman and if there had been a real bomb in the bank and it had exploded, I feel sure that the number of casualties at the scene would have been minimal due to the precautions taken. Not all bomb scares can be resolved by a textbook style operation, however. On another occasion I faced a much more complex situation and, rightly or wrongly, decided on a rather unorthodox approach.

It was just before Christmas when the call was received from the local bus company. A suspect bomb had been found on one of the seats of a double-decker in the town centre and, understandably, after the passengers had rapidly departed the driver had also quit his cab and was refusing to take the vehicle any further. This was bad enough, but the incident itself had occurred after dark right in the middle of the evening rush hour and when I got there I saw that the street was jam-packed with Christmas shoppers and slow moving vehicles.

Boarding the bus with a couple of young constables who had joined me at the scene, I was shown a briefcase lying on a seat on the upper deck. The briefcase was locked and I could hear a distinct clock-like ticking noise coming from inside. Glancing through the window at the crowds streaming past, I felt my throat go dry. So how did I handle this one? Evacuating a main shopping thoroughfare heaving with people is never an easy task, but in the dark with just a handful of bobbies at your disposal (and no prospect of securing reinforcements, due to shift shortages and other major commitments), it is a complete non-starter – coupled with which, there is every likelihood that it will lead to mass panic. But with the bus going nowhere and the chance of getting an army bomb disposal team to the scene in under an hour very remote, I also had to take into account the fact that if the briefcase *did* contain an explosive device it could go off at any minute, taking half the shoppers with it.

As my brain started cartwheeling around inside my head, I was joined by a third bobby and the next moment I found myself staring at three pale expectant faces. 'What do we do now, sarge?' one of them queried, voicing the thoughts of all three. For a moment I just stared at him. So what *did* we do? Well that in itself was the million dollar question, but the three stripes on my arm meant I had to come up with the answer, so I went for it.

Whether the decision I took was the right one or not is a matter of conjecture for latter-day armchair critics, but faced with that 'devil you do, devil you don't' situation, I plumped for the only real option I felt was open to me at that moment. Reassured by the fact that the briefcase had been carried on to the bus in the first place – which suggested that if it did contain a bomb, the device itself was not sensitive to movement (a logical assumption that in subsequent explosive awareness training turned out to be badly flawed) – I decided that, since the bus could not be removed from the scene, then the solution to the problem was to remove the briefcase from the bus.

There were no volunteers for the job, but my colleagues did agree – once they saw that the briefcase was not going to explode – to clear the way ahead of me as I carefully carried it back to the station via a virtually empty arcade and deposited it in the specially provided sandbagged pit at the rear of the building.

It was only after the bomb disposal team had attended that we found all the fuss had been for nothing. There was no trace whatsoever of any explosive in the briefcase. Apart from some very ordinary business papers, it actually contained nothing more life-threatening than an office Dictaphone loaded with an expired tape, which was ticking irritably because someone had forgotten to switch it off.

Once again our so-called bomb call had amounted to nothing, but I for one was not in the least bit disappointed by the outcome and although the incident had become just another false alarm, no blame was attached to the bus crew for sending the balloon up in the first place. They had acted with the very best of intentions and to have failed to call for police attendance in such circumstances would have been nothing short of irresponsible in those dark days.

Unfortunately, not all the suspect bomb calls we received were good-intentioned. With the tragedy of Ulster very much in the news, a new kind of sick prankster had emerged from the woodwork to plague the already overstretched emergency services. Very often the culprit was a juvenile who thought that dialling '999' to say that there was a bomb in a shop or school was excellent entertainment, especially when fire, police and ambulance units turned out in force. But sometimes an adult tried it on, maybe because he or she nursed a grudge against someone or simply because they were drunk or had got out of bed on the wrong side.

Hoax calls were the bane of our lives, because they frequently involved the mass evacuation and lengthy searches of premises, sometimes tying up emergency service personnel for hours on end, delaying responses to other legitimate calls and causing massive disruption to local businesses, schools and transport. If caught, hoaxers could expect to receive no mercy whatsoever from the police and they were invariably prosecuted. The trouble was that they were actually quite difficult to catch; making their calls from isolated telephone kiosks and disappearing well before these could be traced, leaving the police with no alternative but to wait until they unwittingly gave themselves away or tired of their stupid game. It was all very frustrating and the hoaxer was about the only one who was able to see the joke.

Having said that, there were a couple of occasions when we did see the funny side of things. One prankster dropped himself right in it when he made his call to our police control room, for in the course of passing his hoax message he inadvertently revealed his true identity as a sort of automatic reflex action – only to express absolute astonishment when the police turned up to cart him away.

Even funnier was the case of the Irishman who took it into his head to ring a local business to make his threat after everyone had gone home for the weekend and ended up leaving his message on the answering machine. 'There's a bomb in your factory,' he said in a voice laced with menace, 'and it's going to go off at twelve.' There was a half click as the receiver was almost returned to its cradle and then the same voice was back in a rush, scuppering any chance of being taken seriously. 'That's twelve in the afternoon!' he explained helpfully.

CHAPTER 16

CHEVRONS AND SHENANIGANS

In the police service, leadership ability is a vital prerequisite of both supervisory and management rank, and because the work itself is largely reactive, those on the ground – particularly inexperienced probationers – tend to look to those above them for quick decisive action in operational situations. Snap decisions are not always appropriate, however, and sometimes it is better to take a more measured approach in order to achieve the right result.

I was presented with just such a situation the day I was sent with a young unit beat officer, named Mick, to a house on the outskirts of Reading, this time to assist a doctor with a disturbed male patient who was due to be committed to a mental hospital for treatment.

When we were admitted to the house, we found the doctor waiting for us in the hall and the patient restlessly pacing up and down in the kitchen. It was quite obvious that the man had worked himself up into a severe state of nervous tension and he was likely to lose control at any second. The problem was what action to take without exacerbating the situation, particularly as our man had a large knife to hand, which he had placed on the nearby kitchen table.

As I saw the situation, we had two alternatives. We could forcibly restrain him while the doctor administered a sedative by means of an injection and then help the waiting ambulance men to get him into their vehicle or we could try to persuade him to go with the ambulance crew voluntarily.

It didn't take me long to decide that persuasion was the best option, for his wife and young children were tearfully watching the proceedings from the staircase behind us and there was just no way I was going to cause them unnecessary distress by resorting to heavy-handed tactics unless I had to. The doctor was in full agreement with this sort of approach and after we had persuaded the patient to sit down at the kitchen table with us, we did our best to talk through the man's problems, keeping a wary eye on the knife at the same time.

They say talk is cheap, but it is also very tiring – especially if you have to keep the conversation going for almost two hours, as we did. We were only partially successful too, for although we did manage to calm our man down quite a lot, we were still unable to get him to go with the ambulance crew voluntarily. In the end forcible restraint did become necessary and we had quite a struggle with him before the doctor was able to administer the required injection, which was rather disappointing after all our hard work.

As it turned out, however, our efforts were very much appreciated and that appreciation came from a most unexpected quarter. Several weeks after the incident, the doctor wrote to our chief superintendent, bringing to his notice a letter he had received from his patient, thanking us for our patience and kindness in the way he had been treated.

That letter was certainly a very nice gesture and it made everything we had done seem worthwhile, but we were only too conscious of the fact that things could have been a lot different. Few incidents involving mentally or emotionally disturbed people tend to end quite so amicably and there is an even chance that the police officer called to the scene will be assaulted in some way, with personnel from the other emergency services running a similar risk.

A colleague of mine who went to another house around about the same period to assist fellow officers and an ambulance crew with a mentally unstable man armed with a knife nearly lost his life as a result. Before the man could be overpowered, he managed to stab the sergeant in the chest and one of the ambulance men in the stomach. Both eventually recovered from their injuries, but it was a close run thing and even today the case provides a keen reminder to those responsible for dealing with people suffering from similar problems that nothing should ever be taken for granted.

Having said that, from an emergency services perspective, one of the main difficulties associated with mental or emotional instability is that a particular condition may not always be apparent to start with. An individual may show no obvious signs of irrational behaviour and is likely to be seen going about his or her everyday life in a perfectly normal way until something triggers the violence that is lurking just beneath the surface.

That is exactly what happened in one never to be forgotten case, which started out as a fairly routine complaint of harassment and ended in a horrific tragedy that left my colleagues and myself completely stunned. When a quiet mild-mannered young man working at a shop in the town developed an unwanted crush on a pretty young woman managing a late night café and started pestering her and sending her unsolicited gifts, no one thought he could actually be capable of violence. However, following her rejection of his advances, which was reinforced by a police warning regarding his future conduct, something must have snapped inside him, for he responded to the situation by lying in wait for her one night as she shut up shop to go home and throwing acid in her face. He was quickly arrested of course and, after his trial, was put away for a very long time, but that did not help his innocent victim, for she suffered massive disfiguring burns to both her face and her body, which as far as I am aware, she had to carry with her for the rest of her life.

What made that attack so much worse than the violence I had previously encountered in my career was that it had been a calculated rather than a spontaneous act. Even after nine years in the job, I still found it difficult to believe that one human being could actually plan to do such a dreadful thing to another. Reading was to further my street education with quite a few nasty surprises though and one of these nearly cost me a lot more than any man would be prepared to pay.

The incident itself involved a disturbance at a girl's probation hostel just after midnight and once again I attended with a young patrolman to sort things out. On our arrival we were confronted by a young woman armed with a long-bladed knife who had been in an argument with another inmate. She was trembling and in such an excitable frightened state that it took a lot of persuasion to get her to part with the knife. But if I thought that was the end of the matter I was in for a big surprise. When I tried to prevent further trouble by advising her former antagonist to obey an instruction by the hostel staff to go indoors, I mistakenly went for the Dutch uncle approach and with one of the staff attempted to steer her gently by the elbow in the appropriate direction. Before I knew what was happening she had pushed me violently in the chest, shouting and swearing, and brought her knee up between my legs in an agonising jab.

She had to come in for that, of course, and when she appeared at court she was convicted of assault and sent away for a few months. To my surprise, she refused to let things rest there, however, and after a failed appeal process to the crown court, she took the matter to the Queen's Bench Division of the High Courts of Justice, only to have her appeal finally dismissed and the conviction upheld.

The legal process certainly took long enough to run its course, but at least in this respect the outcome was a satisfactory one and amounted to a resounding endorsement of the actions I had been forced to take on the night of the disturbance. Furthermore, as a spin-off to it all, the case and its judgement joined previous judgements in official archives as a legal precedent (or 'stated case'), earning me a tiny place in legal history and opening the door to calls from various senior colleagues and training officers seeking to use it to support their own legal arguments or illustrate a particular training scenario. But there was a down side to it all too, for although my claim to fame lasted for about a week (even overturning Andy Warhol's theory that everyone would be famous for just fifteen minutes), the discomfort in my nether regions as a result of that assault stayed with me for a great deal longer, raising serious doubts in my mind as to whether the pain really had been worth the gain!

Assaults on police were not uncommon on the Reading beat and there were some quite nasty cases while I was stationed in the so-called 'Biscuit Town' – including one where a woman police officer suffered substantial injuries when she was thrown down a shopping centre escalator. The workload was also much higher than any other station in which I had served, with shouts for a police response to incidents involving serious crime, violent street offences, domestics and traffic accidents often running at a frenetic rate. This generated mountains of paperwork and supervisors had an uphill task checking the dozens of potential prosecution files that were submitted almost on a daily basis, as well as trying to ensure that their officers kept abreast of the unpopular job of report writing in the first place. Checks on the dockets where officers kept their incomplete files were regularly carried out, castigations issued for delayed work and lengthy guidance given to inexperienced probationers on the preparation of the multitude of different kinds of file that had to be put together – and all this on top of the supervisory responsibilities that had to be carried out on the street.

Travelling as I was from my home in Maidenhead every day – a round trip of some twenty-five miles – and coping with early, late and night turn shifts, as well as three quick changeovers a month (which meant, for example, finishing a week of night turns at 6am on the Monday and starting again for a week of late turns at 2pm the same day), I found the work totally exhausting. Nevertheless, I loved every minute of it and, surprising though it may seem, I couldn't wait to get back on duty to confront the same hassle each day. But that was while I was working as a patrol sergeant and unfortunately my situation was set to change yet again – and not for the better either. Sadly, nothing stays the same for very long in the police service, especially if you happen to be enjoying yourself.

I didn't ask to be station sergeant – the position was thrust upon me with the appointment of the regular skipper to the temporary rank of acting inspector – and my heart sank when the chief inspector broke the news to me, especially as he finished up with that same hackneyed and by now very familiar 'all good experience' line. Despite my dismay, however, I had no choice but to accept my 'sentence' and try to make the best of it – even if it did mean that I would have to adopt the lifestyle of a troglodyte for the next few months.

During my time in the force, the role of station sergeant (or custody officer as the job came to be called) was traditionally a very important one, particularly in the larger police stations where, in the eyes of operational officers, the postholder was seen as not just the person who ran the administrative side of the nick, but the nick itself. The rank of station sergeant was actually no higher up the ladder than that of patrol sergeant, but the nature of the job lent it an extra unofficial authority few were prepared to dispute. Unfortunately, with the status came heavy responsibilities, coupled with a working environment, which at Reading really took some managing.

This was especially true with regard to the care and custody of prisoners, which had to be carried out in accordance with very strict rules that were not only enshrined in legislation, but reinforced by the requirements of the force's own bible (or standing orders) as well. The searching of prisoners and the removal of their personal property while in custody was of prime importance, each item being listed on the detainee's detention sheet and locked away in a plastic bag sealed with a numbered tag. This was done not simply to safeguard their property or to preserve any evidence found in their possession, but to prevent them injuring themselves or anyone else, or effecting their escape with anything they might have hidden away. It was vital that nothing was overlooked, for it was the station sergeant who ultimately carried the can if one of the officers completing the searching failed to do the job properly.

It was not an easy task though, for it is a fact that accomplished criminals and those in the special risk category, like drug addicts, potential suicides and people with mental health problems, have a tendency to hide things in the most unlikely places. Razor blades taped under a man's scrotum, drugs concealed inside a woman's vagina – everything has been tried at one time or another. We even had one biker who was found to have pushed a flick knife up inside his anus. When the horrified searching officer tackled the man about it he gave a typically slow grin and said in a deep halting voice: 'I ain't stupid, you know. I put it in the other way round!' The mind boggles.

As well as being an onerous job, searching prisoners could also be a very unpleasant business – something I had learned only too well during my days as a beat bobby. This was especially the case when a prisoner was drunk and had defecated in their trousers or vomited all over themselves, and I witnessed many a young constable blanch at the prospect of dipping a hand into a badly soiled pocket or bending down to release a pair of cycle clips...

Coupled with the unpleasantness of it all, there was the hidden risk factor that always needed to be borne in mind. Some of the people picked up off the street had infectious diseases and this was not always appreciated until it was too late. A vagrant brought into the then charge office at Reading during my stint as station sergeant gave everyone quite a scare in this respect. At first we took no notice of his persistent racking cough, thinking that he had nothing more than a chest cold. That all changed when he suddenly collapsed on the floor, for, after he had been rushed to hospital, he was found to be suffering from highly infectious tuberculosis. The hospital promptly put the unfortunate man into isolation and advised us all to consult our own doctors as a precautionary measure after a six month period, which was apparently the normal incubation period for the bacillus. In due course we found that we were in the clear, but that had to be one of the longest and most worrying waits I have ever had to endure.

The tuberculosis incident was not the only scare I had in relation to infectious prisoners either and it was followed by exposure to other equally unpleasant diseases, including AIDS, scabies, hepatitis, syphilis and a nasty blood condition called Australian Antigen. Luckily I escaped any sort of infection, but after a few such scares, I found myself constantly living in dread of picking up something and taking it home to my wife and family. This certainly focused my mind in relation to the manner in which body searches were carried out.

Unfortunately, while every effort was made to minimise the health risks associated with custodial duties by sticking rigidly to the book, in a big station like Reading caution sometimes had to be balanced with expediency, for the sheer number of prisoners requiring processing at any one time could be mind-blowing.

Monday to Friday on early turn presented the biggest headache, especially if the local Magistrates Court and the Crown Court were both sitting at the same time, for then, in addition to prisoners arrested by our own patrols and placed in the cells the previous night, there were others arriving in prison wagons on remand from penal institutions all over the place. On one early turn, for example, I was landed with twenty-six prisoners and when I abandoned my breakfast and raced up to the charge office after a frantic call from one of my station duty officers, at least half of these were lined up with their prison officer escorts in the corridor leading to the charge office; all waiting to be documented, searched, fed and placed in cells that were already bulging with detainees for production at court within an hour and a half.

Prisoners were not the only worry either. I soon found that, as station sergeant, you had a multitude of other responsibilities too, all designed to help you reel through your day with the maximum amount of hassle.

Almost as a badge of office, you were provided with a huge set of keys, which opened virtually all the important doors, cupboards and drawers in the station. These keys could be a real pain in a lot more ways than one. The places they accessed, like the cell block and the station sergeant's safe – which held amongst other things travel warrants and the station's petty cash float – were in constant use and you were forever in demand to attend to each request personally. To lose the keys was unthinkable as they had to be handed over at the end of each duty tour from sergeant to sergeant, but one day I did the next worst thing.

I had had a very trying morning and because it was midsummer, the office was like a hothouse. I couldn't wait to get home and have a bath, so when my relief arrived I briefed him on the day's events, then left the station for the quarter of a mile walk to the Huntley & Palmers biscuit factory where the local police had permission to park their private cars. I became aware of the pounding feet halfway to my objective and, turning quickly, I was presented with an astonishing sight. I was being pursued by the chief inspector, the relief sergeant and one of the station duty constables – all of whom were shouting at the top of their voices in the sort of panic-stricken manner that suggested someone must have just planted a bomb in the nick. It turned out to be almost as serious – I had actually walked off with the station sergeant's keys.

Without a doubt, one of the station sergeant's most time-consuming responsibilities was the station duty office with its busy front counter handling public enquiries. When not in the cell block, charge office or carrying out essential administrative tasks – like checking prisoner's custody sheets and station registers or answering telephones that never seemed to stop ringing – you invariably ended up dealing with those awkward complaints and queries from the public that the officers manning the front counter could not resolve themselves and politely, but firmly pushed your way. These could be anything, including requests to visit prisoners held in the cells, complaints against individual police officers, advice sought in relation to neighbour disputes or reports of serious crime.

On one of my night duties a young couple came to the enquiry desk carrying a tiny baby girl wrapped in a blanket. They looked pale and shaken, while the baby was obviously in a great deal of distress, and I soon found out why. Apparently the couple had driven to some woodland late at night for a romantic liaison when they saw the baby crawling across the ground in front of their car, trailing her nappy. On examination of the child, they found that she appeared to have injuries to her private parts and was not only bleeding quite a lot, but obviously in a state of shock. All she could do was to croak like some distressed animal and when I stared into that white face and those big wide eyes, my blood boiled. To think that someone could have actually abandoned a tiny injured baby and left her in the woods at the mercy of foxes and other wild animals was beyond my comprehension – and there was also the burning question in my mind as to how the child had come by such horrendous injuries in the first place. It was like something out of a fictional horror story. We took the little girl from the couple and rushed her to hospital where I gather her injuries had to be stitched. Social services were contacted and serious crime enquiries started by CID in an effort to trace the parents. The job being what it was, I had no further involvement in things, but I shall never forget the expression on that child's face for as long as I live.

My time at Reading as a newly promoted sergeant was certainly an experience, providing me with much more than a cursory insight into the raw underside of a tough urban environment, but as well as the practical side of things, it presented me with an unexpected opportunity that had absolutely nothing to do with my role as a uniformed sergeant.

The whole thing began with a summons to the office of the superintendent and when with some trepidation I attended, it was to be offered a very unusual 'just' job. The editor of the town's main newspaper *The Reading Evening Post* had expressed a keen interest in running a weekly police news and advice column for his readers and because of my interest in freelance writing and my earlier success in the *Queen's Police Gold Medal Essay Competition*, the superintendent thought I was 'just the chap to take the job on'. The offer was a nice compliment, but having never written a press column before and mindful of the pressure I would be under trying to meet a weekly deadline while working shifts, I must admit I hesitated. In the end, however, the temptation to actually write for a newspaper was too strong and as a result, *Police Talk* was born and became the very first police chat column to be produced in the Thames Valley Police area.

I thoroughly enjoyed the writing over the next twelve

months, but the task proved to be even more of a challenge than I had expected. To start with, meeting a weekly deadline while working long unsocial hours, coupled with the added strain of three quick changeovers a month and a twenty-five mile round trip between my home and the newspaper offices, proved very difficult. Home computers and email were a thing of the future then and I had to make do with a manual typewriter for the purpose – afterwards delivering the finished product to the newspaper personally before the agreed weekly deadline. I couldn't afford to miss a single edition either so whether I was sick, called in for extra duty or on holiday, the column still had to be submitted as usual, which sometimes meant writing two or three columns in advance to cover any periods I anticipated being away. To make things even more difficult, extracting information from my naturally reticent dyed in the wool police colleagues about cases they were dealing with was a bit like trying to draw King Arthur's sword from the stone. Inherently suspicious of anything involving the newspaper industry, they were very reluctant to pass anything on to me at all and for a while I was faced with a major bridge-building exercise. When a few police appeals to the public produced some leads, however, the attitude of my colleagues began to change and they started to appreciate the importance of publicity – so much so, that on occasions I ended up being bombarded with information and had to make some hard decisions as to what could be included in any particular week.

In due course, the column became a very useful link between the police and the public, but more importantly as far as I was concerned, it also served to mark a new era of cooperation between the police and the press, and for me that was what really made all my months of hard work worthwhile. *Police Talk* and similar columns in other newspapers, which unbeknown to me at the time were to follow, didn't do my career any harm either, but I didn't find that out until much later in my service. In the meantime, I had a series of further moves to contend with and the first was to a sleepy riverside town just a few miles outside Reading.

CHAPTER 17

REGATTAS AND ROADSTERS

The river drifted lazily under the ancient stone bridge, stirring the cabin cruisers at their moorings. Children with ice-creams raced excitedly among the mix of elderly tourists and bikini clad girls thronging the towpath, while in the town centre antique shops and old-fashioned tea rooms watched the world go by through dusty windows. It seemed incredible that the hustle and bustle of Reading could be just a short drive away, but this was Henley-On-Thames – the other side of the Thames Valley coin – and though people usually only came to this delightful riverside resort on holiday, I was actually being paid for the privilege of working here.

After two years at one of the busiest stations in the force, I found Henley a real change. There was still plenty to do, of course, especially in the summer season, but generally the work tended to be lower key stuff, like investigating reports of petty thieving and vandalism or dealing with traffic offences and road accidents, and there wasn't that relentless pressure to put up with all the time. As a result, I managed to get out and about on foot to talk to people and I found that the police had a much more personal relationship with the locals who were not shy to refer to them by their Christian names. Shades of the old Kencot days, I thought.

As for the nick, it was probably as old as the town itself, occupying a corner position near the market, and a lot of the bobbies had been there a long time. Despite amalgamation they still thought of themselves as part of the now extinct Oxfordshire Constabulary and they wanted as little to do with the new regime as possible. Having come from Reading, which was frowned upon as a sort of *Sodom and Gomorrah* place, I had to tread warily at first because I represented change and change itself was regarded as a virtual declaration of war. But when it became apparent that I had no intention of challenging Henley's own particular brand of UDI or of trying to impose big town ideas on everything that moved, I gained a sort of grudging acceptance. 'We do things different here,' one stalwart advised. 'We don't rush around like they do at the other place.' That was true enough, but then, in view of the town's slower pace of life, they could afford to adopt such a philosophy. Instead of an intense parade briefing of around sixteen officers constantly interrupted by radio calls for them to go here, there and everywhere, each of the Henley shifts managed a civilised chat over a pot of tea for four.

As with most places, the town did have its moments, of course – like the call I received to a boarding kennels just outside the town, which had been torched by an arsonist. Such incidents were the exception rather than the rule, however, and as a result, it was not difficult to be seduced by the apparent tranquillity of the town and lulled into a false sense of security – which is exactly what happened to me during one quiet late turn tour.

I should have been on patrol in Henley itself, but convinced that not much was happening, I decided to sneak a visit to my parents living in the nearby village of Highmoor Cross. Halfway through a very welcome cuppa my personal radio blasted, despatching me to an armed robbery in

191

progress at a local petrol filling station at Nettlebed, just a couple of miles down the road. Due to my illicit social visit, I could not have been closer to the crime scene and I took off like a rocket. But the arrest of the year was not to be had, for as it turned out, I missed the alleged gunman by seconds. This was a real let-down for me at the time, considering the rarity of such incidents in a place like Henley, but on reflection maybe it wasn't such a bad thing, bearing in mind what could have happened if I had managed to confront the offender actually in the commission of his crime.

But if armed robberies were not a major problem at Henley, one other type of crime was – and that was the incidence of burglary. The police area boasted a large number of what were categorised as 'good class dwellings' – expensive houses owned by people with money to burn – and these were frequently targeted by criminals. The problem for the police was that those responsible for the break-ins were seldom local opportunist thieves, but professional villains from other parts of the country, which made them a lot more difficult to catch. Furthermore, the value of their haul – in terms of cash, jewellery and/or antiques – could often be measured in the thousands rather than hundreds of pounds, which pushed the local crime figures up into the hyper league and put CID under heavy pressure.

Because of the problem, uniformed patrols spent a lot of time checking vulnerable premises – from chocolate box cottages to rambling mansions – especially when the owners were away on holiday. It was a pretty routine task, but it could sometimes turn into an unnerving experience. As in my days at Kencot, the officer doing the checking was usually alone and because of the size of the area and the isolated locations of many of the houses, there was little prospect of any back-up if an intruder were to be discovered.

Once again night duty was the loneliest tour of all and shocks were easy to come by. In the grounds of one house I nearly jumped out of my Y-fronts when a ghostly shape materialised from a hollow in the moonlight and stared at me with bulging eyes before bounding off into encircling woodland. It was only a deer and the woods around the outlying villages were full of them, but it gave me a nasty jolt just the same – especially as I knew from past experience that there was always the risk of stumbling upon something a lot more lethal when venturing inside the gates of a big country house at night.

In fact, I had actually been presented with just such a scenario while responding to an emergency 'intruders on premises' call with a colleague on an earlier, rather more memorable occasion. A young woman staying in her friend's isolated house while they were out had telephoned the police control room claiming she had been awakened by suspicious noises coming from downstairs. We raced to the incident in a patrol car, but as the five-bar gate giving access to the premises turned out to be securely locked, we were forced to climb over it and make our way on foot up the long drive to the house. Unfortunately, what the caller had neglected to tell our control room operator after dialling '999' was that a large Doberman pinscher dog was running loose in the grounds. But we were not long kept in ignorance, for halfway up the driveway the beast burst from some thick shrubbery behind us and we only just about made it to the front door in time. Seeing that big black apparition loping after us had come as quite a shock, but at least after checking round inside the house and finding everything to be in order we were able to positively assure our frightened caller that if there had been an intruder, with 'Fido' wandering around to welcome guests, her nocturnal visitor was unlikely to be doing much intruding in the foreseeable future.

That didn't help our own position, however, for we still had to work out how we were going to get back to our car without becoming the dog's next meal. Declaring our little problem to the police control room didn't seem like a good idea, for we knew we would never live the thing down afterwards, but trying to outrun the Dobermann was not even a close option. 'She's not really vicious, you know,' the lady promised. 'She won't come anywhere near you if you're facing her. It's only if you happen to turn your back on her that she'll come after you.' Somehow it didn't help us much to learn that the animal had a yellow streak, especially as it was not her dog in the first place, but belonged to the people who owned the house.

In the end, we decided we had no choice but to take her at her word and try to bluff our way back to the gate – which is exactly what we did, with the Doberman stalking us every inch of the way and forcing us to wheel and face the thing with our torches every time it tried to rush us from the cover of the shrubbery bordering the driveway. The last few yards were the worst bit, for by then the animal had grown a lot bolder and become much less intimidated by our blazing torches. Finally, no doubt sensing that it was fast running out of opportunities to take a chunk out of one or other of its visitors, it suddenly launched itself at us in a last desperate attempt to secure a trophy. I have never been any good at athletics, particularly pole-vaulting, but I distinguished myself that night and went over the gate in one leap, clearing the topmost bar by several inches – even ahead of my younger fitter companion who was certainly keen to ensure that he wasn't left behind. We didn't hang about afterwards either, for the Dobermann seemed determined to continue the chase beyond the boundary of the property. Even as we climbed back into our patrol car, the animal was venting its frustration on the bars of the gate itself and I remember thinking as we drove away that if these were the actions of a cowardly Dobermann I'd hate to meet a courageous one.

Although much of the patrol work at Henley did involve fairly routine tasks, like the checking of vulnerable premises, the town did have one claim to fame and that was its famous regatta. Over a period of several days the crowds converged on the place in their thousands to watch or participate in one of the main boating events of the year and the roads into the town sometimes became a solid mass of revving, honking motor vehicles stretching for several miles in each direction. This meant that, like it or not, the small station had to accept manpower assistance from Reading and several other stations as part of a major operation. The event itself was a colourful occasion, celebrated by flags and bunting and with a proliferation of striped blazers, yachting caps and straw boaters among the restless mass of humanity cramming the river bridge and the regatta site itself.

From a police point of view, however, the regatta meant road accidents, petty crime, people jumping or being thrown into the river and moneyed yobs (the 'Hooray Henrys') from so-called upper class families becoming a real pain in the rectum after downing too many glasses of Pimm's.

My job the year I fell for regatta duty was to supervise the uniformed bobbies who had been assigned to static traffic points to prevent snarl-ups. It was a thankless task and, as always, there were one or two motorists who seemed to regard the sight of a police officer standing in the middle of the road as a challenge to do the exact opposite to what was required. Taking over one of the traffic points myself, I was confronted by an objectionable young woman who sat in the queue at the end of the day's events repeatedly pumping the horn of her flashy sports car to indicate her displeasure at being kept waiting. It had been raining heavily for some time and I was so wet that bubbles issued from the lace-holes of my boots at every single squelching movement. That horn was the last straw and I walked grimly over to the motorist and told her politely to stop being so impatient, warning her that misusing her horn was an offence for which she could be prosecuted. 'Balls!' she said pleasantly. 'Do you realise I have been here for fifteen minutes?' This was a gross exaggeration, but I didn't bother to argue the point. Instead, I replied tightly, 'Yes, madam, and I have been here all day!' She was so surprised by the retort that she simply sat there staring at me with open-mouthed astonishment as I turned on my heel and returned to my point. Maybe Daddy hadn't told her that engaging in repartee was not the sole privilege of the self-appointed upper classes.

Dealing with moneyed people I had long ago discovered could sometimes be a more disagreeable task than sorting out the yob element, especially as many of them were well-connected socially and could call upon influential friends – including high ranking police officers – to intervene if they considered they were not getting the sort of service that befitted their station. Unfortunately, the Henley area seemed to attract rather a lot of such people and it was not difficult to rub some individuals up the wrong way; a dubious skill I had acquired from my rural beat days at Kencot, when I had crossed swords with a number of local dignitaries over their mistaken belief that they were major 'shareholders' in their local police service and could therefore dictate how it should be run. But police work is all about extremes and there were people at the other end of the social scale who posed problems of a different sort.

I came across just such a character one black moonless night and the circumstances of our meeting were unusual to say the least. I was driving along the A423 Maidenhead to Henley road when the headlights of the police car picked out something directly in my path. I pulled up quickly and got out to have a look – only to discover that it was an old rickety pram piled high with clothing and what looked like cooking utensils. I was still standing there staring at the thing in absolute astonishment when I heard footsteps slowly approaching me through the darkness. Moments later a bent figure appeared at my elbow and a cracked voice said politely: 'Evening, officer.' The speaker was an old tramp and he was evidently the owner of the pram, for the next moment he set off back the way he had come, pushing it in front of him.

Too surprised even to ask the obvious question, I returned to my car and carried on towards Henley, overtaking the bent figure on the way. But I didn't get far before I was confronted by another pram in the middle of the road. The tramp joined me, still pushing the first pram as I was trying to push the second one into the kerb. 'Evening, officer,' he said again and, abandoning the pram he was pushing, began to shuffle away with the second one. I was beginning to feel a bit out of my depth now, but made an effort to get to grips with the situation. 'Just a minute,' I called after him. 'Are both these prams yours?' He stopped and half-turned towards me. 'All my worldly goods, officer,' he replied. 'But this is a busy traffic route,' I exclaimed, surprised that no vehicles had actually passed us in the last few minutes. 'Don't

197

you think it's a bit daft pushing a pram along here in the dark while you leave another one in the middle of the road?' He considered that for a moment, scratching his chin, then chuckled. 'Not half as daft as trying to push two at once,' he retorted, deliberately missing the point. I closed my eyes tightly for a second in resignation, wondering if it was me. 'I don't suppose you have another pram round the corner?' I continued sarcastically. 'Another one?' he echoed. 'What would I want with three prams? It's enough bother with two!' Then, before I could think of a suitable reply, he and the second pram abruptly faded into the darkness, leaving me no alternative but to let him go on his way.

Like the old tramp I had arrested on the Kencot beat all those years before, this particular character turned out to be something of a local celebrity and he was often to be seen laboriously pushing his prams along the A423. He also had a habit of setting up camp in the woods close to the road itself and his log fire must have presented an eerie spectacle to passing motorists in the early hours of the morning, perhaps even prompting them to drive a little faster when they glimpsed that elfin glow among the trees. Sadly, however, my own acquaintance with him was cut short soon after that very first meeting. As I had feared would happen, he was knocked down and killed on another dark night when a car's headlights failed to pick him out until it was too late. A tragic end for a true gentleman of the road who became just another fatal accident statistic to chalk up to the motor car.

CHAPTER 18

SPIES AND SPEEDERS

Tragedy on our overcrowded roads has actually become a depressingly common feature of everyday life over the years, rivalling even the consequences of violent crime, and after my tour at Henley and a brief period as acting inspector back at Reading, I was thrust into the forefront of it all with a surprise, and almost instant, posting to the southern traffic area at Taplow, near Maidenhead.

I had always fancied a job on traffic ever since my probationary days at Didcot when, as part of my two years training, I had to spend a fortnight attached to the forerunners of the present day traffic department, then called 'mobile'. They had used beautiful black Austin Westminster cars for patrol work in those days and the crews were nicknamed 'The Brylcream Boys' (a slightly less derogatory term than 'The Black Rats' as traffic officers later came to be called). The job was much more wide-ranging than it is today and as the eight patrol cars with which the force was equipped were attached to local divisional stations rather than to separate traffic bases, they responded to almost every type of police commitment – from road accidents to burglaries.

I well remember going with the crew to check an outlying petrol station after it had closed for the night and nearly jumping out of my uniform trousers when a huge Alsatian hurled itself at the glass doors the moment I shook the door handle. My colleagues had neglected to tell me about the dog, but at least my reaction lived up to their expectations and gave them something to laugh about for the rest of the tour.

The intrepid pair had another laugh at my expense too. Caught short in the Boars Hill area of Oxford I asked for a comfort stop. They obliged immediately and told me to relieve myself on the edge of a roundabout while they shielded me with their car. I should have realised what was going to happen, but being young and naive, I took them on trust. Big mistake. I was in full flood when they drove off and for the next minute and a half I was subjected to the blast of horns from late night revellers driving home from pubs and theatres as they pinpointed me in their headlights. Talk about humiliation; I was just so grateful it was too dark for them to spot my red face.

The practical jokes did not put me off traffic, however, but while I enjoyed the patrol car experience, the thrill of riding a high performance police motor cycle was what particularly appealed to me. I did actually manage to pass the police test for lightweight machines after about three years too, but sadly, the nearest I ever got to fulfilling my ambition was the occasional use of one of the curious water-cooled Velocettes allocated to the local Blewbury beat.

Referred to disparagingly by all and sundry as 'Noddy Bikes' – possibly because the policeman in Enid Blyton's childrens' stories about *Noddy and Big Ears* had had a penchant for riding one – the grey stand-up-and-beg abortions looked as if they had been constructed from a Meccano set. Sitting astride that ridiculous looking contraption with my feet placed squarely on the running board did my macho reputation no good at all, especially when overtaken by fast-peddling cyclists.

My interest in the traffic department itself, however, and the vital role it performed in operational policing never really left me, even though my enthusiasm for a transfer to the department began to wane over time as each application for advertised vacancies was met with rejection. When the official posting to the department arrived on my desk out of the blue during my time at Henley, I could hardly believe my luck. Unbeknown to me at the time, however, while the transfer had been arranged with the best of intentions, someone in high places had handed me a poisoned chalice.

I actually got an inkling of what I was heading into on my very first day. The atmosphere at Taplow was distinctly cool when I reported for duty and though I was treated to the standard welcome every new arrival received, I detected a definite sense of resentment among the traffic crews I met. This should have come as no real surprise to me, for I had already been warned that gaining acceptance on the base was going to be a difficult process.

In the first place, I had never been on traffic as a constable so I had no traffic experience; secondly, I had not been through the usual interview procedure; and, most important of all, I had not passed the advanced traffic driving course normally required as a prerequisite to appointment. I was fully authorised to drive standard police vehicles, of course, and had done plenty of fast driving in my service, particularly on the support group where car pursuits had been a regular event, but I had not earned the advanced driving ticket so prized by traffic officers and I would now have to take the necessary training course *after* joining the department instead of before, which was unheard of. Through no fault of my own then I was seen as an interloper and someone for whom the rules had been bent to suit the occasion. As I found out later, that was not so far from the truth either.

In fact, my appointment had been made in a hurry and on a specific recommendation, due to pressure from above to create a position for me, but having anonymous friends in high places can sometimes be a disadvantage when you are trying to settle into a new job and I was caught in the middle of an internal political battle between the hardened élitist traffic managers who were determined to prove a point and their high level bosses who were equally determined that their decision would stand.

To reinforce my position, I was given the job of training the traffic crews on new legislation that was about to come into force, requiring the fitting of tachographs (the so-called 'spy in the cab' devices) to certain goods vehicles as a means of recording their driving hours, and I was sent away on an intensive course to Birmingham to learn the ropes. But even with this qualification under my belt, I faced an uphill struggle and when I attempted to deliver the courses, I was met with hostility from some long-serving officers who objected to a non-traffic sergeant lecturing them on such a technical traffic subject.

Nevertheless, I persevered and out on the ground I worked hard to improve my credibility among the rank and file of the department, after a while managing to gain some grudging respect for my supervisory style and my determination to get my hands dirty. Dirty jobs were not difficult to come by on traffic either – and I am not just talking about crawling under lorries and cars to carry out vehicle examinations. During my time on the department I attended several horrific fatal accidents and one in particular I will always remember.

A young local man walking across a bridge straddling the then A423(M) with his girlfriend had decided to climb over the edge of the bridge parapet as a gesture of bravado. What happened after that is anyone's guess, but he ended up falling from the bridge into the path of several vehicles travelling at high speed along the carriageway and he was killed instantly. As a result of the accident, the A423(M) had to be closed and diversions put in place to re-route the traffic on the roundabout where it joined the M4 motorway. My colleagues and myself were there for most of the night, enforcing the closure and recovering the dead man's remains, which were not all in the same place! It was a vile task and involved a careful fingertip search of the carriageway with the aid of powerful spotlights to ensure nothing was left behind and we all felt pretty sick at the end of it.

What made things even worse was the attitude of some of the motoring public. Despite police road closure and diversion signs across the mouth of the junction, overhead lighting and the presence of uniformed officers wearing reflective jackets, many drivers seemed incapable of under-standing why they couldn't be allowed through.

One particular driver in a flashy Jaguar actually protested that the diversion would make him late for an engagement – and this even after he had already been told that there had been a fatal accident. I remember standing by the traffic cones in the blaze of the spotlights as he drove off and thinking back to all the other serious incidents – railway accidents, fires, suspect bombs and major crime – I had attended over the years and wondering why it was that the mere sight of a road or premises coned off by police should engender such public indignation. Was I missing something or were some people so bereft of common sense that they were either incapable of grasping the obvious or simply wanted to be obstructive for the sake of it? Whatever the truth was, after a few hours on that grim exposed site without so much as a drink to fortify the soul, biting the tongue certainly became a mammoth exercise in self-control.

Dealing with obstructive or antagonistic motorists is all part of the job on traffic, and it was a real eye-opener for me to see just how much hostility the public reserved for traffic officers as opposed to the ordinary bobby on the beat. Things have got a lot worse since my time on the department too and if I were to hazard a guess, I would probably lay the blame for this at the door of speed enforcement. Today the car is king and any attempt to restrict its potential is seen by many as nothing less than prejudice against drivers – even if the purpose of speed cameras and safety partnerships is to save lives. To be frank, the majority of motorists will accept that if someone is prosecuted for driving at sixty miles an hour in a thirty mile an hour zone they deserve all they get. What people cannot accept is the zero tolerance policy that has been employed by some forces, which results in a normally law-abiding motorist being pilloried for straying just a couple of miles over a limit. A degree of common sense is therefore necessary if speed enforcement is to retain its credibility and not be seen simply as another means of grabbing revenue for the Exchequer.

Catching speeders was certainly a bread and butter job for the traffic crews at Taplow, with radar traps and an onboard computer system called VASCAR the mainstay of their enforcement armoury. The highly accurate speed cameras and the CCTV vans operated by safety partnerships today were not even an emerging gleam on the horizon then and the issue of speeding was not the high profile thing that it has now become. But although speed enforcement was only one of the multitude of responsibilities down to the department, I found the almost daily diet of road accidents, drunk drivers, speeders and defective vehicles infuriatingly repetitive after the sheer variety of work I had experienced on more general police duties. Patrolling the motorway with committed traffic officers, whose fixation with motoring offences and enthusiasm for the performance characteristics of different cars or motor cycles, drove me to distraction. While I had every respect for the department and the job it had to do and couldn't help but admire the superb driving skill of my colleagues, I was fast coming to the conclusion that traffic was not the job for me.

After an uncomfortable advanced driving course, which left me feeling dismembered and disillusioned at the end of it, I made one of the most difficult and potentially damaging decisions of my service and applied to come off the department to return to general police duties in my home town of Maidenhead. My request received a very frosty reception at headquarters, but after an interview with the chief superintendent in charge of the traffic department, my request was reluctantly granted and I found myself back at Maidenhead, first as patrol and then station sergeant.

It was great to be back on familiar territory and I was flattered when shortly after my arrival I was asked to write a similar weekly police news and advice column for the local newspaper, the *Maidenhead Advertiser*, as I had done for the *Reading Evening Post*. It was a lot easier doing this at Maidenhead too, since Elizabeth and I were still living in the area, and dropping the finished copy into the newspaper offices in time for the weekly deadline involved just a ten minute trip across town.

But I was still unsure as to whether I had made a massive career blunder by asking to come off traffic in the first place, especially as my application to leave this highly prized department must have upset the political applecart at headquarters and caused a certain loss of face among those high-ranking officers who had made the original decision to post me there against so much grassroots opposition. My fear was that I had made some powerful enemies as a result and, feeling vulnerable and with no real idea as to where my career was now heading, I was frustrated and confused.

But things were destined to get a lot better. A few months later I managed to obtain vital information from a local informant as to the main source of heroin supply in the area, which I passed to the drug squad. Following a very successful operation, the principal offenders were arrested and a substantial quantity of illegal narcotics seized. I received a mention in despatches and very shortly afterwards I was approached by a detective superintendent who, despite my obvious lack of CID experience, asked me if I would be interested in a job with the regional crime squad. Why he had singled me out in this rather unorthodox way I had no idea, but thinking of my appointment to traffic I had more than a touch of *déjà vu*. The opportunity to join the squad was certainly an exciting prospect – that went without saying – but knowing how things worked, I recognised that there was also a downside to accepting such a posting. If I moved to the RCS I would have to cut my teeth on yet another new department, which meant it was likely to be a long time before I could be considered for advancement to the next rank. Yet to refuse the offer was likely to offend and I certainly couldn't afford to do that – again! Fortunately, I didn't have to make a decision either way, for even as I was mulling it over, I passed the next promotion board and suddenly found myself heading for the big multi-cultural town of Slough to take up the post of uniformed shift inspector. Evidently, despite upsetting the applecart by applying to come off 'the cream' of departments, the gods were still smiling down on me.

CHAPTER 19

PIPS AND GURDWARAS

'You'll have to wash your neck now, governor.' The normally taciturn civilian in force clothing stores really stretched himself this time and he chuckled as he handed me the bundle of white shirts to place on top of the pile of new uniform with which I had just been issued. Nowadays, all police officers wear white shirts irrespective of their position on the ladder, but at the time of my promotion to the first level of junior management white was reserved for those of inspector rank and above. Constables and sergeants wore air force blue and it was a long-standing joke among the rank and file that they could make their shirts last a lot longer than their bosses, because they didn't get dirty as quickly.

Inspector rank, however, carried with it a lot more than a change of shirt colour and two bath stars (or pips) on my epaulettes instead of three stripes. In the service vernacular, I was no longer just a skipper, but a governor and that was quite a jump in terms of responsibility and decision-making. I now headed my own team (or shift) of sergeants and constables and was personally responsible for their deployment and supervision on the Slough section during the eight hour tours of night, late and early turn duties.

The responsibility could be a pretty challenging one too. Like Reading, most of the constables on my team were either probationers or semi-rookies with just a fraction more service and because the shifts were smaller and the station was also plagued by a constant shortage of personnel there were fewer of them to go round anyway. Covering all the designated foot beats and panda car areas could often be a major headache and meeting all the commitments that came in well nigh impossible. During one particular night duty week, for example, we were so short that for two of the nights I was left with just a couple of probationers and a sergeant to cover the whole town and ended up on patrol in one of the panda cars myself in an effort to provide some sort of minimum coverage. Fortunately, both nights were relatively quiet, so we managed well enough, but the residents of the town would have had a fit if they had known about it.

In this sort of situation morale could be a real problem, for shortages in personnel invariably meant more work and less time off for those at the sharp end, coupled with which the town was not the most attractive of its kind to police and certainly not the most popular posting in the force. Unlike Reading, which despite its size and continuing expansion still retained some of its old charm, Slough came across as a cold grey unwelcoming place with no identifiable centre and very little to commend it aesthetically. On first acquaintance, you couldn't help dismissing it as nothing more than a vast acreage of concrete made up of sprawling housing estates, modern shops and grim looking industrial premises, dissected by the broad slash of the busy A4 Bath Road with its linked lights and massive roundabouts. The town's sole claim to fame seemed to be the giant Slough Trading Estate, which was said to be one of the biggest of its kind in north-west Europe, and it was hard not to empathise just a little with the feelings of Sir John Betjeman when he wrote: 'Come friendly bombs and rain on Slough; it isn't fit for humans now...'*

But in reality, there was a lot more to Slough than there at first appeared to be. Like Reading – or any other major conurbation for that matter – it did suffer from its fair share of crime, with violent assaults, robberies and burglaries quite a regular occurrence, but there was also a strong sense of civic pride and community spirit about the place, particularly among the ethnic minority communities who at that time made up around a quarter of the total population.

Policing a multi-cultural environment was not exactly a new experience for me. During my time at Reading and – to a lesser extent – Maidenhead, I had worked in communities with substantial ethnic minority populations. But then my contact with the different cultural groups had been restricted to everyday patrol duties. Community relations as a specific issue had been a matter for someone else higher up the ladder and not something for me to concern myself with, apart from its impact on individual street incidents. As an inspector at Slough, however, I found myself in a much more high profile management position and with racial discrimination now very high on the political agenda and already starting to develop into a whole new social 'industry', I had no choice but to get more directly involved.

Ultimately, that led to my being appointed divisional police community liaison officer, initially as deputy to one of the station's chief inspectors who was already in post. The job brought with it ex-officio membership of the Slough Community Relations Council and although it threw up some awkward problems, I enjoyed the experience

* 'Slough,' from Continual Dew. Collected Works of Sir John Betjeman, 1937

immensely; in the main receiving nothing but courtesy from the Sikh, Moslem and Afro-Caribbean communities with whom I talked on a regular basis.

The work involved a lot of talking too, for in most cases community members were simply seeking an explanation or reassurance over a particular incident and when they got it they were quite happy. The complaints they made were usually quite minor ones as well and though the spectre of racism did rear its ugly head from time to time, it wasn't the serious issue that it is in some towns and cities today. Overall, Slough had an enviable reputation in that quarter and was proud of the harmony that existed between its different communities; the vast majority of problems that did occur being due more to a misunderstanding or poor communication than anything else.

There was another side to things though, for while the majority of those I dealt with were genuine people, seeking only the same sort of fair equal treatment from society as the rest of the population, there were others for whom playing the 'race card' to gain an advantage or concession was second nature. Arresting, summonsing or even checking some members of the ethnic minority community could be fraught with aggravation in this respect and the indignant cry 'You're only picking on me 'cause I'm black' was used almost as a standard response by some young tearaways who seemed to think that their ethnic status gave them a *carte blanche* right to do anything they liked.

As a result, I soon found I had a very difficult political tightrope to walk. On the one hand, there were those who complained that they were being discriminated against because of their ethnicity and maintained that a policeman like myself would do nothing about it anyway as I was bound to be prejudiced in favour of my own officers. On the other, there were the cynical bobbies at Slough police station who firmly believed that the ethnic minorities received preferential treatment because of their colour and that, as community liaison officer, I would always take their side against my own colleagues in order to secure more brownie points with the powers-that-be. Trying to maintain my own credibility in both camps was sometimes a near impossible task and it often left me feeling impotent and frustrated.

The job itself did have its lighter moments though and I well remember my first invitation to address the local *gurdwara* (or temple) to reassure the Sikh community that the police would pay special attention to the area after a group of white youths had hurled insults at Sikh women and children making their way there on foot from neighbouring houses. On arrival, I was astonished to see scores of discarded shoes lying on the floor just inside the main entrance and I was pondering the question of how the worshippers would ever be able to find their own footwear again after they had finished their devotions when my smiling host suddenly asked me to remove my own shoes and leave them with the others before proceeding any further. That certainly wiped the indulgent smile off my face.

Dressed as I was in full uniform, the prospect of parting with my shiny black shoes on an occasion when authority and dignity were so important to the image I was trying to convey did not exactly boost my confidence. Furthermore, I couldn't help wondering what I would do if I was unable to find my shoes among the multitude of others when I came out again. The thought of having to drive back to the nick in my sock soles was the sort of stuff nightmares were made of. Nevertheless, I knew that to avoid causing offence I had no

212

choice but to do as I had been asked. Unfortunately, Fate seemed determined to rub my nose in it, for as I followed my host into the inner sanctum, I discovered to my horror that I had a more immediate problem; there was hole in one of the socks through which my big toe was protruding with a sort of grotesque determination.

Now feeling completely ridiculous, but trying to muster as much dignity as I could, I marched up the aisle between the rows of impassive worshippers with a resolute air. But my face was as red as the saris some of the women were wearing and partially trying to curl my toe under my foot as I went in an effort to hide the hole, I only succeeded in affecting a limp that must have attracted more than a cursory glance from the people on either side and certainly drew a curious frown from my host as he led me up on to the dais where I was to give my address.

Despite my misgivings, however, all turned out well in the end. My little speech was actually very well received and I also found my shoes without difficulty when finally making my departure, but I certainly learned a lesson from that embarrassing experience and ensured there wasn't the slightest suggestion of a hole in any of my socks before going on duty in the future.

As for the actual reason for my visit, a firm warning from the local beat officer to the youngsters who had been harassing the Sikh worshippers – reinforced by regular police attention to the area – soon put a stop to the misbehaviour and averted the very real threat of retaliatory action by the Sikhs themselves.

Sadly, not all community problems were as easy to resolve as that. During one particularly anxious week, despite its overall reputation for community tolerance and peaceful coexistence, Slough itself teetered on the very brink of serious public disorder and the irony was that the situation the police ended up confronting had nothing to do with local issues at all, but was nothing more than copycat aggravation imported from other cities where so-called race riots had erupted.

Rumour was the biggest enemy on this occasion and the 'disinformation brigade' began deliberately stoking up the fires at the very first opportunity, warning local people of impending race riots that had never been on the agenda until the whisperers started their mischievous campaign. Word quickly spread throughout the town too and, despite the best efforts of local beat officers to dispel community anxieties, the belief that there was going to be big trouble soon took hold. To make matters worse, some shopkeepers in the town centre gave way to panic and, contrary to police advice, actually started boarding up their premises, which served only to legitimise the warnings and add to the deteriorating situation.

It wasn't long before the rumour machine succeeded in doing what it had set out to do either and the first indications we had that something nasty was going down came with reports of milk bottles being stolen from doorsteps and a local dairy, and petrol being siphoned from cars or drained from the residue left in petrol pump hoses after garages had closed in the evening. You didn't have to be a brain surgeon to work out that someone somewhere had decided to turn their hand to making Molotov cocktails and the suspicion that a violent element in the town was readying itself for major disorder gained weight when a van was spotted leaving a local building site with a haul of stolen bricks and rubble on board.

All police time off was cancelled and officers put on twelve instead of eight hour shifts to increase the number of bobbies on duty. At the same time normal police patrols were removed from the streets and formed into mobile teams – or immediate response units – using specially protected Ford Transit vans to cover the designated foot beats and panda car areas.

Put in charge of one of those Transits, I found myself cruising an area that had become strangely unfamiliar to me. The boarded up shop windows and almost empty streets gave the place the feel of a Third World city on the eve of the revolution and the odd group of youngsters melting away into a side street on our approach added an unmistakable sense of menace to it all. The tension was palpable and the officers in the vehicle with me were unusually quiet. 'Calm before the storm,' the bobby at the wheel remarked dryly. He was right. As dusk fell reports of sporadic disorder in various parts of the town started to come in. Most of the calls were malicious and when police units got to the scene there was nothing happening there at all. It was all part of the wind-up process that was designed to keep us racing from one commitment to another, heightening street tension at the same time. But some of the reports were genuine and on a number of occasions missiles were thrown at police vehicles – once smashing through a Transit windscreen and hitting a sergeant colleague in the face, causing him some nasty injuries.

Things finally came to a head when the would-be rioters tried to march on the town centre, but the attempt was foiled almost as soon the mob left the housing estate where they had formed up. Anticipating the orgy of vandalism and full-scale looting that would take place if they got to their objective, the superintendent in command of the police operation made the only realistic decision he could under the circumstances and ordered us to stop them with a baton charge. The mob itself heavily outnumbered the police, but as with any rabble confronted by a disciplined force, the rioters fell back in a panic before breaking up into small groups and disappearing into the side streets from which they had originally emerged. Those that decided to argue the point or were a bit slower on the uptake than the others were quickly arrested and deposited in the cells at Slough police station to await an appearance at what turned out to be a very unsympathetic court. As for the anticipated rioting, despite all the malicious rumours and the efforts of a few determined troublemakers to stir up a devil's brew, it never really happened and the town actually returned to normal within just a few hours. But Slough had certainly come close on that occasion and that was something none of those on duty at the time would ever forget.

There was an interesting spin-off to those frightening events too. As part of my community liaison job, I had to pay regular visits to local schools to talk about law and order and deal with the inevitable complaints that came up regarding the attitude of the police towards ethnic minorities. On such occasions I was often told about an incident which had allegedly occurred, involving some unknown bobby who had been violent or abusive towards an unnamed friend of a friend on an unknown date at an unknown location. When such allegations are made, as a senior police officer you are on a hiding to nothing, because you can never disprove what has been said and you are seldom given enough information to be able to follow up the allegation; anyone can say anything if they don't have to back it up with real facts. But mud tends to stick, as they say, and what is claimed by a pupil in a classroom – whether true or false – will be believed anyway by the rest of their friends, which is another nail in the coffin of police community relations.

On one particular school visit shortly after the Slough disorders, however, I found myself in a much better position to rebut one of these allegations. I had just given my usual talk to a packed class when a young black girl stood up and told me how her boyfriend had been picked on and abused by racist policemen as he walked innocently along the road. Ordinarily, I would have had no chance of disputing such a story, but this time I was given much more detailed information about the incident than was usually the case, including the day, the location and the fact that the policemen had been travelling in the back of a Ford Transit van. Coincidentally, it had been the afternoon of the build-up to the Slough street disorders and I had not only been in charge of this particular Transit at the time, but remembered the incident very well. Far from being an innocent victim, her boyfriend had actually been guilty of disorderly behaviour and had been quite properly dealt with.

I have to admit I did rather enjoy shooting her down in flames and as I left the school and her chortling classmates behind me, I couldn't help wondering what she would say to her boyfriend later about the lurid and highly imaginative story he must have related to her.

Talking to schools is seldom an easy task, especially when you are faced with anti-authority teenagers who have little interest in what you are trying to tell them, and I have every sympathy for teachers who have to do the job every day. One of the most important points to remember is not to let the youngsters wind you up or get the better of you when you are on your feet, so dignity is a vital prerequisite. Unfortunately, as with my inaugural visit to the *gurdwara*, things don't always go according to plan and after what happened to me on one disastrous school visit, the hole in the sock episode paled into absolute insignificance.

I had been asked to talk to two pre-leaver classes about a career in the police force and to illustrate my talk I had brought along a projector and slides. The event was to be held in the school hall and tables had been provided for the projector and screen. It was an excellent venue and I felt quite confident about things when I began setting up the equipment – confident, that is, until I bent down to pick up the heavy projector. Fortunately, no one was within earshot to hear the loud splitting sound, but I was pretty sure what had happened and carefully feeling the seat of my trousers under my tunic, my worst fears were confirmed; I had split the seam all the way up and the lining was now hanging out the back.

For a moment my mind just froze. How on earth could I talk to thirty odd teenagers in that condition? I wouldn't be able to hear myself speak above the hysterical laughter. Yet my talk was only minutes away, which meant that there was insufficient time for me to return home for a replacement pair of trousers. Then I had a brainwave. It was a cold day outside so I was wearing a short overcoat over my tunic. All I had to do was keep it on and no one would be any the wiser – and that is exactly what I did, sweating it out in an environment that had almost as many radiators as a Kew Gardens hothouse. When I finally made it back to Slough police station my shirt and underwear were literally sticking to me, with the perspiration running in rivulets down my face and neck. 'Do you want a bit of a hand with that, governor?' one of my more muscular patrols called as I staggered through the door with the offending projector in my arms. I nodded, panting heavily at the exertion. He grinned as he took it from me. 'You want to be careful lugging things like that about on your own,' he said. 'You could easily do yourself a mischief!'

CHAPTER 20

SPILLS AND THRILLS

Even without disasters like ripped trousers and holed socks, public speaking is never a job for the faint-hearted and whether those waiting on your words are a class of adolescents or a group of merchant bankers, the whole thing can be a real ordeal.

Prior to joining the police service at the tender age of twenty, my own experience of getting on my feet in front of people had been restricted to family birthday parties and even then the prospect had terrified me. But a few years in the police made all the difference to my confidence, which was just as well, for as shift inspector at Slough I found myself not only speaking to schools and Sikh temples, but actually prosecuting cases in the local magistrates court.

Today, all court prosecuting work is carried out by legally qualified crown prosecuting solicitors, but then routine cases at magistrates court level were a police responsibility and down to the early turn shift inspector. It could be a pretty heavy one too. There was at least a couple of hours of pre-court file preparation to get through even before you got to court, followed by a long tiring day presenting the evidence and questioning both witnesses and defendants against volleys of protest from defence solicitors who would naturally use every trick in the book to get their clients acquitted.

Sometimes vital evidence would turn out to be missing from a file, resulting in a last minute panic to try and get hold of it before it was too late. On other occasions the file itself would decide to arrive from the police prosecuting department just as the court was about to sit, which meant trying to scan the evidence between other hearings, praying fervently that everything was there and the facts were not too complicated. Then, when the court adjourned for lunch or completed its business for the day, it was a question of dashing back into the police station next door to find out what had been happening on your shift while you were away and attempting to resolve any outstanding issues before handing over to the late turn inspector at 1.45pm.

The whole experience could be quite stressful, particularly if you happened to be nominated as prosecutor for several days in the same week, because that meant your shift 'In' tray would soon be overflowing with paperwork you had not had a chance to look at, while other important operational responsibilities that were down to you would end up being neglected.

To try and keep on top of things I started taking my prosecution files home with me so that I could go through them the day before; that way I could be more or less on the ball the morning of the court and could use the first two to three hours of early turn duty for shift paperwork and supervision instead of court preparation. It was technically against the rules to take files home (though some of the other inspectors did the same thing) and it also amounted to extra unpaid duty, which for obvious reasons could not be claimed back, but I reasoned that if it made my life easier then it was worth doing. Unfortunately, on one occasion my strategy had exactly the opposite effect.

It had been snowing heavily in the night and when I got up to go on early turn duty, it took me nearly fifteen minutes to clear the snow off my car in the driveway. When I finally arrived at Slough police station after a ten mile drive from Maidenhead, it was to find the cells virtually fully of prisoners, night turn officers still tied up with road accidents, which had occurred all over the place, and only half my own shift able to make it to work. Relieved that I had vetted my prosecution files the night before and could therefore deal with some of the operational problems now facing me, I grabbed my mug of tea and headed for the inspector's office for shift hand-over. An hour and a half later, with most of the problems I had inherited from the previous shift resolved, I decided to grab some breakfast and carry out a last minute check of my prosecution files so that I was fully prepared for court in two and a half hours time. But I was in for a nasty shock, for when I checked my desk it instantly became apparent that the bundle of court papers was missing. In a panic I raced out to my car in the police station car park and went through it with the same painstaking thoroughness as a fingertip search of a murder scene, but there was not a trace of so much as a paper clip or an elastic band.

Involuntarily, my mind started to retrace my steps. Yes, I had definitely carried the papers out to my car that morning after cleaning all the snow off the vehicle – the files under one arm and my briefcase in the other hand. Then I had put the briefcase on the ground to search for my ignition keys in my pocket and while doing that had placed the bundle of files...on the car roof!

Suddenly I felt sick to the stomach and, as the snow whirled in surreal flurries around me, I visualised my court papers spread along several miles of the A4 Bath Road and at the same time saw my own career crumble into the same feathery particles that were once more beginning to bury my car. There was just one slender chance and, dashing back to my office, I frantically dialled my home telephone number.

Getting your wife out of a nice warm bed on a bitterly cold morning and asking her to search several square feet of snow for a bundle of court papers is not exactly calculated to aid marital bliss, but the risk paid off. Clad in my wellington boots and with a coat over her nightdress, Elizabeth set to with a garden shovel and, after several minutes searching, managed to find the files in the driveway outside the house almost completely buried in the snow.

I had practically eaten my fingernails by the time her call came through and my stress levels weren't helped by the fact that I ended up in the morning rush hour as I headed back home along an accident littered A4. But luck was with me once again, for I made the magistrates court with just minutes to spare and with no one save my wife and myself any the wiser for my embarrassing *faux pas*. As for the files themselves, I have to admit that when I finally returned them to the prosecutions department later that day, some did appear to be in a rather stained and still slightly damp condition, but as far as I know none of the booking-in staff noticed a thing when I dropped the bundle in the appropriate tray – and I made no effort to enlighten them.

Prosecuting work could certainly be a real hassle at times and whether the aggravation encountered was actually self-inflicted – like dropping confidential files off the roofs of cars – or simply due to the nature of the job itself, you rarely looked on your day in court with any real enthusiasm. The only consolation was that this particular responsibility accounted for just a fraction of the month's rostered duties and there were plenty of other things to keep you 'amused' for the rest of the time.

Like Reading, Slough seldom disappointed in this respect and it was easy to get caught napping – which is exactly what happened to me on one memorable occasion and in the most private of places. It had been a fairly busy late turn shift and I had snatched a few moments to have a quiet sit-down with the local newspaper in the toilet when the station tannoy nearly blasted me off the seat with an urgent summons to the control room. When I got there it was to learn that there had been a 'Hazchem' incident in nearby Langley.

In the language of the emergency services 'Hazchem' meant hazardous chemicals and a 'Hazchem' incident usually meant a spillage of some sort, which could present a risk to life and property. Not surprisingly therefore, I didn't hang about, but headed straight for the scene and on my arrival found that the road had already been coned off, closing it to all traffic and pedestrians, and that a number of my colleagues, together with fire and ambulance personnel, were there ahead of me.

The incident turned out to have involved just one vehicle, a Bedford flatbed lorry, which had shed two of its load of twenty-two drums, disgorging a substantial amount of white powder from one of them on to the road surface. The driver had apparently been trying to shovel up the powder when the first police patrols and fire service units had arrived, professing he had no idea what the stuff was, but his clear-up job turned out to be a very bad idea and I soon found out why. One of the firemen wearing breathing apparatus came over to me as I stared at the pile of powder from what I had regarded as a safe distance and handed me a face mask. 'Better put that on, guv'nor,' he said calmly, nodding towards the spillage. 'We've been told it's cyanide.'

I backed off pretty quickly after that, but even with twenty yards and several parked vehicles between myself and the stuff I felt far from happy. After all, I had probably inhaled some of it already and it didn't make me feel any better when I saw more firemen donning full protective clothing and breathing apparatus beside the fire engine parked several yards away.

Nevertheless, I had a job to do, so leaving the fire crew trying to sort out the safest way of neutralising the poisonous spillage and arranging for its disposal, I got on with the business of managing the police operation with the small number of officers I had at my disposal. This involved keeping the public well away from the scene, visiting adjacent houses and a local convent situated directly opposite the spillage to make sure people stayed indoors with their windows closed, and setting up the necessary traffic diversions to prevent snarl-ups in the middle of what had become a very heavy rush hour.

Unfortunately, because different chemicals have their own special characteristics and therefore have to be handled in different ways, the clean-up operation was not just a simple process of shovelling the powder into a skip and dumping it on the local council tip. The manufacturers had to be contacted, not only to confirm exactly what it was, but to seek advice on its disposal, and it was just our luck for their headquarters to be located in Geneva in Switzerland. As a result, the whole operation took a lot longer than anticipated and it was just over six hours before the road could be reopened and everyone stood down.

Even then the ordeal was not over for some of us. Because several of the emergency services personnel, including yours truly, had got a bit too close to the site of the spillage without breathing apparatus, we were despatched to the local hospital's casualty unit for a precautionary check-up before being allowed home. In my case it was getting on for midnight by the time I reached the hospital and, due to other accident emergencies, well into the early hours of the morning before I could be seen and discharged. But if, like my colleagues, I thought I had a decent night's sleep to look forward to I was sadly mistaken. The advice from the hospital was that we should try to stay awake for the next twelve hours or if we couldn't, to make sure we were woken up at two-hourly intervals just in case we had unwittingly inhaled any of the chemical's harmful dust, which might result in respiratory failure.

Thankfully, neither my colleagues nor myself suffered any apparent ill effects from the spillage – though the driver of the lorry and his company did not do too well out of the accident as they were both prosecuted for insecure load – and it turned out that the risk to public health had not been as great as had at first been thought. Evidently the substance itself was at its most dangerous when in contact with moisture, since it could then turn into a lethal vapour, which had potentially fatal consequences if inhaled. Fortunately for us and the local residents, the offending lorry had chosen a clear dry day to shed its load, so much of the flap had been for nothing, but to think that while digging my garden that morning I had actually been praying for rain!

As an operational inspector with a huge trading estate on your doorstep and other smaller industrial sites dotted all around the area, the possibility of a chemical accident involving cyanide, acid, paint or some other equally nasty substance is always at the back of your mind, but it is

225

something you learn to live with and during my time as shift inspector I found myself attending any number of spillages and fires, some relatively small, others much larger and posing a significant threat to public safety. In one potentially lethal situation, however, the culprit was not some frightening industrial chemical like cyanide, but a substance most of us use every day and take for granted as an essential part of modern living – petrol.

Few motorists realise just how volatile vehicle fuel can be – you only have to see drivers filling up their cars at garages with lighted cigarettes or mobile telephones in their hands to appreciate this – and when there is a major leak of the stuff, all it takes is one small spark to cause a massive explosion and loss of life.

The scene was set for just such a calamity on another of my late turn duties when a tanker driver delivering fuel to a petrol filling station on the outskirts of Slough tried to pump a quart into a pint pot, with the result that the petrol overflowed from the underground tanks, saturating a wide area and seeping into the drains under a local housing estate.

As soon as I arrived on the scene with as many police and fire service units as could be mustered, we faced the mammoth task of visiting every house in the immediate vicinity to warn householders to extinguish all naked lights, for we knew that it could take just one lighted match dropped down a toilet pan to turn the estate into a fireball. There was then the even more difficult logistical problem of evacuating a large number of residents, many of whom were elderly or infirm, to a local hall and social club well away from the site of the spillage. Senior staff from the borough's sewage plant turned out to monitor the situation and for a time it looked as though the main sewage system to the centre of Slough would be contaminated. As it turned out, the petrol was eventually dispersed and the residents of the estate allowed to return home, but the police officers manning the control room at Slough who were acutely aware of what could be flowing through the network of drains beneath the station passed an anxious few hours before they got the all-clear.

Incidents like this always receive maximum publicity and the press love to resort to dramatic scaremongering tactics whenever they can – after all, that is what sells newspapers. Yet there are a multitude of other potentially serious incidents that attract a lot less attention, but which can be just as frightening to deal with. Such incidents are not always home-grown either, but can be the result of something that has happened elsewhere in the country. This is particularly true of major crime and I found myself in just such a situation the day I met up with an army bomb disposal man on a platform at Slough railway station. With the so-called 'Troubles' still ongoing in Northern Ireland and IRA cells active on mainland Britain, an explosion at a main postal sorting office in London had prompted an immediate check of all mailbags in the same batch. It was discovered that one bag was missing and it was just my luck for it to turn up at Slough railway station during my tour of duty.

The problem was that every letter and package in the bag had to be examined *in situ* and it was not feasible to leave it to the army man to go through it on his own. But at the same time it was not reasonable to ask any of the other officers at the scene to do the job, which meant I had to get stuck in myself, gingerly lifting each item out of the bag in turn so that the bomb disposal man could physically check it with his specialist equipment. The contents of the bag did turn out to be clean in the end, but by the time we had finished I freely admit that I was suffering from a significant perspiration problem and it wasn't simply due to the heat of the day.

Slough was certainly a good career move for me, enabling me to build on all the varied experience I had gained at Reading, and it marked another run of good luck too. During my five years on the sub-division I found myself once again writing a police news and advice column. This time it was called *Patrol Point* and it appeared weekly in the local *Slough Express* newspaper, mirroring the columns I had previously started in Reading and Maidenhead. To my astonishment, I also managed further successes in the Queen's Police Gold Medal Essay Competition, gaining second and third prizes in two successive years and earning a double quota of brownie points for myself with the divisional hierarchy.

My perceived writing skills had an unexpected knock-on effect too, which I did not entirely welcome at the time, but which later in service proved to be of considerable benefit. Summoned to my chief superintendent's office, I was presented with a lengthy article that had been sent down from the assistant chief constable, support at headquarters for rewriting. The article was factually accurate, but needed to be put into what was whimsically referred to as 'proper journalese' before it could be offered for publication.

'You're a bit of a wordsmith, so we want you to do the job,' the boss said, fixing me with his steely eye. I gulped, suddenly feeling totally inadequate. Writing competition essays and a series of small columns for local newspapers was one thing, but this was an entirely different ball game, requiring the sort of professional copywriting/editing experience I just did not have. I started to blurt out what was on my mind, but he silenced me with a benign smile and a dismissive wave of the hand. 'Every confidence in you, Mr Hodges,' he said and that was that.

I did actually complete the rewrite, but it was a hard time-consuming job that took up quite a bit of my spare time and when, with some trepidation, I finally dropped the finished product into the chief super's tray, I anticipated that it would soon wing its way back to me from headquarters with a string of criticisms. But to my surprise I never saw the article again, nor did I receive any kind of official acknowledgement or feedback about what I had submitted, apart from an oblique reference to my work by the chief superintendent as being 'excellent stuff'. But unbeknown to me at the time, that particular 'just' job had earned me the right kind of notice in the place that it really mattered – which perhaps explains why one of the 'gods' at the big house decided I should be given an even greater test.

Not that it was put to me quite like that; the whole thing was broached in a very casual way and in the most unusual of places. I was on early turn at the time and making my way across the rear car park at Slough police sation when I was confronted by the chief superintendent who asked me quite abruptly if I would accept a temporary posting. When I asked what the posting was he shook his head firmly and said: 'I'm not playing silly games with you. Do you want it or not?' My curiosity aroused, I took a chance and agreed to take it – only to gape in disbelief when he grinned and said: 'Headquarters housing and buildings department.'

Plainly amused by my incredulous expression, he went on to explain that the department in question had a heavy backlog of paperwork and despite the fact that I had no experience whatsoever of either housing or buildings, for some reason I was seen by the assistant chief constable, support as having the necessary skills to help sort out the mess.

I felt numb. To be taken off operational duties and moved to some headquarters administrative job seemed to me like a classic kick in the teeth, however it was dressed up by my boss, and it didn't occur to me that there could be more to the temporary posting than was immediately apparent. That being said, I was well and truly snookered anyway. Not only had I been neatly tricked into accepting the posting already, but it was pretty obvious that even if I had turned it down, I would have been going to housing and buildings anyway; assistant chief constables tend not to change their minds very often.

As a result, almost before I could catch my breath I was heading up the motorway on the first of what became a daily seventy mile round trip from my home in Maidenhead to the force's headquarters near Oxford and embarking on one of the steepest learning curves of my service.

And what a learning curve it was too. Instead of managing an operational shift and dealing with criminal assaults, burglaries, chemical spills and serious road accidents, I found myself liaising with county architects and struggling through mountains of files on such mind-boggling issues as the redecoration of police houses, the siting and maintenance of radio masts and the unplugging of blocked drainage systems. Nevertheless, encouraged by a very supportive and well qualified civilian team who provided as much advice and guidance as possible, I got stuck into the task, determined to do the best job I could – and it paid dividends too. When, after what turned out to be a manic few months, I went back to division, it was with a nice pat on the back from the manager of the department and a real sense of satisfaction over what I had been able to achieve in the face of one of the most unusual challenges I had encountered in my career so far.

Despite my original reservations, the headquarters posting did not seem to have done my operational credibility any harm either. Soon after settling back into my former role as shift inspector, I was appointed sector commander of the sub-division's smaller satellite station at Langley – still in the rank of inspector, but with vastly increased responsibilities, which included managing four uniformed shifts and a busy CID department, as well as the day-to-day running of the station. A temporary spell as acting chief inspector and second in command of the sub-division followed and even as I reluctantly returned to my substantive inspector role – now feeling strangely unsettled after savouring the responsibilities of the next rank – promotion boards for chief inspector vacancies were advertised in the force's weekly order sheets. Not that confident about my chances of being recommended for interview, since it had taken me several attempts to pass both my sergeant and inspector boards, I nervously submitted my application and waited for it to bounce back – but it didn't.

CHAPTER 21

PRESS AND POLITICS

The promotion interview was far too relaxed. It was almost as if the three members of the board were playing a game with me. At previous interviews I had always felt uptight and under pressure, with contentious questions coming at me from all sides, but this time the whole thing was managed like an informal chat as if the selection panel was just going through the motions. Aware that there were just two or three vacancies to be filled and having already seen the long list of candidates and identified at least a dozen names that I knew were bound to be front runners, I drove away from headquarters afterwards in a very downbeat mood, knowing instinctively that I had failed. But this time my pessimism proved to be way off beam, for a few weeks later a green slip of paper signed by the chief constable landed in my docket, giving me the news that I had never expected to hear – I had actually passed the promotion board and would be considered for a future chief inspector post when a vacancy arose.

In fact, that vacancy came a lot quicker than I had anticipated and within a couple of months I was offered and had accepted the post of chief inspector managing the prosecutions department at Banbury, right at the other end of the force area.

The posting could not have come at a better time, for less

than a year before Elizabeth and I had moved from our red brick semi in Maidenhead to a nice upmarket chalet bungalow on a new development near the village of Cookham, only to find, like a lot of other young couples then, that the increased mortgage left our finances uncomfortably tight. Promotion meant a substantial rise in salary and coming as it did at the end of October, it was the best pre-Christmas present we could ever have received.

But although the promotion was a financial life-saver, it came with strings attached and this only became apparent when I received a pointed telephone call from the chief superintendent, personnel, 'strongly advising' me to buy a house in the small market town of Bicester rather than in Banbury itself so that I would be more centrally placed for any further move that might arise. Though phrased as advice, it was obvious that I was being given a polite instruction, but I was too preoccupied with all the arrangements for my move to think too much about what I was being told or why it was being said. With no real idea at that stage where Elizabeth and myself were going to live, there was no profit in trying to argue the point anyway. So I did exactly as 'advised', buying a house on a new development just outside the town, securing places for our two children in local schools and starting at Banbury prosecutions department one Monday morning in the certain knowledge that I would be there for at least a couple of years. As I very shortly discovered, however, I could not have been more hopelessly off the mark.

Banbury actually turned out to be the shortest posting of my career and I had hardly got my feet under the table before the assistant chief constable, support, on a visit from headquarters, poked his head round the door of my office one morning and said, 'How would you like to be my force press officer?'

To say I was staggered would be an understatement. The job of press public relations officer (or PRO) was part of Thames Valley's newly created community liaison department and was regarded as one of the most challenging high profile chief inspector positions in the force. As someone so keenly interested in writing and the world of publicity, it was also a job I had coveted for years without ever dreaming it would actually come my way. But now it had been offered another more spooky realisation dawned on me. My name had obviously been in the frame for the job well before my arrival at Banbury prosecutions and someone must have been monitoring my performance a lot further back than that – hence the reason I had landed the copywriting job for ACC, support and the temporary posting to HQ housing and buildings department. It also explained why I had been pressured to relocate to Bicester, which was a lot closer to headquarters than Banbury. Obviously there had never been any question of my remaining in prosecutions; that had only been a convenient slot for me until the press office job had become vacant. In short, I had been led by the nose all the way without knowing the slightest thing about it.

Later, imparting my suspicions to an old friend and senior colleague, I was rewarded with a thin smile. 'Welcome to the "Magic Roundabout", Dave,' he said. 'From now on, it's politics all the way!'

How right he was too. The moment I walked into the press office I could sense the atmosphere. The smiles that greeted me were superficial and there was a wary expression in the eyes of each of the four office staff that told me I was on probation again and in a completely different ball game. 'Be strong,' one ex-press officer warned me, 'and always watch your back.' I had good cause to remember that warning in the months which followed, for I discovered that a police PRO is in a very vulnerable exposed position and, much like a police community liaison officer, is in the unenviable position of being sandwiched between opposing interests. On the one side, I was seen by the media as part of the establishment and a slave to the party line, while on the other, by many of my colleagues as a renegade who had gone over to the 'enemy'. Worse still, because I had the ear of the chief constable and implemented press policy on his behalf, I attracted resentment from some very senior officers – particularly one or two divisional commanders and heads of department who objected to being advised by someone two ranks down the scale, even if it was done in the most respectful manner.

On the plus side, the chief constable at that time was a very astute progressive individual who saw the news media as an important communication link between the police and the public and consequently had ruled the traditional 'no comment' response to press enquiries as out of order, except in specific circumstances; for example, where the release of information was prohibited by law. This gave me the necessary authority to try and build up a positive working relationship with the industry. Unfortunately, however, not all the chief's senior officers agreed with his policy and behind the scenes some simply refused to cooperate at all – a bit like the feudal barons in Mediaeval times when the king issued an edict and the barons greeted his messenger with a truculent, 'I will if I want'.

The trouble was that the mistrust of the media, which had built up in the police service over so many years due to the reprehensible tactics of a few unscrupulous journalists, had become very deep-seated and it was not about to change in our force area simply because we had a progressive new chief constable who wanted to foster a more open relationship. The sad fact was that, apart from a cadre of old hacks who had managed to gain the right level of trust among the senior ranks by respecting 'off the record' comments and striving for accuracy in the copy they filed, journalists as a breed were seen by most police officers as the lowest of the low; interested only in a good story, regardless of the facts, and prepared to use any shady tactic to get it – even if that did mean distorting a quote, breaking a confidence or rubbishing someone else's reputation in the process.

Prejudiced stereotyping this may have been, but at that time it was a widely held view, which led to some high level intransigence over the release of information and put me in a very difficult position with senior elements of the media themselves. As a departmental manager, I could hardly go running to the chief like some disgruntled schoolboy every time I faced an impasse between a police manager and a newspaper editor – that would have done my career prospects no good at all. So I just had to try to overcome each problem as best I could, relying on persuasion and a little guile where necessary to achieve the right result. Usually this worked well, but occasionally I was put in a position where, regardless of my junior rank, I was left with no alternative but to assert my position as PRO to ensure that the force's press policy was adhered to – and this inevitably led to one or two unpleasant confrontations.

Perhaps the worst of these resulted from the action I took when I was called out to deal with the press following the discovery of a badly burned body in a patch of remote woodland in North Oxfordshire. The reporters on the scene had already been given basic information about the incident, which later turned out to be a tragic suicide, but the regional television company needed the same information to be supplied to them in visual form for their evening news bulletin, which meant an interview with a police spokesperson. The press-hating senior police investigating officer (SIO) who had since left the scene had apparently refused to allow any form of interview to be given and he refused to change his mind when I telephoned him. This put me in a very difficult position, since there was no justifiable reason why information already released to the newspapers could not be repeated in front of a camera.

Faced with an extremely disgruntled news team and not only the prospect of media antagonism on site, but the threat of some very bad press later, I stuck my neck out and agreed to do the interview myself. The TV crew jumped at the opportunity and when they finally left the scene with my two minute contribution they could not have been happier. Not everyone felt the same way, however, and on my return to headquarters I was promptly carpeted by my chief superintendent, following a furious complaint by the senior investigating officer that I had deliberately disobeyed his instructions. At first things didn't look too good for me, but fortunately common sense prevailed in the end. After listening to both sides of the story and viewing a tape of the actual interview, the chief super decided that I had acted fully in accordance with force press policy and without in any way compromising the police investigation.

I was in the clear. Yet I felt no sense of triumph – only relief that my decision to give the interview had been upheld – for I knew full well that, while my actions had managed to keep the TV crew happy, they had won me no favours with one particular SIO. That was the name of the game, however. It was all a delicate balancing act and sometimes things did not work out as well as they should have done. But at the end of the day a press policy has to be credible and consistent if the media are to be expected to cooperate with it, otherwise everything degenerates into a free-for-all where nobody wins.

Cooperation is particularly important at a major incident or crime scene, for if reporters and camera crews suspect that they are being short-changed on information, they will be all over the police like a rash, impeding the operation and unwittingly destroying vital evidence. Effective dialogue costs nothing, but it can pay dividends in the long run.

This was brilliantly demonstrated on another of my press call-outs when police units homed in on a wooded site to investigate the suspicious death of a young boy. Because of the age of the victim there was intense media interest and hoards of reporters and TV crews besieged the police incident post, which had been set up some distance away. Anxious to prevent them becoming a major headache to the investigation team, the local area commander not only agreed to a full press conference, but also provided a couple of police Transit vans to convey a limited number of TV crews and press photographers to the spot where the body had been found so that pictures of the taped off scene could be obtained from a satisfactory distance. The outcome could not have been better. The media got what they wanted and therefore left the police to concentrate on their investigation without hindrance, while the police themselves gained all the publicity they could have wished for to help them with their enquiries. A real case of *quid pro quo*!

This level of mutual back-scratching did not happen that often though and on a day-to-day basis the press office usually faced a frustrating uphill struggle to keep the cooperation going. This situation wasn't helped when someone on the ground actually neglected to tell us about a particular incident that was in progress, leading to media allegations that our open press policy was nothing more than a sham, or an unscrupulous reporter chose to breach a confidence and compromise a police investigation, which only served to reinforce the hostility of the force's anti-press lobby.

The problems we encountered were not new, of course, and the previous head of the department had undoubtedly suffered the same sort of headaches during his term in office, but that didn't lessen the challenge for me as a novice PRO and it soon became apparent that, unlike most headquarters jobs, the headaches didn't stop at 5pm. Call-outs in the middle of the night were not uncommon and though my press office assistant, who was an experienced journalist, shared this responsibility, there were times when more than one press officer was required to cover different commitments, which meant that I had to get into the habit of sleeping with one ear open, listening for the strident ringing of the telephone beside my bed and hoping that I would manage to lift the receiver before the thing woke up the whole house. Weekends were not sacrosanct either and though again the cover duty was shared, I could not go anywhere without my electronic bleep just in case something happened.

To add insult to injury, some elements of the press actually managed to get hold of my home telephone number too and even when I was officially off duty they had no hesitation in calling me if they thought it would help them get a better 'in' on a breaking story or they were having problems extracting information from a local police station. Despite the fact that this was well out of order, I always did my best to resolve the problem for the sake of the force's image, but sometimes even this was seen as not enough and I well remember a particularly aggressive call I received one Saturday from an independent news agency. I was off duty and on the point of taking the family out for the day when the reporter telephoned and complained angrily about the lack of cooperation he was getting from one of our police control rooms over a breaking news story. As it turned out, control room staff were not being uncooperative at all, but because of the nature of the incident and the fact that the investigation had only just begun, they were only able to give him the barest of details. He was not at all happy when I gave him the bad news and his agency later followed up his complaint with a nasty missive direct to the chief constable, suggesting I personally had given them poor service.

Acutely conscious of the fact that I had spent several hours of my own time looking into his complaint and had had to cancel my family's day out as a result, I felt pretty upset by what I saw as a deliberate vindictive attempt to drop me in the mire. Fortunately, it didn't work on this occasion and the only hassle it created for me was that of having to submit a detailed report to my chief superintendent on the circumstances. But the episode left me with an unpleasant taste in my mouth and gave me a much better appreciation as to why so many of my colleagues, suffering similar bruising encounters with journalists, nursed such animosity towards the media.

Nevertheless, I did not allow my own encounter – or the many other encounters I had with unprincipled journalists over the next three years – to prejudice my commitment towards better police/media relations, which I firmly believed to be the only way forward if we were to improve our communication with the public and elicit their help – much as my weekly press columns had tried to do in their small way at Reading, Maidenhead and Slough. The hard work of our tiny press team paid dividends too. In a number of serious crime enquiries – including the murder of a student whose body was found in woodland on a country estate in Oxfordshire and the kidnapping and murder of a small boy who was snatched at a fairground in Berkshire – the news media could not have given more support to the police investigations. Not only did they keep the crimes 'alive' through a process of long-term publicity, but also provided coverage of police reconstructions and in some cases actually helped in the production of publicity material, like posters, to raise public awareness.

For me this demonstrated in a very practical way that the advantages to be gained from working more openly with the media by far outweighed the disadvantages, but the *pièce de résistance* in this respect came with the force's commitment to the development of BBC Television's exciting new *Crime Watch UK* series, which had the strong personal support of our chief constable in his role as secretary of the Association of Chief Police Officers' (ACPO) Crime Committee. The series itself, which was designed to elicit the help of the viewing public in solving crime and bringing wanted criminals to book, was an immediate success, but very few viewers at that time would have had any real idea how much planning and preparation had gone into things before the very first programme appeared on their screens.

As force press officer, I found myself in the thick of it all, liaising with the producer, Peter Chaffer, and presenters Sue

Cook and Nick Ross, as well as other police forces, trawling for suitable material for the forthcoming launch and setting up relevant locations for filming. The work involved a considerable amount of chasing around and meant several visits to the BBC's studios in London, but I was in my element. As a would-be writer, being given the opportunity of working with producers, presenters and film crews seemed too good to be true so I certainly made the most of it and when I was invited to participate in the launch of the series and take part in the very first programme, I felt a tremendous sense of pride knowing that my own force – and our chief constable in particular – had been one of the prime movers in getting the project off the ground in the first place and that on the personal front, I myself had actually been involved in such a historic achievement in police/media cooperation.

CHAPTER 22

HOSTING AND GHOSTING

The job of a police PRO is certainly one of extremes. One minute you are practically fighting for your own survival and the next sailing on a virtual cloud of euphoria. But though media liaison is one of the key responsibilities of any PRO, it became apparent to me at a very early stage in my introduction to the role that there was a lot more to it than simply dealing with press enquiries. When I was not trapped in the office, helping my staff with the scores of calls that came in almost every working day or out on the ground, trying to keep the journalists and photographers off the back of one of my senior colleagues at a major incident or crime scene, I was hosting visits to the force, 'ghost-writing' speeches and drafting sensitive letters to councillors, members of parliament or government departments on behalf of individual chief officers. Then there were the press releases and news features to write, media complaints to look into, television and radio interviews to be provided and talks to be given – both to police training courses and outside organisations. For a time, I even found myself providing an input into public order training courses for senior and chief officers at the Police Staff College, Bramshill – and that was a real education in itself.

All in all then, a pretty varied job portfolio, keeping me very much on my toes, and the incredible thing about it was that, like my predecessors, I had received no relevant training at all prior to taking up the appointment. That didn't come until I was several months into the post, which clearly indicated that someone somewhere had seriously underestimated the level of professional expertise the job required.

The public relations side of things was a case in point, for clangers dropped in this area were likely to have far-reaching consequences, not only for the PRO personally, but for the force itself. This was particularly true where powerful or influential people were involved and I quickly realised that while the role certainly demanded an outgoing approach and good communication skills, tact, diplomacy and a sound measure of political awareness were of equal, if not greater, importance.

Essentially, this part of the job was all about marketing an image – presenting Thames Valley Police in the best possible light and looking for openings to capitalise on good news stories about the force and its activities. I found myself in regular contact with other UK forces, plus a whole variety of public bodies and government departments – including the Central Office of Information, the Foreign Office and Home Office, and occasionally even the press office at Buckingham Palace. It was fascinating work and it also brought with it the opportunity to host visits to the force by all kinds of people and organisations – from county councillors and members of parliament to schools and writers' circles.

The visits I enjoyed hosting the most were those from overseas police forces and during my term in office I found myself welcoming parties not only from European countries like France, Denmark and the Netherlands, but also the USA, Brazil and parts of the African continent. What made these events so rewarding was the esteem in which the British police service seemed to be held worldwide and I made the most of each visit by waxing lyrical about the force and its achievements, knowing full well that I was not only more or less preaching to the converted, but doing my patriotic bit to enhance the reputation of the UK on a truly international scale. For a committed Queen and Country nationalist like myself, that was an opportunity too good to miss.

In the main, as a result of detailed planning, the majority of visits went well and I received some very nice letters of appreciation from both the forces concerned and the Central Office of Information which had set them up, but there was also the odd visit that became indelibly etched on my memory for all the wrong reasons and one in particular left me with a very red face indeed.

The police party on this occasion had come from the Netherlands and a full programme had been arranged in liaison with the chief superintendent commanding the force operations department. All went well until the chief superintendent decided on a photograph or two of our guests to commemorate their visit and, in the absence of a professional photographer, he charged me with the task. Unfortunately, my knowledge of photography could easily have been accommodated on the back of a single negative and, with hindsight, I should never have taken on the job at all. The professional reputation of the force appeared to be at stake, however, so I felt I had no choice – and anyway, taking a few snapshots did not seem to me at the time to be such a big deal.

As it turned out, I did the PR bit rather well and even though I say so myself, I also managed to take some nicely posed shots of the Dutch police officers in their smart uniforms to mark the auspicious event. But that was as far as it went and it was only when I got back to my office after the party had left that my gaffe became evident. Opening the back of the camera, I found to my horror that there was no film inside! The press office assistant I had left with the job of loading and checking the camera had let me down big time.

I suppose I managed to keep the chief superintendent off my back for about three weeks in total, even though his query as to when his pictures would be developed became more and more insistent. But in the end I had to face the unpleasant job of telling him that there weren't actually any pictures *to be* developed and that was not an easy thing to do with this particular chief superintendent whose colourful verbal repertoire was almost legendary. 'No pics?' he said, frowning. 'Why's that, David? Forget to put a film in, did you?' I swallowed hard. 'There was a problem with the camera, sir,' I replied mildly, which in a way was quite true, since any camera without a film inside would be a problem. He grunted. 'So you did forget to put a film in,' he growled, fixing me with a hard stare before adding dismissively: 'Dick-head!'

Luckily the meet and greet function only called for the force PRO to dub as official photographer on very rare occasions as there was usually someone from the force photographic or scenes of crime department to do the honours. This meant that my camera handling skills – or lack of them – were never actually put to the test again, but I was not quite so fortunate in other areas of professional expertise.

One responsibility that demanded a whole basket of specialist skills was the production of the force newspaper, *Thames View*, which enjoyed wide external as well as internal circulation and was the force's very own shop window. In the past, this eight page tabloid had not presented too much of a problem for the force PRO, since the job of editor had fallen to the department's deputy press officer who was always a trained journalist, but it was just my luck for that worthy individual to leave the department for pastures new just a few months after my arrival. As a result, I suddenly found myself saddled with the job until a replacement could be found. That meant desperately trying to meet the next publication deadline while struggling to master a whole range of new skills like proofreading, sub-editing, layout and design, which, despite my avowed interest in creative writing, were about as familiar to me as plumbing or aircraft maintenance.

To add to my difficulties, in those days the newspaper was produced the old-fashioned way. There was no sophisticated computer equipped with a state of the art desktop publishing system, turning out formatted copy-ready disks for digital printing. Apart from my long-suffering clerical assistant's newly acquired electronic typewriter and a so-called 'message switch' in the general office, which connected us with the rest of the force like a telex machine, the technological revolution had not touched the department at all, with the result that everything had to be done manually.

In such an environment, getting the newspaper out on a regular basis could be an intensely frustrating, head-banging process – especially when a deadline was missed or a major textual error was overlooked at the proofreading stage – and though it was always very satisfying to see the printed bundles finally arrive in the press office for distribution, knowing that I had actually put the finished product together in the first place, my satisfaction was tempered with the knowledge that the publication of one edition signified it was time to start on the next. Small wonder therefore that with all my other responsibilities as force PRO, it was not long before the business of producing a corporate newspaper began to lose its appeal and I could not have felt more relieved when a new deputy press officer was finally appointed and my eight month stint as *Thames View*'s editor came to an end.

My brief sortie into the corporate newspaper world was certainly an eye-opener, but despite all the hassle accompanying the experience I learned a lot of new skills I would never otherwise have acquired. Nevertheless, when I vacated the 'editor's chair', it was with one thing very clear in my mind: if for any reason my future police career did not quite work out as I'd hoped, newspaper publishing was definitely not something I would want to pursue as an alternative.

But if my interest in newspaper production was dealt a terminal blow by my *Thames View* experience, my enthusiasm for creative writing remained as strong as ever and those in high places were not slow to capitalise on this – pushing lengthy features, speeches and articles my way as ghost-writing assignments whenever they could or with a wry smile and the comment 'you're a bit of a writer, aren't you?' appointing me as secretary of a working party with the boring job of taking the minutes and drafting the final working party report.

On one occasion my enthusiasm for writing was acknowledged in a rather more unusual way when the chief constable himself actually invited me to join him and some guests for lunch. I was certainly flattered, particularly when I learned that his guests were well-known fiction writers, whom he thought I would like to meet. I spent a very enjoyable couple of hours in the officer's mess talking to the 'professionals' and came away on a real high, but unbeknown to me at the time, the chief's invitation had a sting in the tail. Several days later I received a lunch bill from his staff officer, asking me to share the cost of the meal. Talk about being hoist by my own petard! Nevertheless, it was all worth it in the long run, for as a result of that lunch I forged a long-term friendship with two of the writers who took to telephoning me regularly on points of police procedure and in return provided me with invaluable advice on detective fiction writing. Once again a clear case of *quid pro quo*.

My penchant for the written word also resulted in one or two very nice press office assignments being put my way and my proudest achievement in this respect was, with the professional assistance of the force photographer and printing department, designing, writing and producing the first all-colour PR brochure for the force, entitled *Serving The Community*, which attracted widespread interest and was circulated both at home and abroad.

Unfortunately, as well as being a personal success story, which undoubtedly earned me a mega quota of brownie points, indirectly the brochure itself was also my undoing and actually influenced me into making the first of two very bad career decisions.

I could not have been happier when I was selected for a prestigious command course at the Police Staff College, Bramshill – the police service's own university – seeing it as a significant boost to my career, but after successfully completing the course and returning to my force, I allowed my writing aspirations to cloud my judgement. Offered a change of post from force PRO to operational chief inspector at Oxford, I went against the advice of the chief superintendent, personnel and elected to remain in the press office so that I could see through the force PR brochure project, which at that time was only half completed.

It was a bad mistake, for shortly after the brochure came out Thames Valley lost its reigning chief constable to a top police post in another force and the last thing the new chief constable needed was a change of PRO. As a result, I not only missed a valuable opportunity to gain middle management experience on an operational area, but faced the prospect of staying in the press office for a lot longer than I had originally anticipated.

My wake-up call came when my previous selection for the promotion board to superintendent was overturned by the incoming regime and the new chief constable then ruled that future superintendent posts would be filled by a process of individual selection rather than by the promotion board system. Suddenly I saw a deep pit opening up before me with my future promotion prospects subsiding into it, and decided that a move to an operational position was vital if I was to demonstrate I had sufficient management experience for the next rank. This was when I made my second mistake.

Submitting a report to the new chief constable requesting a move, I was shaken rigid by both the speed with which the report came back and the fact that it bore just the one word reply to my request in large black letters: 'No!' Prudence dictated that I left the issue there, swallowed my disappointment and tried again a few months down the road, but I had the bit between my teeth and was in no mood to listen to inner voices urging caution. Consequently, I did the unthinkable by appealing against the decision and asking for a career interview with the chief superintendent, personnel, to put my case. That was my really big mistake and I learned sometime afterwards from a confidant in high places that I could not have committed career hara-kiri more effectively.

In short, if you wanted to get on in the police service, you didn't alienate the chief constable by questioning him over one of his decisions!

I did get my move in the end, but things certainly did not work out to my advantage. To start with, my career interview was conducted in an atmosphere of tangible hostility. Then I fell into what I suspect was a carefully laid trap. Instead of being asked what sort of posting I was seeking, the question was quite the opposite; in short, what would I *not* like. With hindsight, I should have adopted the tactics of *Brer Rabbit* in that famous fable in which he pleaded with *Brer Fox* not to throw him into the briar bush, secretly hoping that his enemy would do just that and enable him to escape. But I didn't and naively thinking that an effort was being made to accommodate me, I said I did not particularly want the position of chief inspector in prosecutions or a posting to Aylesbury – essentially because it was the furthest accessible station from my home that I could legitimately be sent to. The chief superintendent nodded with apparent understanding, but I must have misread the signals, for when I saw him a few weeks later there seemed to be more than a hint of relish in his expression when he told me that the only posting on offer was chief inspector, prosecutions at Aylesbury.

Whether that posting actually was the only one available or the powers that be had simply offered it to me in the belief that I would turn it down and stay where I was, I will never know, but if the offer was a carefully contrived set-up it didn't work, for I reluctantly accepted it and prepared myself for what I suspected would be the most frustrating soul-destroying job of my career. I was not disappointed.

CHAPTER 23

PURGATORY AND PROTECTION

One of the essays that had earned me the second prize in the Queen's Police Gold Medal Essay Competition had been entitled *The Role of Police in the Prosecution of Offenders* and in it I had concluded that the decision whether or not to prosecute in criminal cases should be removed from the police altogether and handed to an independent legally qualified body like an attorney general's department. Staring at the 'In' tray on my desk in the divisional prosecution department at Aylesbury, I could only regret that this had not already happened. The two or three tier plastic paperwork trays used by most organisations are designed to hold a reasonable amount, but never the mountain of files that this one held. It must have measured sixteen inches in height and some of the topmost files had already cascaded on to my desk, a couple of them even lying on the floor by my chair.

This was my first day managing the department, following a short period of settling in under the watchful eye of the previous incumbent who had finally left wearing the sort of relieved grin a lifer exhibits when the prison gates open for him after thirty years of incarceration. And the sight which greeted me that morning was to greet me almost every other morning from then on, no matter how successful I was in clearing my paperwork before I went home each night. For me, the job of chief inspector, prosecutions was nothing less than a brain-numbing, soul-destroying taste of purgatory that ate away at my normal resilience like a parasitic worm as I struggled to keep on top of the work that poured in every day from all over the division and wrestled with complicated criminal cases that sometimes involved multiple offences and six, seven, eight or even more alleged offenders. Often the evidence was just not there, with the result that a file had to go back for further work to be done, and on other occasions the relevant legislation had to be checked or legal precedents considered, which meant hours pouring over law books written in the sort of gobbledegook that seemed designed to turn your brain inside out. Furthermore, as head of the department you were in a very vulnerable position, for your every decision could be questioned at any time by virtually anybody and if you could not justify why a case had been dropped or, conversely, recommended for prosecution, your head could easily be on the block with no one around to champion your cause.

The position also brought with it managerial responsibility for thirty odd civilian staff and two experienced police inspectors who had been in the department so long that they had forgotten more than I could ever hope to learn in the few years I expected to be in post. Being both the governor and the rookie at the same time is never an easy situation to handle and it was made a lot harder by the fact that my natural motivation to do the job was just not there. I hated every minute I spent in the department, positive that I had been dumped on for no more heinous a crime than asking for a career development move against the wishes of the chief constable, and I nursed a secret dread that I might end up staying in my small office at the top of the building until retirement. Chief inspector, prosecutions, was one of the most unpopular jobs in the force and I could not see anyone voluntarily applying for the post, except perhaps an eager young inspector seeking early promotion.

In this negative frame of mind it would have been so easy to have allowed resentment and bitterness to rule my head completely, pushing me into resigning from the police service altogether and looking for a completely different career. I certainly came close to doing just that in the months that followed too. But personal pride and a strong determination to confound those at the top, who I firmly believed had deliberately set me up to fail as a form of self-inflicted punishment, I stuck with the job, as with previous jobs I had not particularly liked, and kept my head down for the duration.

That was not as long as I had expected either. In under two years there was a major shake-up of the whole criminal justice system in Britain with the introduction of the Prosecution of Offences Act. This resulted in responsibility for prosecution decisions passing from the police to a brand new independent crown prosecution service, or CPS, staffed by qualified criminal lawyers. This was a rather ironic thing to happen while I was still chief inspector, prosecutions, since I had been one of those to propose such a step in that runner-up gold medal essay of mine a few years before – never dreaming at the time that the very process I was recommending would one day be my ticket out of a department I had come to dislike to much.

There was a further irony too. After spending my last few months in post, seeing through the initial stages of transition on the division, I actually vacated my chair with a degree of satisfaction that I would never at one time have thought possible – not because I had finally 'escaped' and was turning my back on the department for good, but because, despite a hard core of opposition and professional rivalry on both sides, I had finally managed to set up a liaison process between the department and the fledgling CPS that was acknowledged as one of the best in the force.

As a result, rather than leaving under a bitter personal cloud, I went with a morale-boosting sense of achievement and that wasn't the only thing to restore my faith in myself and my future career prospects either. About the same time I learned that I had chalked up another, much more prestigious achievement, something I had been striving for virtually all my service, and it had absolutely nothing to do with prosecutions whatsoever. In short, after three previous runner-up awards, I had actually won the first prize and gold medal in the Queen's Police Gold Medal Essay Competition.

The 'wires' certainly hummed after that and as the congratulatory letters started arriving from colleagues all over the force, I was invited to the Home Office with my wife and two daughters to receive my medal from the Home Secretary, the Rt Hon Douglas Hurd MP, at a ceremony also attended by my own chief constable who had made a special, and much appreciated, effort to be there. It was a really thrilling occasion – for my family, as well as myself – and when we all got back on the underground to head home, my wife carrying the biggest bouquet I had ever seen, I knew that this was a day I would remember for the rest of my service.

I soon came down to earth, however. Contrary to my hopes, earning my gold medal did not set me on the path to glory or promotion to superintendent rank. Quite the opposite, in fact, for after relinquishing my role as chief inspector, prosecutions, I found myself on just another sideways move. This time it was to a post bearing the vague uninspiring title of chief inspector, support – a job that brought with it wide-ranging administrative responsibilities on behalf of the divisional chief superintendent, including such 'exciting' tasks as managing the overtime and allowances budget for divisional HQ staff, supervising the sale of unclaimed found property by auction and monitoring and updating the division's operational orders.

At first sight then my new position did not appear to be much of an improvement on my previous job as chief inspector, prosecutions, but the reality was a lot different. Unlike the chief inspector support roles on most other divisions, this one carried with it unique and very important responsibilities: the security of the prime minister's residence at Chequers and the deployment of a firearms trained 'divisional team' – established to provide tactical support to the armed police unit guarding the premises round the clock and a rapid response to any reported incidents.

For me Chequers was like a lifeline thrown to a drowning man and the closest I was able to get to the hands-on operational role I so desperately wanted – especially since the chair of the sub-divisional chief inspector directly responsible for the physical policing of the Aylesbury area was already occupied and was likely to remain like that for quite some time. Furthermore, the job gave me a legitimate reason for quitting my small office on the divisional headquarters floor – with its daily workload of overtime and expense claims, found property queries and requests for statistical returns – and head out into the country for a couple of hours to check on the security coverage of the Chequers estate and cadge a cuppa off the crew on duty there.

If I am honest, that was about as far as this aspect of my support role went too, for the bobbies looking after the PM's isolated retreat were highly professional and took their job very seriously indeed. As a result, apart from one or two false alarms over suspect vehicles seen in the vicinity of the premises or ramblers found trespassing on the edge of the grounds after wandering off adjoining public footpaths by mistake, nothing untoward happened there during my time in post – which was just as well really, for an incident involving what would have been seen as a failure of security at the official residence of such a high profile figure as the prime minister would not simply have added to my career woes, but actually put paid to my job altogether.

As for the divisional team, though in great demand as back-up to the bobbies on the beat when one or other of the individual 'parties' that made up the unit was not specifically engaged on Chequers duty, they were disciplined enough to operate with the minimum of supervision. My main role as chief inspector, support was to ensure through the individual party sergeants that they were used effectively when requests for their services were made by sub-divisional stations or a major incident room, rather than physically patrolling with them.

The only occasion I did actually find myself working with them on the ground was during a major criminal trial at Aylesbury Crown Court when the chief superintendent gave me the job of setting up an operation to provide security coverage of the court building. Reliable intelligence had been received that a gang of violent criminals might either attempt to 'spring' one of their associates, who was on trial for shooting and seriously wounding another man after an argument at a club, or otherwise try to harm the key witness in the case. It soon became apparent that fears over a possible criminal assault in the court room might be well founded too, for during the trial several suspected gang members were actually spotted in the vicinity of the building and there were some tense moments for all of us throughout that long operation, including the mysterious disappearance of a set of crown court keys. Things were made a lot worse by the fact that some of the gang were known to carry firearms, whereas we were not allowed to be armed whilst in the precincts of the court and it did not help to ease our minds when our divisional chief superintendent tried to reassure us by saying that the gang would probably do nothing as they would believe we were carrying concealed firearms anyway. Some reassurance that was under the circumstances.

In the event, however, nothing actually happened, for the case itself subsequently collapsed when an important witness failed to turn up to give evidence. As a result, the accused man had to be acquitted and the key witness was whisked away to safety by his police escort. This was a very disappointing end to an operation that had taken so much time and effort to set up, but at least the work of myself and my team did not go unnoticed. A short time afterwards a very nice letter of appreciation regarding the operation was sent to my chief superintendent from the force prosecuting the case, which certainly helped to ease our feelings of frustration. Sadly, however, it wasn't the last time that the man accused of the shooting came to notice. Some months later he was arrested in another force area after being involved in a bungled armed robbery in which an off duty police officer was blasted to death when he tried to intervene. This time the case against him did not founder and he was put behind bars where he belonged but it was all too late for his innocent victim and I cannot help but wonder whether the murdered man might still have been alive today if that witness had decided to turn up at Aylesbury Crown Court to give evidence.

Apart from that crown court operation and its tragic sequel, my first three years at Aylesbury was not a period that would ordinarily have committed itself to my memory. That it did had nothing to do with the job itself, but rather what happened to me as a result of it and what it taught me about myself and my priorities.

The catalyst was actually another case of murder – a young girl found naked and strangled in an isolated barn at Bledlow Ridge in Buckinghamshire. This prompted one of the biggest police manhunts the county had ever seen, which required someone of senior rank to manage the administrative side of things; including the provision of equipment and personnel resources, the rostering of duties and the approval of overtime and expense claims for over seventy officers. Desperate to get out of the rut in which I felt I had been dumped, I volunteered for the job and that proved to be another big mistake, for I soon discovered that I was not only expected to manage this logistical nightmare, but look after my own divisional duties as well. This meant travelling to the incident room at High Wycombe police station early in the morning to carry out my admin role and then returning to Aylesbury to deal with my normal responsibilities later in the day. To make matters even worse, about the same time sod's law dictated that the sub-divisional chief inspector at Aylesbury should be involved in a nasty road accident and be packed off on long-term sick leave, with the result that I found myself having to give a weather eye to the responsibilities of his post as well.

They say that pride goes before a fall and it certainly did

on this occasion. Working on average between twelve and sixteen hours a day for weeks on end without any chance of time off, drinking gallons of coffee, bolting my meals and managing only five hours sleep each night, I became a walking disaster waiting to happen and it finally *happened* in a toilet at Aylesbury police station of all places, when I collapsed with an internal haemorrhage.

Hospital corridors immediately beckoned and following a series of uncomfortable and worryingly inconclusive tests, I spent seven long weeks off sick, stewing myself not only about what might be going on in my insides, but what effect my collapse might have on my future career. The doctor had made the sobering observation that my haemorrhage amounted to a 'gypsy's warning' and he advised me to review my manic approach to my job before it was too late. But as a senior police officer, I knew that such advice would not be so easy to put into practice. Applying the brakes halfway up the ladder would have been seen as an admission that I was unable to cope and that was the last thing I needed to be suggested on my next promotion appraisal form. Not that all my previous dedication and hard work seemed to have been appreciated anyway, for despite all I had done, none of the divisional hierarchy showed any inclination to call and see me. In all the time that I was off sick I was visited only by the sub-divisional chief inspector (now recovered from his road accident) who brought me a basket of fruit and drank my whisky. Otherwise, it was as though, from a force point of view, I no longer existed.

In the end, I did make a slow recovery and no serious health problems were identified from the hospital tests – physical stress they said sagely – but the affair had quite an impact on me psychologically. I felt hurt and totally let down by those for whom I had worked so hard and the old adage about the graveyards being full of indispensable people seemed cruelly pertinent. I returned to work in a very bitter negative mood, determined that from that moment on I would do the absolute minimum and sod the lot of them! But my newly acquired militancy did not last long; it just wasn't me. Like it or not, I had to knuckle down and get on with the job. No matter how bruised or embittered I felt, my own pride would not let me do anything else. And I got my reward for battling on very shortly afterwards. It came with the announcement by the sub-divisional chief inspector at Aylesbury that he had finally decided to retire from the job and take up a new career with the local authority. Almost before the ink in his resignation report had had time to dry, my application for the post was winging its way to the chief superintendent and a few weeks later I found myself sitting in his chair as second-in-command of the sub-division.

At last I was operational again, doing what I had actually joined the police service to do, and for the first time in three years I felt that, like the tube train starting off after being held up in a tunnel during the rush hour, my career was once more on the move. But not all my disappointments were over and I received another smarting rebuff when the sub-divisional superintendent also retired and, in spite of running the station on my own without any problem for several weeks, a new sub-divisional commander was promoted to the top chair over my head.

Looking back on things now, it must have been a very difficult moment for the new man when he first walked into his office, knowing that the person he would have to rely on in the future as his deputy had been passed over for a position he had been managing unofficially for a substantial period already. It was to his credit though that he took the bull by the horns and brought the issue out into the open straight away, as a result of which an excellent working relationship was established between the two of us right from the start.

My time as second-in-command on the Aylesbury sub-division was probably one of the most stimulating experiences of my service and even though my new boss was the archetypal action man – proposing initiative after initiative in his relentless pursuit of change – he had the sort of natural charisma that drew the best out of people and made even the punishing twelve hour days I worked on a regular basis seem worthwhile. For the first time in so many years I found that new ideas were greeted with genuine interest instead of being rejected outright as 'rocking the boat' and I got immediate backing for several projects of my own.

One of these involved setting up a police post in a busy town centre shopping mall to provide a better service for the public who normally had to traipse over a mile to the divisional headquarters site on the outskirts of Aylesbury. Though this particular service had to be abandoned after a few months due to lack of available manpower, it certainly established the need for a permanent police presence in the town centre. It also later resulted in the decision to base members of the police community liaison department and traffic wardens in the old and long since vacated borough police station as a means of 'showing the flag'.

The project that gave me the most satisfaction, however, was the creation of the town's first alcohol-free 'public house' to pull the youngsters in off the streets and keep them out of trouble. Setting up a small voluntary committee of churchmen and professional people with the aid of a Christian evangelist and a local minister, I used what influence I had as a senior police officer to persuade the district council to come up with some suitable accommodation and to my delight they agreed to set aside a derelict public house for our use. Then it was a case of embarking on a massive fund-raising campaign to secure enough money to renovate the building and pay for a permanent live-in manager. It took months for our little committee to get anywhere and for a time it even began to look as though the project would fail. But the will was there and after a competition to find an imaginative name for the new premises, a local lad came up with the winning entry. A few months later *Alcatraz*, with its twenties American Prohibition décor, was born.

Sadly, *Alcatraz* has long since disappeared from the streets of Aylesbury – a casualty of a subsequent road development scheme. The project did run successfully for several years, however, gaining a bronze award in the Queen's Royal Anniversary Challenge and winning the Scottish Widows Regional Award for Community Innovation, and I like to think that it served an important local need at the time – maybe, just maybe keeping some vulnerable youngster out of trouble, at least for a while...

CHAPTER 24

HOSTAGES AND HAZCHEM

Aside from community initiatives, Aylesbury threw up plenty of operational challenges too, including royal visits, public order problems, firearms incidents and some pretty heavy crime – each challenge demanding a different type of approach. Some, like royal visits and major entertainment events, were known about well in advance and as such were more a test of planning, resourcing and management skills than anything else, but others happened spontaneously and on these occasions strong leadership and the ability to make decisions on the hoof were of much greater importance.

One particularly nasty incident I attended with the super-intendent soon after I had taken over my sub-divisional role had actually started off as a routine domestic dispute. By the time we got to the scene, however, it had degenerated into something a lot more serious, with an unstable knife-wielding man holding a child hostage over a bath of scalding water. It was the sort of nightmare scenario that even the most devious police trainer would have had difficulty devising – a situation so unpredictable that the slightest error of judgment was likely to have the most horrific conse-quences. Rushing the offender, though obviously an option, was clearly out of the question under the circumstances, but holding off had its drawbacks too, for there was a very real chance that the man could flip completely or accidentally lose his grip on the infant, with fatal consequences.

In the end, negotiation was considered to be the best approach and while I managed the overall police operation, including pulling in more resources and securing the area, the superintendent and another senior officer spent an anxious time reasoning with the offender until the child could be rescued and the man taken into custody. When he was finally sentenced at the crown court, the difficult situation the police had faced at the time was directly commented on by the judge who went to the extent of commending us all for our 'restraint, good sense and patience' – which made a very welcome change from the criticism my colleagues and myself were so used to receiving from people in high places.

As said before, dealing with any domestic issue where children are said to be at risk is always difficult, for such situations are rarely clear-cut. With emotions running at fever pitch and family members playing for the highest stakes, you never know who to believe or how real the level of risk actually is. Another incident I attended some months later was certainly like that and from the initial complaint, which was certainly well-intentioned, I fully expected the business to end in a dreadful tragedy.

The whole thing started off as a heated argument between a couple in the throes of suing for divorce, with their two-year-old daughter caught up in the middle, and it culminated in the mother walking out on her husband and taking the child with her to stay at the grandmother's house just outside Aylesbury. Later the same day the father 'allegedly' snatched the child from the grandmother's home while his wife was out and promptly disappeared. The balloon went up when the wife frantically telephoned the police to say that her husband was suicidal and was armed with a shotgun.

To add credence to her story, a police check revealed that he was indeed the holder of a shotgun certificate and a search of the marital home failed to find any trace of a shotgun, which suggested he had the weapon with him. The welfare of the child uppermost in my mind, I immediately initiated a full-scale search of the area, including checks on all known friends and relatives, and had the make and number of his car widely circulated. It did not take us long to track him down though, for even as we began our checks on likely addresses, his car was spotted parked outside his mother's house on the other side of town.

As with the previous hostage incident, charging in through the front door of the premises was not a viable proposition under the circumstances – the potential risk, especially to the child, was far too great – so I arranged for the scene to be kept under close surveillance while I considered what options we had. As luck would have it, shortly after the surveillance had been set up our man left the house we were watching and returned to his car. The little girl was not with him and it was apparent that he was not carrying a weapon of any sort so we promptly moved in and detained him on the spot.

A search of the house then revealed that his daughter was safe and well inside and there was no evidence whatsoever to suggest that he had intended to harm her in the first place. According to his version of events, he had simply taken her to the address for her own good. As for the shotgun, it transpired that this had actually been lodged at the house of a friend some time before and the weapon was later seized by police officers and the relevant shotgun certificate revoked.

From my perspective as the operational police commander, the incident could not have had a better

266

outcome. In human terms, of course, the affair still had its tragic side with the poor little mite at the centre of the marital break-up facing an uncertain future as yet another referral for social services intervention. But at least she had been found unharmed, no one had been injured and no firearm had been discharged, so in this respect at least the police operation had been a complete success.

In fact, contrary to the popular perception of the general public who are regularly bombarded with a depressing litany of violent crime by sensationalist newspaper reports and reality television programmes, most domestic disputes attended by the police usually end in peaceful resolution and though – like that first murder I attended as a probationary constable at Didcot years before – some incidents do end in tragedy, this is the exception rather than the rule.

Unfortunately, it is a fact that it is usually the incident that goes wrong that makes the headlines and all too often success is based on a police shooting or a dramatic arrest. 'Non-events' seldom feature in statistical returns, even though incidents which come to nothing can take just as much – if not more – police time to resolve than those resulting in high profile action. Like it or not, police effectiveness will always be about detections, arrests and offences reported, because that is the way the system works and how government ministers use statistics (and sometimes doctor them) to hang on to power.

Take the 'armed siege' I inherited from a colleague on a neighbouring division, for example. It came at a time when the sub-divisional superintendent was away on a lengthy course and I was put in charge of the sub-division as acting superintendent. The information I was given was that a local High Wycombe girl had been twice threatened by her jilted boyfriend with a handgun and it was known that the boyfriend had now returned to his home in a village just outside the town, which happened to be on the Aylesbury sub-divisional area. Officers keeping watch on the house saw what appeared to be the man in question walking past a lighted window in the living room with what looked like a rifle or shotgun in his hands and I found myself under pressure to authorise a raid on the premises.

After considering the issues involved, I firmly resisted the clamour for direct action, firstly, because we had no definite evidence that the man in question was actually in possession of a firearm or in a position to cause harm to anyone. Secondly, the thought of armed police officers crashing through the front door of a private house in the dark on the sketchy information we had acquired just did not bear thinking about – especially in terms of the possible risk both to the officers concerned and anyone else who happened to be in the house at the time. Instead, against a lot of disgruntled opposition from those on the ground, I instructed that we would maintain a watching brief until daylight to see how things developed.

It was quite a long night though and I finally finished at 3am – after a total of fourteen hours continuous duty – to go home and get my head down for a few hours before returning to work at 8.30am. When I did resume duty, in the absence of any declared threat, an officer was sent to knock on the door of the house to see whether our man was actually inside. He was and he came to the door, wearing the grin of the century. It had all been a game to him. He had seen the officers outside his home the previous night and had played along with their suspicions, deliberately walking past the lighted window – not with a shotgun or rifle, but a simple broom handle. His grin only faded when he learned how close he had come to facing police officers armed with real firearms and to this day I shudder to think what could have happened if I had buckled to pressure and persuaded the assistant chief constable, operations, to authorise one of our armed teams to go in instead of waiting for the dawn. A man shot dead in his own home for waving a broomstick about is the sort of incident that nightmares are made of.

My appointment as acting superintendent only lasted around three months, but during that time I gained plenty of operational command experience, dealing with a variety of major commitments, including firearms incidents, a royal visit to the town and the tragic death of one of my own officers who collapsed while on duty in the rural station next door to his home and was found by his young son. The policeman's death came as a terrible shock to his family and I tried to give them as much support as I could during the weeks that followed, particularly on the day of the funeral, which proved to be a very harrowing experience, not only for them, but also for the officer's colleagues who attended to pay their respects to a man who had been such a popular member of the sub-division.

Tragedy manifests itself in different ways, however, and one equally tragic event was the air crash I attended near the Oxfordshire village of Chinnor when a helicopter *en route* from Navenby, Lincolnshire to Blackbush in Hampshire, ploughed into a tree in thick woodland. The pilot, who was apparently on a routine business trip when he was killed in the crash, was found still strapped in his seat in the cockpit several hours later, following a sighting of the wreckage by the police helicopter, and a police guard had to be set up overnight to keep the scene secure until the air accident investigators could attend the next day.

I well remember scrambling through the undergrowth to the site of the crash to liaise with the officers already at the scene and thinking how awful it was that the man should lose his life in such a way and wondering whether he had died instantly or sat there alone and badly injured for several hours in the remains of that cockpit, waiting for the help that never came.

A serious accident like an air crash can obviously happen anywhere and we were lucky when the helicopter went down that it didn't do so in a densely populated area like Aylesbury or High Wycombe, for then we could have been talking in terms of multiple deaths rather than the one – particularly if the machine had exploded on impact in the middle of a housing estate or after hitting something like a chemical factory or petrol refinery. The potential for this kind of catastrophe is always on the cards, and when Fate points the finger it could just as easily be at a sleepy village in the Cotswolds as a sprawling development in the middle of London – a fact horrifically illustrated by the infamous Lockerbie disaster.

Conscious of the need to always be prepared for such disasters, emergency services across the country are constantly planning for the unthinkable, producing major accident plans to deal with the aftermath of every kind of disaster they can visualise and testing the effectiveness of their own response through joint make-believe exercises. This is a very sensible approach too, but only provided the exercise itself is not pre-empted by the real thing – which is precisely what happened out of the blue during my command 'apprenticeship' at Aylesbury.

The exercise we had been planning for several months

had been due to take place in the village of Wendover and was set to involve a petrol tanker overturning in the main street and decanting its load of fuel into the street drains and the cellars of an adjacent public house. That the exercise never took place was due entirely to the fact that, just days before the planned event, a thirty-eight ton petrol tanker overturned while negotiating a small roundabout on the A41 in Aylesbury and crashed into a lamp standard. The accident ruptured the tanker's fuel tanks and thousands of litres of neat petrol poured out on to the road surface and into the main drainage system of the town.

Miraculously, the only person slightly injured as a result of the accident was the driver of the tanker who managed to climb out of the vehicle through the smashed windscreen, suffering from just shock and a few cuts and bruises, but when I got to the scene to marshal the police units attending from all over the division, I realised with a sinking feeling in my stomach that the situation was critical. Although the fire service with their usual speed of response had arrived within minutes and had been able to reduce the risk of a fire or explosion – first by spraying the tanker with foam and later by laying down multiple tons of sand supplied by the Highways Department – their explosi-metres were registering 100% readings in the petrol flooded drains. All it needed was for someone to drop a lighted match and a substantial part of Aylesbury would have disappeared in a huge fireball.

With around a dozen fully manned fire tenders and some 40 odd police units on the scene, plus a fleet of ambulances on close stand-by, this was one of the biggest major incidents I had ever dealt with and I was acutely conscious of the fact that this time the buck stopped with me as operational commander. Not that I had much time to think about that, for I had too much else on my mind. Amongst other things a police control point, rendezvous point and dedicated radio channel had to be set up, road closures and traffic diversions introduced and buildings within a quarter of a mile radius evacuated, including not only the residents of a nearby housing estate, but an entire commercial site flanking the accident scene, which comprised major retail outlets full of customers. Because of the risk of a spark from vehicle ignitions, the large car park serving the commercial site also had to be sealed and motorists prohibited from starting their engines. Then there were security patrols to be deployed to stop any looting of empty premises and unattended vehicles, and the press and general public to be prevented from accessing the scene.

The inconvenience to residents, shoppers and motorists alike was considerable, but it was unavoidable under the circumstances and a rest centre was set up away from the scene to accommodate as many displaced people as possible. There was worse to come, however. On the advice of the fire service it was decided that the electricity power to the area would have to be shut down as a safety measure and this produced another set of problems.

Firstly, some of the premises had emergency generators, which were automatically programmed to kick-in the moment the power failed, producing the very sparks we were trying to avoid, so arrangements had to be made to disable these in advance. Secondly, the decision to turn off the power drew howls of protest from some of the businesses on the commercial site. This was hardly surprising under the circumstances, for they included a supermarket and a cold store, both of which faced the prospect of losing thousands of pounds worth of frozen and sell-by date goods if the power were to be turned off. In the end to try and resolve the problem, they were given authority to transfer as much of their perishable produce as possible to other branches, using a convoy of diesel lorries for the purpose, subject to their electrically powered refrigerated units being switched off while the vehicles were inside the restricted area. Trying to supervise this operation, manage traffic diversions, provide on-site security and deal with the evacuation process, while at the same time liaising not only with the fire and ambulance service, but with other key organisations, such as British Telecom, the water, gas and electricity utilities, the National Rivers Authority and various departments of the county and district council, was certainly no easy task, but it was tremendously satisfying to see all the different organisations working so well together and to find that the major accident plan that everyone had put so much effort into producing actually worked.

The incident and subsequent clean-up operation, using special environmental tankers to cart away hundreds of tons of contaminated earth and other waste material, actually lasted almost three days and though I was exhausted at the end of it all I felt a real sense of achievement that everything had gone so well. My chief superintendent was pretty pleased too and I was put forward for a chief constable's commendation in recognition of my successful management of the operation. It was a nice gesture, which I greatly appreciated, but I was also rather embarrassed by it, for I felt that my contribution to things had been no greater than that of anyone else involved in the incident. We had all worked together as a team and not only did I feel it was inappropriate for me to be singled out for special mention, but I was conscious of the fact that such an award was likely to cause a great deal of resentment among my colleagues. I said as much when approached about the proposal and fortunately the hierarchy took exactly the same view – as a result of which I ended up with a nice letter of congratulation instead.

The ditching of my commendation didn't do me any harm either, for a few weeks later I received a summons to head-quarters to see the assistant chief constable in charge of personnel and I arrived in his office to find two other chief inspector colleagues already there. 'You're all going to see the chief today to be promoted,' the ACC said gruffly. 'Congratulations.' A few minutes later I left the chief constable's office as a substantive superintendent – though not as the officer in command of a sub-division, as I had expected, but as the manager of the force computer department of all things.

CHAPTER 25

MARS AND BEYOND

It was as though I had been banished to another planet – a distant world on the far side of the solar system, which had its own unique galactic culture and an alien language that could only be interpreted by someone like Captain Kirk of the old Starship Enterprise*, who might well have described it as 'life, but not as we know it'!

My arrival as the new manager of the force computer development department was greeted with a mixture of astonishment and resentment by the thirty odd technical staff who made up this little civilian empire – astonishment when the techies learned just how little their new boss knew about information technology and resentment because it had long been assumed that the job would go to the highly qualified and experienced senior techie on the department, who, on paper, stayed as my deputy.

I was absolutely delighted with my promotion – still could hardly believe it – but as head of computer development, I was not simply out of my depth, but at serious risk of drowning. I just could not fathom why the chief – in his infinite wisdom – had decided that I was the most appropriate person for such a highly technical job when I had spent most of my police service in operational roles and

---

* 'Star Trek' television series, created by Gene Roddenberry, 1996

would have been a lot more comfortable back on division. The official view of the personnel department was that I had shown my ability to adapt to a variety of different positions during my service (housing and buildings department, for example) and therefore should have no difficulty in adapting to this one. Maybe that was how the chief saw it too, but there again maybe, as one wag confided, he was just 'having a laugh'. If he was, then that laugh had the potential for being a pretty expensive one.

The department's budget allocation was very serious money indeed, catering as it did for the information technology requirement right across the force area and it needed someone at the top with the right sort of IT experience to be in control of the purse-strings. Unfortunately, I didn't see myself as fitting that particular bill. Although keyboard proficient, I had never actually used a computer in my life before – I was the original Luddite with no real interest in technology whatsoever. It was only a few months before that I had finally replaced the manual typewriter I had been using at home with an electronic version and even installing the right channels on a new television or using the timer recording facility on a video left me cold.

Small wonder that I found the prospect of managing the force's entire computer development strategy so terrifying and although I set to with a will, doing my best to knock back all I could on the bewildering subject of mainframes, stand-alones, networks, systems analysis and so forth, it soon dawned on me that the best way to deal with the problem was to get out from under it altogether. It had already been mooted that my new post would one day be civilianised and, with my so-called deputy (who in practice actually ran the department for me) only too willing to offer his support, I pushed hard for this to happen. Fortunately, the penny didn't take long to drop in the minds of the headquarters hierarchy and in just seven months the department, and my deputy in particular, got what they wanted and I finally managed to escape – as I had from the divisional prosecutions department a few years before – to a job much more up my street.

My new posting brought with it yet another dose of *déjà vu*, for I now headed the very same community liaison department I had once been part of as force press officer. Now though, in addition to press, public relations, I was responsible for such diverse areas as crime prevention and reduction, drug and solvent abuse, community relations and the force's burglar alarm policy. The job was essentially that of an overseer as each section of the department had its own small team to deal with its individual responsibilities and it was very much a case of keeping a finger on the pulse to make sure everything came together under the one umbrella and operated as effectively as possible. There were hands-on opportunities too, however, especially where major initiatives were concerned and I had a key liaison role in the Safer Communities Partnership project, where the police and other leading organisations, such as the probation service, social services and local councils, came together to provide a unified approach to tackling crime and anti-social behaviour throughout the force area.

Some of the projects led to very interesting spin-offs as well. In the course of carrying out research into drug abuse, I spent time with the drug squad and other agencies in the city of Liverpool, looking at what was then a very innovative approach to tackling the spread of infectious diseases among addicts using dirty syringes. The Liverpool scheme was innovative because it actually encouraged addicts to come forward and disclose their illegal habit by handing in used syringes at special clinics, rather than re-using them or abandoning them in parks and other public places, and receiving clean syringes in exchange. Initially, the very idea of handing out free syringes to illegal drug users at tax-payers' expense went against everything I thought I believed in, especially as it seemed to be actually encouraging drug abuse in the first place, but after a brief insight into the twilight world of the scouse user, I came back to Thames Valley with an entirely different view, accepting that unsavoury social problems had to be faced and dealt with in a practical way, instead of being ignored in the belief that they would eventually go away.

Researching community initiatives took me a lot further than Liverpool too. When a young constable put forward a proposal to reduce crime in car parks by issuing car park operators with gold, silver and bronze awards to mark the level of security they had achieved, in line with an approved crime prevention criteria, I was appointed chairman of the working group managing the project. This led not only to establishing a viable *Secured Car Parks* scheme for the force and persuading essential sponsors to back the idea, but helping to develop it nationwide through a regional committee made up of a large number of other forces. The scheme was later fully approved by the Association of Chief Police Officers and that was a satisfying result in itself, but I was flabbergasted when I then received an invitation to address an international congress on parking in Amsterdam, attended by police forces and civil authorities from all over the world. I felt really honoured to be invited to represent the UK police service in this way, but though excited at the prospect, I boarded my flight to Schipol Airport with some trepidation, praying that my prepared speech would be equal to the task.

In fact, it all went very well indeed and aside from the actual congress, which was an experience in itself, my brief trip across the water was one of the more enjoyable police duties I had had to perform in my twenty-five years' service. More than that, it was the very first time I had been on one of the so-called 'jollies' I had heard so much about – where police officers are sent off on paid trips abroad to share information or carry out research on a variety of projects with dubious value to their own forces and end up having a whale of a time at the taxpayers' expense.

To be fair, this particular trip was in no way dubious and it did have distinct benefits on both sides of the water, simply because tackling car park crime was of major concern to police forces and local authorities everywhere and the exchange of ideas could not but be beneficial to all concerned. Furthermore, a great deal of work went into my presentation, so I felt I justified the expense incurred, but the trip was still a 'jolly' and I certainly made the most of it – especially the hotel, which offered the kind of comfort that would have cost me an arm and a leg if I had had to pay for it and gave me a rare insight into the way the other half lived. Its position could not have been better either. Situated on a confluence of canals, affording a superb view of the waterfront through a massive picture window, it gave immediate access to the city's lively centre – though after what happened to me when I decided to take a nocturnal stroll one evening, this turned out to be somewhat of a mixed blessing.

Unfamiliar with the geography of Amsterdam or where it was wise and not so wise to venture, I left my hotel after dinner for a breath of fresh air and soon found myself in a labyrinth of narrow streets with brilliantly lit windows. I had been to Amsterdam as a tourist with the family a few years before (our first holiday abroad), when we had stayed with a Dutch police officer and his wife, but then the sights we had been shown were strictly confined to canals, windmills and cheese markets. This time though I stumbled upon entertainment of an entirely different kind and one for which Amsterdam was equally famous.

I had passed the lighted window without thinking and I was brought to an abrupt halt by this almost surreal vision of a slender dusky lady, dressed in a thong, thigh length black boots and nothing else, standing in the middle of a sparsely furnished room and staring straight at me with the sort of seductive smile that melts chocolate.

I must have stood there gaping for several seconds before her imperious beckoning broke the spell and with the shocked realisation that I was being propositioned I stumbled back from the window in alarm, shaking my head furiously to make it abundantly clear that I was not interested. Like most people, I had heard all about Amsterdam's notorious Red Light District, but I had never expected my plush hotel to actually back on to it and it struck me that the sensible thing to do under the circumstances was to make a smart about turn and head back to the sanctuary of the hotel bar while I had the chance. As a senior police officer representing my country abroad, the last thing I could afford was the sort of scandal that would arise from a disastrous sexual encounter with a lady of the night on the streets of the host city. It would have curdled the milk on the chief constable's breakfast cereal – not to mention the effect it would have had on my own marital bliss.

Unfortunately, however, the dusky maiden was not so

easily put off and as I started to retrace my steps with as much dignity as I could manage, I heard the sharp clicking of high heels on the pavement behind me. Glancing over my shoulder, I saw to my astonishment that my half-naked admirer had actually left the house and was striding purposefully after me, the long legs in the thigh length boots quickly closing the gap between us as she graphically described at the top of her voice – both in broken English and what I took to be her own native tongue – precisely what she could do for me at 'a very good price'.

During almost thirty years police service I had stood my ground in the face of armed criminals, rioting mobs and homicidal farm animals, but every man has his breaking point and mine was six foot of aggressive bare-breasted womanhood in hot pursuit of a prospective client along a deserted Amsterdam street. Casting my dignity to the cobbles, I literally took to my heels and fled, hardly drawing breath until I was safely back inside the hotel bar with a double whisky in front of me and at least a dozen people between me and the door.

Thankfully 'Attila the Hen' did not pursue me any further and I was able to finish my drink in peace, but the incident certainly made me think twice about venturing out of the hotel after dark again and I was not that sorry when I caught my flight home the following day.

My brush with Amsterdam's seedy side did not end there either, for just a few months later I was back in the city, this time with my boss, the assistant chief constable, support. Apparently the chief constable had expressed a keen interest in the Netherlands' criminal justice system and its youth offending programme, so as head of the force's community liaison department I was the natural choice to accompany the

ACC on a fact-finding visit. We were only in the Netherlands for a few days, but we were able to cram a surprising amount into the trip, not only looking at Amsterdam, but the country's famous port of Rotterdam too. As a result, we managed to gain a brief but useful insight into crime and punishment Dutch style. This included the country's controversial, and by now well documented, approach to drug abuse, together with their trail-blazing HALT initiative. Here young offenders dressed in distinctive uniforms were made to carry out manual work in the community, including cleaning streets and tidying up parks, as an alternative to detention – much like our own community service orders introduced a few years later, but which, unlike HALT, have now become such a cynical joke.

The trip was not all work, of course, and we did manage to get out and about a bit in the evenings to sample the local hospitality, but after my previous Amsterdam experience, I made sure that one particular part of the city stayed off our agreed itinerary. To my intense relief, no dusky bare-breasted maidens accosted us on our travels, while the only red lights we saw were those displayed by traffic lights and passing motor vehicles, which meant that I was able to catch the flight home and face my wife, Elizabeth, with a completely clear conscience, but I did get the feeling that my boss was more than a little disappointed.

That second trip to Amsterdam proved to be the last of my jollies with the firm, for the clock was already ticking towards retirement and I remember thinking as I flew home from Schipol that getting on for thirty years police service had flashed by almost without notice and, incredible as it seemed, I had less than two and a half years left to do before I could claim my police pension.

Despite the fact that my time as a police officer was gradually coming to an end, however, I had no intention of coasting through the final months and slowly easing myself into obscurity. I wanted to go out with a sense of achievement – to feel that I had been able to make a difference – and, luckily for me, the powers that be were only to happy to oblige. Button-holed one day at an official function by the deputy chief constable, I was quietly offered the job of setting up a brand new corporate communication department from scratch and pulling under its umbrella those other units and departments I considered relevant to its operation.

Not surprisingly, I nearly bit his hand off and within weeks I handed over the community liaison department to another superintendent and moved into my new office located in a converted farmhouse at the rear of the headquarters building. It was only then, when I got the chance of looking a lot closer at the task I had been given, that my euphoria started to fade and the sheer enormity of what I had taken on actually hit me. When the deputy chief constable had told me that the new department would have to be set up from scratch that had been no exaggeration. Apart from a borrowed office with just a single chair, desk and filing cabinet, I had nothing else; no staff, no equipment – not even the semblance of a departmental mandate. Worse still, there was no budget for it all and that could not be applied for until I came up with the *raison d'être* for the department, together with its proposed structure, staffing and accommodation requirements. I felt isolated and vulnerable and it didn't help matters when every time I approached my new boss to point out that I needed staff, equipment and a budget before I could do the job, I was treated to his most benign smile and what turned out to be his favourite expression:

'Every faith in you, David, every faith in you'.

Fortunately, despite his outwardly good-humoured but dismissive air, he did eventually heed my concerns and within a few weeks I was allocated a chief inspector as my deputy with the old force legal library provided for her use as an office. Linda, my number two, was magic as far as I was concerned – a truly round peg in a round hole. An academic with a keen analytical mind and a penchant for the written word, she was just what I needed to move things along and we hit it off right from the start.

There were still mountains to move, however, particularly political ones. Snatching staff and specialist units from other departments and securing offices on a site where accommodation was at a premium was never going to be an easy task and there was a lot of 'blood on the floor' before I managed to get my own way.

Communication services as it was initially called was finally established in a nice suite of offices at the front of the main headquarters building and though it was an ideal location as far as I was concerned, not everyone was happy with the arrangement. The offices had formerly been occupied by the operations department and the chief superintendent, operations, was not at all pleased with her enforced move to new quarters, especially since I had chosen to approach the chief constable with my recommendations for the acquisition of the accommodation after she had gone on leave!

My popularity was not enhanced by what were seen as piratical raids on other departments either – my most notable acquisitions being the headquarters press public relations office and the audio visual unit based in the force training centre at Sulhamstead. In fact, I was accused by more than one colleague of nothing more than empire building – particularly when I also successfully applied for a modest increase in staff, including the appointment of a professional photographer and an administrator, as well as the supply of essential office equipment to resource that empire. But I firmly believe that in the end I confounded most of my critics and doubters and the fledgling department established itself as a vital organ of communication, both inside and outside the force.

Sadly, however, communication services was the last project I was to manage, for my enthusiasm for change had begun to wane as the job I had come to love and respect so much gradually degenerated into farce. Political correctness had already gained a foothold and now, bit by bit, it was infecting every aspect of police work like some contagious disease, destroying all tradition, humour and common sense with its spread. Suddenly all police officers were labelled racist, sexist and authoritarian and referring to a female colleague as 'love' or asking for 'black' coffee instead of coffee without milk incurred as much censure as committing a criminal offence. Discipline was disappearing out of the window faster than air from a ruptured tyre and proposals were even being discussed to encourage the use of first names between the ranks instead of observing the customary rank titles.

The police service was certainly not the job I had joined as an eager twenty year old in the sixties and despite my continued determination to try and promote the best possible image of my own force while I was still in post, deep down I felt that, like most forces, we had lost the plot and were not delivering the service we had been created for.

Policing itself seemed to be no longer about positive law enforcement on the streets: targeting and locking up criminals, dispersing yobs and protecting the public. It was all about heavily publicised multi-agency partnerships, crime reduction projects and community initiatives, supported by glossy pamphlets packed with clever slogans, bar charts and tables of statistics. Buzz words, like 'down-sizing', 'scoping' and 'outsourcing', had become the order of the day and every senior officer in the force seemed to be preparing a discussion paper on something or other or wrestling with complicated budgets and performance targets that had little to do with real police work, but helped the Home Office to demonstrate to the public that the police service was being made more accountable.

Then there were the interminable training days, residential courses and seminars on virtually every subject under the sun – from racial awareness and equal opportunities to support skills and management of change – where guest speakers seemed to talk total gobbledegook for hours on end and those attending sagely nodded their heads in agreement with everything that was said to avoid being labelled intellectually inferior. It was all a bit like the well-known fable *The Emperor's New Clothes* where fraudsters sold a non-existent suit to the esteemed ruler, and his subjects, not wishing to appear fools by querying the fact that there was no suit there at all, allowed him to cavort in public wearing nothing but a smile. In the story it took a small boy, uninfluenced by such considerations as image and status, to finally blow the gaff on the fraud and in a flash (to pardon the pun) to suddenly bring home to the emperor's subjects that he had been sold a pup and was actually parading in front of them stark naked.

In the ethereal new world that was developing around me, I couldn't help remembering that fable and feeling a lot like the small boy in question – the only difference being that few of those in high places were prepared to listen to my increasingly critical views, because they themselves were an integral part of the problem and would have been put firmly on the spot if they had had to justify anything. As one more down to earth colleague said to me after a particularly wordy but almost content-free seminar: 'How can you expect them to explain to you what they mean, Dave, when they don't even know themselves?'

What made things even worse was the fact that, as the force's head of communication, I was heavily involved in arranging many of the seminars that I regarded as such a waste of time and resources. This made me feel a total hypocrite, but it came with the territory, so like it or not, I just had to get on with it.

And I *did* get on with it for a while, but my resolve did not last long. After the third senior officer's seminar in a row – with my backside numb from sitting for hours on end on a hard plastic chair, my brain dulled by the drivel that was being communicated by speaker after speaker and my senses driven to distraction by the so-called focus group discussions that followed practically every lecture – I came to a momentous decision. I was past my sell-by date and it was time for me to grab my pension and run.

I had always intended retiring after completing the usual thirty years service anyway, but as a superintendent, I had earned the right to freeze my pension and stay on for a further ten years until the age of sixty, which, under a different regime, I may well have opted to do. But with the spectre of political correctness now sweeping through the service and the prospect of a further decade of senior officer's seminars, gobbledegook and focus groups to look forward to, the thought of staying on was just too awful to contemplate.

My farewell party came along with surprising speed and I was astonished by the huge number of people of all ranks who turned up at headquarters from all over the force area to, as one chief officer put it with a broad grin, 'see me off the premises'. Maybe it had something to do with the fact that free food and a free first round of drinks was on offer or, as another colleague suggested, 'Hodges was buying his first round in thirty years', but I like to think there was a much better reason than that and I had a lump in my throat as the deputy chief constable said the usual goodbyes on behalf of the service.

It was raining when Elizabeth, myself and my family left the building – which, despite my decision to retire, was strangely in tune with my own nostalgic mood – and as I drove out of the gates of headquarters for the very last time, my mind was far away; peeling back the years like some manic automatic slide projector. Incidents, places, faces all flashed before me in a hopeless jumble; good times and bad; successes and failures; things I should have done and things I shouldn't. A large part of my life gone, just like that. Yet despite all the knocks and setbacks I had received along the way, I had no regrets, for the journey itself had been well worthwhile. In fact, overall, I felt that this was one Essex secondary modern school boy who had every reason to be proud of what he had achieved on two GCE O'levels and a score of six out of a hundred for mathematics. Strangely enough, however, as the car's headlights blazed a path for home and towards a new life, it wasn't my career successes that sprang so readily to mind, but the day when, as a naive lad of twenty, I had stepped out on to the streets of Didcot for the very first time, wearing big creaking boots and a tall funny hat.